BORN TO SING

BORN TO SING

An Interpretation and
World Survey of Bird Song

CHARLES HARTSHORNE

Indiana University Press

BLOOMINGTON   LONDON

Parts of Chapters 2 and 3 appeared in *Ibis* (1958), of Chapter 4 in *The Oriole* (1961), of Chapter 5 in the *Emory University Quarterly* (1956), and of Chapter 7 in *Auk* (1956).

Permissions have been given by various publishers, authors, or journals to reproduce or quote certain materials, as follows: Epigraphs: by Julian Huxley, from *Animal Language*, copyright © 1964, permission granted by Grosset & Dunlap, Inc.; and by E. M. Nicholson, from *How Birds Live*, copyright © 1929, by Williams and Norgate. In Chapter 5: graph by Aretas A. Saunders, from *A Guide to Bird Songs*, copyright © 1935, 1951 by Aretas A. Saunders, reproduced by permission of Doubleday & Co., Inc.; notations by F. S. Mathews, from *Field Book of Wild Birds and Their Music*, copyright © 1921 by G. P. Putnam's Sons; and notations by T. Hold, from *Ibis*, 1970, reproduced by permission of British Ornithologists' Union. In Chapter 8A: passages from *Bird-Song*, by S. M. Morris, copyright © 1925, quoted by permission of H. F. and G. Witherby. In Appendix C: notations by A. V. Arlton, reproduced by permission of Roland Arlton. In Appendix D: spectrograms by L. Irby Davis, reproduced by permission of *Southwestern Naturalist*.

Published in Canada by Fitzhenry & Whiteside Limited, Don Mills, Ontario

Library of Congress catalog card number: 72–75392

ISBN: 0–253–10800–4

MANUFACTURED IN THE UNITED STATES OF AMERICA

To those, in many countries, who have helped me to find and identify singing birds, and to those, in some cases the same persons, who with great skill and patience have recorded or precisely described songs so that all of us can enjoy or study them at leisure and in detail.

Whenever any activity of an animal involves consciousness, there are always two answers to our questions about it. One is an immediate answer in terms of psychology, the other a more remote answer in terms of biological function. And each answer is a correct answer. Very often the creature itself cannot be aware of the biological function. . . . I believe that deliberate sound will almost always have an emotional basis.

> —JULIAN HUXLEY, in *Animal Language*.

Birds are all temperament and emotion . . . [their] language expressing apparently not thoughts but feelings. . . .

With no complexes . . . no morality . . . and no future to consider, birds lead a sort of life not easy for us to imagine, though not, I think, absolutely unimaginable. . . . The approach . . . must always be from without, from the external manifestations, and not from the bird itself; . . . learning from what it does and not from what it is.

> —E. M. NICHOLSON, in *How Birds Live*.

To know is to measure.

> —ENRICO FERMI, as quoted by a colleague.

Contents

❦

Contents

FIGURES

TABLES

Preface

❦

The primary aim of this book is to advance what P. Szöke has well called biomusicology, the study of music not just in man but in musical or singing animals generally. Szöke reasonably holds that to work in this field one should be expert both in musicology and in the appropriate branches of biology, especially ornithology. Few persons can altogether meet these requirements. The deficiency I feel most painfully is in music.

Robert Ardrey and Aldous Huxley have made the territorial function of songs known to many besides specialists. But we face an enormous range of degrees and kinds of bird music. To understand something of the meaning of this variety we need more than the single idea of territory, which itself has many forms. Also, while songs do help to make territorial spacing possible, this scarcely tells us how the bird experiences its songs. Copulation enables a species to persist, but no one supposes that a copulating animal is aiming at that result. Cause and effect are less obscurely connected in the territorial case. Still, birds are not ornithologists, and what singing is for them, in their scarcely imaginable naiveté, has yet to be dealt with in the light even of the data now available. I have been investigating this difficult matter during most of a long lifetime.

The two expert modern studies of bird song, those by William H. Thorpe (1961) and Edward A. Armstrong (1963), as Thorpe says, do not so much compete with as complement each other, the one giving a lucid account of experimental work in the subject, and the other summarizing with great learning the results of fieldwork done by observers all over the world. My book, I hope, will play a further complementary role. For one thing, though these works are free from provincialism, their authors have done most of their observing in Britain, whereas I have done much of mine in various widely separated parts of the United States, and have spent over seven years all told in many other countries. Also, I have had access to numerous recordings, including some scores that I made myself (with inadequate equipment and skill) of otherwise unrecorded species.

I have tried, first of all, to cover bird song globally, to reckon seriously with the totality of songs by the 5,000 or more species that could, without stretching the term to the utmost, be said to "sing." Taken without qualification, the project is of course an impossibility. Until recently it could not seriously be entertained. But with the aid of planes, tape recorders, audiospectrographs, the constantly growing international literature, and the Fulbright program, an attempt of this kind, granted its limitations, seems worth risking.

There are both scientific and recreational reasons for attempting global coverage. To take an unduly exalted precedent, natural selection was discovered, not by considering British animals only but chiefly by looking at tropical species—by Darwin, especially in the Americas, and by Wallace in Asia. Life is much more abundant in tropical areas, and things may become obvious there which are more difficult to see in Europe. Also, each continent has distinctive features. Some generalizations about song, as about many other things, are less plausible when viewed in global perspective.

As for the recreational reasons—the day is approaching when the other side of the world will be accessible between breakfast and dinner. Men on various missions are already speeding in a day or less from one zoological region to a radically different one. So long as the impression prevails that the musical songsters are largely confined to the northern parts of the world, so long will even that minority of persons with some feeling for nature be likely to race through other areas, especially the tropics, without bothering to stroll about quietly, especially in forest, listening for songs. In the Fijis, to take an example, the planes (not the ships) land in the arid portion of the island Viti Levu. There only insignificant song is to be heard. But take the bus or the local plane to the wetter parts, find a remnant of rain forest (who knows how long there will be any?), and you will hear many interesting and some beautiful sounds. Within a few minutes I myself had heard not only a few raucous (but piquant) bird voices such as one is taught to expect in the tropics, but also an utterly exquisite song, like a simplified

Hermit Thrush, and a quite pretty little flycatcher song. Luckily I had read Fuertes on the voices of tropical birds, so I knew that such things are not uncommon in equatorial regions. But many have not known this. They have been taught in effect to open their eyes but close their ears when traveling to such places.

Many writers, including Thorpe and Armstrong, have dealt intelligently with the question: Do birds express an aesthetic sense in their songs? Or, has the analogy between bird music and human music any biological significance? In exploring this analogy I have drawn upon some results of philosophical and psychological aesthetics and whatever I could find in the facts of bird life that seemed relevant.

A guiding idea of my studies has been the following. There are just two possibilities for evolutionary theory concerning the musical sensibility and capability characterizing man: Either it is entirely unique to human life, or there are precedents or analogies in the older forms of animal life. The search for evidence bearing upon this question is one root of the present book. Another is this: Natural phenomena fall into certain regularities. Nature is not a junk heap of facts. Chance, disorder, there may be, and I believe that the recognition of randomness by physicists is reasonable and that the limitations to causal order are even greater than quantum physics allows. Still, there are at least statistical regularities. So we may ask, what general aspects of order are present in nonhuman singing, that is, the production of musical or music-like sounds? That these sounds rather generally serve to advertise territory and to aid mating and (in birds) cooperation between mates caring for young was made fairly clear long ago. My aim has been to guess and then test additional general truths about animal music, especially bird song. This is the second root of this book. The point here was not to prove this or that generalization rather than any other, but to find some order that obtained comprehensively. Here I was doing what every ornithological researcher does.

The third root of my effort has been the fascination which the concrete details of animal music have had for me. Whatever causal order does or does not obtain in song behavior, I enjoy the songs of birds, and indeed, of frogs and insects. Anyone who shares this feeling may find something to his taste in these chapters, whether or not he agrees with the theories I propose.

The reader may feel a need to know what songs I have personally experienced. I have been observing and reading about singing birds

for more than fifty years (longer than I have been studying my professional subject, philosophy). My most intensive fieldwork has been
done first in eastern, southern, and far western United States (I have
listened to birds in about forty states, including Hawaii), then in
Australia, and later in Japan, India, and Nepal. I have made less intensive but usually rather extensive observations in England and several other European countries, in Middle and South America, Jamaica,
Uganda and Kenya, New Zealand, Fiji, the Philippines, Malaya, Hong
Kong, and Taiwan. What I have missed above all is Siberia and mainland China.

From many parts of the world (not yet from mainland Asia) there
are now good recordings. I possess many of these and have heard
many more, thanks to the Cornell Laboratory of Ornithology, the
French organization *Echo,* various friends who have with great kindness given me copies of their tapes, and commercially available phonograph records from many countries.

In naming birds I try to follow Peters's *Check-list of Birds of the
World* so far as it goes, or standard regional works, e.g., Vaurie's *The
Birds of the Palearctic Fauna,* Eisenmann's *The Species of Middle
American Birds,* or Meyer de Schauensee's *Birds of South America
with Their Distribution.* I do not give the names of those who originally labeled the species, but they can generally be found in these
works. Given the diversity of scientific as well as vernacular or sub-
stantive names for the same species occurring in the world literature,
it has sometimes been difficult to know when two descriptions of a
song refer to the same group of birds and when they do not.

Concerning technical issues in evolutionary theory I offer no opinions. If there is any subject in which the amateur is at a disadvantage
it is this one. I hold a religious view of nature, but I think that one of
the poorest ways to try to recommend this view is to attack neo-
Darwinism, one of the greatest achievements of human intelligence.
That there can be any cosmic order at all (and that there is some order
is assumed but in no way explained by either physics or biology) I
believe can best be understood in religious terms. But exactly what
cosmic order obtains, out of all the conceivable ones, is a question for
science. I deal with those special aspects of this question which can
be affected by the facts of "animal music" and bird song.

Chapters 1, A and B, and 12, B and C, are the least ornithological
and the most philosophical sections. Parts of some other chapters (e.g.,

6, 8) may seem unduly speculative to some scientific readers. Non-ornithological readers may wish to skip some of the details in Chapters 7–11.

Readers who are puzzled by my use of certain words, in some cases standard in ornithology, in some cases more special to my own practice, may find help in the Glossary and in the list of Abbreviations in Chapter 9A. The primary evidences to which I appeal are from studies of what are sometimes called "true Songbirds," but which I call simply Songbirds, not because they all sing, for many do not, but because they all have well-developed organs (syrinxes) for vocalization and because the suborder (Oscines or Passeres) of the order of perching birds (Passeriformes) which they constitute includes a majority of the species that sing and nearly all of those that sing very well. These are the birds that I know best. The numerous species outside the Songbird suborder which show some degree of singing skill are, with two exceptions (the lyrebirds), largely ignored, except in Chapters 7, D and E, and 11, in which I discuss the evidence they furnish relevant to the questions dealt with in this book.

I am grateful to many persons and institutions, especially to Dr. Olin Sewall Pettingill, Jr., my first and excellent and virtually sole teacher in ornithology, and to the University of Michigan Biological Station; to Professor R. K. Selander, whose unwavering encouragement and critical—sometimes brilliantly constructive—comments have been highly valuable; to my friend and neighbor, Edgar B. Kincaid, Jr., who carries in his head a seeming infinity of bird facts. My gratitude goes also to many ornithologists and bird watchers who have helped me to identify singers in numerous countries, e.g., in Japan Kasuke Hoshino and Takeo Mizuno, in Australia Hugh Wilson, in East Africa Myles North (the last two, alas, now dead), in Mexico and Panama Ernest P. Edwards, in Panama James Ambrose, in Costa Rica Alexander F. Skutch, in Nepal Robert Fleming; also to Peter Paul Kellogg and the Library of Natural Sounds at the Cornell Laboratory of Ornithology. My one-time Chicago neighbor, the sagacious and learned Margaret Morse Nice, a sharp critic but warm encourager of my investigations, should also be mentioned.

I am grateful too, and this may surprise them, to editors of journals who rejected several of my manuscripts, which (though not entirely for the reasons they gave) I have come to see were better not published as they stood. I have, I believe, profited by their criticisms. Certainly I have benefited from Edward A. Armstrong's reactions to some of my ideas (in his book, and in correspondence and conversation), for they forced me to work on statistical problems, the difficulties of which, I now realize, I had underestimated. I also thank, for their comments on parts of this book, Professors Peter Marler, Jared Verner, and the University of California statistician Dorothy C. Lowry, whose candid criticisms of a version of Chapter 6 were very helpful. Father James A. Mulligan of St. Louis University read a draft (much longer than the present version) of the entire book, and his unsparing and wise analysis of its defects has been invaluable. W. H. Thorpe read a later draft and I deeply appreciate his many wise suggestions. Finally I could not possibly say enough about my debt to Dorothy C. Hartshorne for editing my writings, and for having always encouraged and sagaciously shared my interest in nature, some aspects of which she understands better than I ever could.

C. H.

August, 1971

1

The Aesthetic Analogy as Scientific Hypothesis

❦

A. Explaining Behavior

In the explanation of nature a "principle of parsimony" is often evoked according to which a complex explanation is accepted only if a simpler yet adequate one is not available. In the study of behavior, or ethology, this principle takes the form: a higher function, more remote from the simplest beginnings of life, is attributed to an animal only if a lower, more primitive function will not account for its actions. Moreover, the simplest—or at least the most clearly objective—description of animal life is the behavioral one. Whatever animals "do," they move parts of their bodies and their bodies as wholes, and these movements are in principle intersubjectively discernible, whereas any sensations or emotions the animals might be thought to experience seem problematic inferences from the movements, the behavior. Thus behaviorism is a plausible form of intellectual parsimony. However, with most philosophers and probably most scientists, I find strict behaviorism inadequate, at least in the study of human beings; moreover, in view of the evolutionary continuity of life, and the ideal of a unitary explanation of nature as a whole, it seems an unsatisfactory dualism to make man a mere exception. (See Thorpe 1963: 3–13, 470.) Hence I deny the final adequacy of a purely behavioral view.

In our culture many people suppose that "aesthetic" ideas concern only subordinate refinements or complications of life, not the essential principles. But this view, as a great logician and experimental scientist

Charles Peirce once suggested, involves a failure to generalize the concepts employed in analyzing aesthetic phenomena, concepts like "harmony," "unity in variety," and "feeling." Taken in their full generality, these concepts do not connote complications, but can have instances as simple as life itself. In a one-sided technological culture this may not be obvious, but it is one of the faults of such a culture, allied with the dangerous sense of lack of meaning now apparent in our midst, that this is so. It is clear enough to me, as to some other philosophers, that we shall never understand ourselves or any other animal in a fully satisfactory way until we see that all activity is motivated by the sense of possible harmonies and by the flight from the twin evils of discord and monotony. The "curiosity" which animals display is relevant here. Novelty is not boring, but it may be either disturbing or pleasing, depending partly upon broadly aesthetic factors of contrast and unity, including contrast and unity between present and in some fashion remembered past experiences.

If specifically human aesthetic responses are beyond the capacity of the other animals, this is not because the responses are aesthetic, but because of the intellectual element which pervades them. I have every sympathy with the caution contemporary ornithologists show regarding any attribution of humanlike thought to birds (in spite of the navigational feats of migratory species), but I distinguish between aesthetic feeling and aesthetic thought. When a baby babbles rhythmically he is not doing much thinking, aesthetic or otherwise; but I believe he is enjoying certain sensations and feelings which I term aesthetic. Thus for me the principle of parsimony does not rule out aesthetic considerations.

If animals are aesthetically enjoying and not merely behaving creatures, there is a double meaning in the request for explanation of a piece of behavior. On the one hand we explain the behavior in its evolutionary origin by showing that it favors reproductive success. On the other hand, we explain it in its present character as the action of an emotional creature by conceiving suitable motivations for which there is behavioral evidence. As Julian Huxley (1964: 17–18) has noted, there is not the slightest incompatibility between these two accounts. Evolution selects for behavior resulting in survival and reproductive success. If such behavior is the external sign of a certain emotional state, then evolution selects for that emotional state. Thus it selects for sexual behavior which internally involves pleasure, and for avoidance of injurious situations which internally involve pain. The animal acts sexually at least partly because it enjoys doing so, yet it has the capacity for the enjoyment, as for the action, because animals deficient in this respect do not propagate their kind. As William James sensibly said, the distribution of pleasures and pains is explicable in evolutionary terms only on the assumption that they have behavioral significance. But it does not follow that this significance exhausts the facts. Sexual behavior, like avoidance behavior, is a mode of feeling as well as of acting.

Although the chief function of bird song is to maintain territory, it does not follow that the chief, still less the sole, emotive meaning of singing for the bird is territorial "hostility." Why not say it is "liking" for the territory, or perhaps at times for the mate that shares the territory? Or why not, part of the time, simple joy in the singing? An utterance informing those whom it may concern that one would be short-tempered with trespassers implies potential, but not necessarily actual, hostility. Military bandsmen can enjoy the music they play, as well as hate possible or actual enemies. Either we rigorously exclude all human analogies and thus miss valuable suggestions and clues, or we consider each one on its merits as helping or hindering us from understanding not only how the animal came—and is able to continue —to be what it is but also what it is. Evolutionary causes of present behavior lie deep in the past, but the animal is living now, and we should like to know what is going on in it from moment to moment. I believe with Heinroth and others that what is going on includes a sequence of emotions, which we can never know precisely; but we might know something about them.

In many or most cases the tendency to sing is closely correlated with the presence of certain male hormones, and hence is maximal in the breeding season. These physical factors must alter not just the behavior but also the feelings of the bird. It does not follow that the bird's feeling is merely an idle accompaniment of the hormonal level. Some drugs cause intensified sensory experiences in human beings; but these experiences have aesthetic aspects which influence behavior. (Indeed the danger of the drugs lies partly in this very fact!) The physical influences on bird behavior must also, I argue, influence its emotional life (and whatever mentality it has—see E. Howard 1935: 14, 50–55), and this in turn influences its behavior. The notion that emotions are mere "idle wheels," or mere epiphenomena, is suspect. So pervasive a factor

in human life must have both evolutionary significance and evolutionary antecedents. (See Thorpe 1965a: 60.) One may ignore this aspect of nature; one may allow speculations about it to swell into anthropomorphic orgies, as our ancestors tended to do; or finally, one
may try to find a reasonable mean between these extremes. This last is
my attempt.

B. Subjective and Objective Aspects of Aesthetic Response

We generalize by noting analogies. Without them thought has little
power; with incautious reliance upon them thought goes astray. The
main theme of this book is the possible scientific uses of the aesthetic
analogy between other animals, especially birds, and man with respect
to music. I shall present facts about bird behavior, some of which had
not been noted before and would not have been noted by me had I
not been pursuing this analogy, but which fall into coherent patterns
by means of it.

It may be objected that bird and animal utterances generally are
primitive forms of language rather than of music. Of course there is
some analogy here also. But note that certain forms of language, the
"poetic," are akin to music. Is bird language poetry or prose? Alarm
notes seem more prosaic than songs. On the other hand, the chatter of
parrots (Chapter 4) seems prosaic. This book is primarily about song,
and I hold that song is best regarded as music, even though it is music
used to convey a message. Once in Paris I asked the significance of a
little tune, played on some sort of pipe, and was told that it was a
street vendor or artisan announcing his business. If that was language
then that is the sense in which animal song is also language.

Language in the normal sense is different. Its parts have separate
conventional meanings. But in music or song the parts (as used in the
song) have no separate denotative or conventional significance. Hence
they can be combined simply in terms of how well they sound together, or how interesting and distinctive the auditory effect is.
Granted a distinctive, interesting, readily recognized and remembered
pattern or style, the message will be conveyed. This is not how sentences function. Their parts have their own meanings, largely retained
in diverse combinations. But the various parts of a complex bird song

all say the same thing, if they say anything, namely, "Here I am, a Mockingbird—or a Brown Thrasher—male, engaged in seeking or keeping a mate and warning intruding members of the same or even related species that the area is not open to them." The human analogy is with music.

The street vendor falls into the habit of announcing himself more or less musically because musical sounds are most readily made distinctive, recognizable, and memorable, and the activity is easier to maintain through long hours or days (as birds maintain their singing) if it has some intrinsic aesthetic character or pattern. Note, too, that both the vendor and the territorial bird need sounds that are distinctive at a distance. We shall see how important this aspect is.

Nicholson (1929: 46–47) speaks for many, perhaps most, ornithologists when he says that natural selection operating on sound production raises "the standard—of efficiency, not necessarily of music." He argues that the evidence is against the Darwinian view of the females selecting the finest singers (but see below, section C), and adds that any musical merits of songs are "mere byproducts" of the evolutionary forces, similar to the visual beauty of birds and other animals. He complains that only "a few highly-developed songsters" give any sign of musical discrimination; also that many songs are "earsplitting," and that the Nightingale's alarm note is extremely "jarring." And finally he asserts that unmusical songs fulfill their functions at least as well as musical ones, "for there is no aesthetic selection in bird song."

I have great respect for Nicholson's wisdom about birds and their songs. But I shall give reasons for thinking that he overstates the difference between efficiency and "musical qualities." (Elsewhere—p. 100 —he himself refers to song as "simply vocalized music.") In certain situations it is musical qualities which are most effective. And he should not, I submit, have taken a harsh alarm note as relevant to the question of musical sensitivity. A human musician may speak harshly to an annoying person without ceasing to possess musical discrimination. Sounding an alarm or expressing annoyance is one thing; producing or enjoying music is another. Also there is much human music that some would object to as earsplitting, or harsh, but which is nevertheless properly classified as music. That some bird utterances functioning as songs do not seem beautiful to us should be compared with the fact that some human music, including much contemporary composition, is often similarly judged. The word "beauty" is too narrow, in its most natural meaning, to cover all of music. Nor should any particular person be expected to like all forms of music.

Philosophy has reached at least one definite insight in value theory which I believe has some importance for ornithology: there may be objective as well as subjective components in valuation. To say, "I like it," and stop there is not to describe the thing liked. But to say, for instance, "I like it because of its complexity" is to imply that the thing is unusually complex. If one has some understanding of the class of things being compared and some way of measuring complexity, this statement raises an issue of fact. If each individual of a species has, on the average, a "repertoire" of six easily distinguishable songs, then its singing is complex when compared to a species which has but two songs—at least if each of the two is in itself no more complex than each of the six songs of the first species. Again if a song is a monotone, just one note repeated many times, in a definite sense (which information theory could make precise) it is less complex than a song on several different pitches. There are many other ways in which bird songs can be compared objectively by attending to what the songs are liked (or not liked) *for,* rather than to the mere liking. And it is fair to ask what behavioral significance, or survival value, if any, do the objective properties in question have? Ornithologists differ remarkably in their willingness or ability to distinguish between the subjective and the objective components in aesthetic responses to bird life. Some are so sure that the former are nearly the whole story that they do not focus on the latter at all. Others do not have this difficulty.

There are several sources of confusion here. First, beauty is the central, not the sole, aesthetic value. Is *King Lear* beautiful? Or is it rather tragic and sublime? Is a pretty girl beautiful, or only pretty? There are, I hold, at least two relatively objective dimensions of aesthetic value: the dimension simple-complex; and the dimension integrated-diversified, or ordered-free. In both dimensions beauty is the mean between extremes. A phenomenon can, for a given observer, seem perfectly ordered and still not beautiful. Running up the scale chromatically for an octave and running down again gives definite order, but not much of a melody. The orderliness is too great, too restrictive of freedom. We have "neatness" rather than beauty. Mere randomness is also not beauty. Freedom must be within limits. Taking the other dimension, that of simplicity-complexity, a musical chord, say the major triad, may be a good balance between unity and diversity, for the three tones contrast yet seem to belong together. However, the scope of the diversity is too slight to produce more than prettiness. Prettiness is an ultrasimple, superficial beauty. Where complexity and intensity are great, "sublime" may be a more suitable term than "beautiful." Here, too, beauty is the comfortable mean between extremes. But deviations from this mean, if not too radical, may still have aesthetic worth. Only the hopelessly unfree or hopelessly chaotic, or (in the other dimension) the hopelessly ultrasimple (and hence trivial) or hopelessly overcomplicated (and hence unintelligible) are totally without such worth. "Hopelessly" means, for a given organism. The following diagram illustrates these relationships.

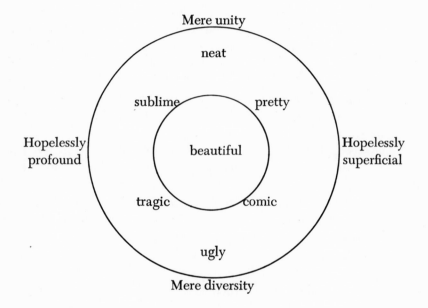

The qualification "for a given perceiving organism" is to be understood throughout. There is of course no absolute aesthetic value in any physical phenomenon, such as a sequence of sounds, which is the same for all types of observers. What is complex or profound for a bird may be ultrasimple for a man. What is ordered for the man may be a meaningless chaos for the bird.

But (and this is an axiom for my thought) higher types of organisms can have some sympathy and understanding for lower types. Were this not so there would be no science of behavior! We human beings can appreciate all the degrees of complexity in animal songs, provided our ears (if necessary aided by slowed-down replay) can perceive this complexity. It is the reverse relation which is not possible. Bird judgment of human music must indeed be hopelessly "subjective" or, to invent a word, *ornithomorphic.*

The outside of the circle represents zero aesthetic value (for a given organism). Inside there is at least some value, even in the ugly. It, too, has its appeal as a stimulus. The entirely valueless aesthetically is not even ugly; indeed it is not noticed at all, and falls outside experience. For immediate "satisfaction," apart from consequences, is the broad definition of aesthetic value, and no organism lives for nothing even for a moment. The bare existence of the organism is a harmony in diversity, and all experience is in some degree an achievement. Beauty is the norm of this achievement, equally far from the four extremes or poles of failure—mere disorder as opposed to mere (lifeless) order; utter triviality as opposed to complexity entirely beyond grasp. All aesthetic value is either beauty or a not too extreme deviation from it in one of the four directions: toward mere chaos *or* lifeless order; toward negligible complexity and intensity *or* baffling complexity, unattainable intensity.

It may seem that only human beings can experience such contrasts as those between the beautiful, the pretty, the sublime, the tragic, the comic, the ugly, the neat. And obviously these terms connote something quite special when used of organisms endowed with the symbolic power centering in language. But consider a newly trapped and caged wild animal: its impulses are thwarted by the cage; it experiences discord to a "tragic" degree. Consider the same animal after long conditioning has in a fashion reconciled it to its cage. Now instead of profound disharmony there is dull contentment. The situation is one of acceptable though not thrilling routine. This corresponds to the "neat" or at best the pretty. Consider also a playful animal mildly excited by some harmless amusement. This is its "comedy." Any observer of animals, including birds, can give examples.

My claim is neither that our aesthetic impressions can duplicate a bird's (not to mention an insect's) nor that one person's can duplicate another's. It is rather that songs are, in varying degrees, objectively aesthetic in the sense of avoiding the utmost extremes of mechanical regularity and mere chance diversity, as well as the ultrasimplicity of mere chirps or squeaks. Also, while we can never entirely cross the gulf between our awareness and a bird's, or entirely agree with one another in our estimates of songs, we can, if we proceed carefully and intelligently, share with each other relevant notions of what is on the other side of the gulf. In particular we can make biologically significant, even though somewhat vague, judgments about the extent to which a song approaches the maximum of enjoyable complexity possible for a bird, as well as the extent to which, for the bird, it approaches that ideal balance between expected repetition and the unexpected, that joint avoidance of monotony and chaos on a sufficient level of complexity, which is beauty.

Stephen C. Pepper (1937, 1970) explains "aesthetic organization" in terms of four principles: design, pattern, type, and dominant emotion. Design is organization so far as "based on the sensory and attentive fatigue processes to avoid monotony and extend interest." Its methods are "contrast, gradation, and theme-and-variation." Pattern is organization "based on the limited span of human attention employed to avoid confusion. . . ." Type is "a system of associated elements recognizable as a whole." Omit the word "human" and the whole of the foregoing can reasonably be applied to all singing animals. They all have sensory processes and are subject to fatiguing of attention through monotony or lack of perceptible patterns or recognizable wholes. And they have emotions. The idea of dominant emotion is difficult to analyze, as Pepper admits, but it, too, might just as well apply to nonhuman as to human animals. Our symbolic or abstract mode of thinking is inessential, so far as the foregoing aesthetic principles are concerned. The dominant emotions of birds, still more of croaking frogs or singing crickets, will of course be widely different from those of man, but not absolutely different or simply incomparable.

C. Beauty and Utility

Some authors have tried to demonstrate an aesthetic sense in birds by arguing that certain songs are more complex or beautiful than mere evolutionary utility would require. Thus Craig (1943) held that the elaborate twilight song of the Eastern Wood Pewee (*Contopus virens*) is functionless. This type of evidence, even where it may be valid, is not for me the main point, which is rather that certain useful modes of behaving require an attitude or feeling in the animal at least remotely analogous to what in us is aesthetic enjoyment. People and, in their fashion, other animals, make love, thereby (in some cases) prolonging the existence of the species, but they do not usually act with their minds on this result. Rather they find some kind and degree of beauty in this activity or experience. Birds and other animals sing and thereby win and keep mates and, in many cases, also territories; but the energetic persistence in singing may be sustained partly by a feeling, however primitive, for the beauty (i.e., the "unity in contrast") of the sounds they are making.

It is now well-established that in many avian species the most vigorous singing comes from males that have territories but lack mates, and that this extra-vigorous singing attracts unmated females. Thus "a female confronted with two singing males may be most likely to choose the one who is singing most persistently" (Marler 1961). What motivates this persistent singing? Is it the idea, "I want a mate"? Is it sensation in the sex organs? Or is it pleasure in singing? To argue that the latter is at least a factor is not to exclude all other factors.

Darwin thought that female selection of mates according to the qualities of their visual or auditory displays was a factor in the evolution of these displays. The subject is still being argued. But we know that some of the extreme criticisms of this view are unjustified (Haldane 1959: 131; Selander 1971). And if the arguments of this and later chapters are sound, it is no objection to Darwin that he assumed some degree of aesthetic sensitivity on the part of females. The human species is different, but not absolutely different. And the varieties of possible aesthetic sensibility are unimaginably great. One form of sexual selection of song may be as follows. Males born the previous season and singing territorially for the first time will not have fully matured their songs, and so presumably will be at a disadvantage. This has survival value to at least this extent: males which have survived into their second breeding season are more likely to excel in adaptive capacity than those which have yet to demonstrate such durability. Also males, whether or not over a year old, which have developed better songs will, if I am correct, have more enthusiasm for singing. It seems likely that this will influence females, and that such males will tend to be generally more vigorous and carry better inheritance.

If we take the animal's pleasure in singing and hearing itself sing, as well as hearing others (Stevenson 1969), to be a reinforcer, we must then ask why this pleasure does not keep the bird singing equally vigorously after a mate is attained, and also outside of the breeding season. Any reinforcer has to compete with other psychological forces. Having a mate releases impulses other than the impulse to sing, and to some extent in rivalry with it. In winter, finding food, migrating, and learning to live in a different area may inhibit any aesthetic impulse the bird has toward music. Musical human beings, too, may sing less when immediate practical needs are greater. But the singers with refined, complex songs are, as we shall see, less readily diverted or inhibited from their musical performances than those with cruder, simpler ones. I hold this to be a statistical fact (Chapters 6 and 8). It is what we should expect from the aesthetic analogy.

The territorial or utilitarian account of singing and the aesthetic account are answers to two distinct questions: "Why does evolution produce and support species that act in a certain way?" and "What is the probable inner state of the individual so acting?" An animal's capacity to growl or make other threatening noises when interfered with is useful, and so is the capacity to sing. They are the natural expressions of two different physiological-psychological states. A musician groaning from sudden great pain or snarling from strong disgust is not a musician at that moment. Neither is a subhuman singer in a similar, even though almost unimaginably more primitive, analogue to this situation. Evolution selects for several kinds of acoustical expression; that they have selective advantages in common does not do away with their emotional differences.

My basic view is Craig's (1918), that animals find their chief pleasure in their essential activities. As Kierkegaard said, birds (some birds) are creatures "who not only sing at their business, but whose business it is to sing." Growling to warn off another animal is not essentially making a certain sound. Essentially it is keeping the other animal away. The sound is incidental. The pleasure is chiefly in getting rid of a hindrance. In many cases song, too, is a warning. But animals, including birds, are not farsighted. There may be no rival near by at the moment, and no mate to appeal to. So I argue that often the singing itself must to a considerable extent be its own reward. This means that it becomes music to the animal. Perhaps this is not entirely and always untrue even of growling. But there is at least a distinction of emphasis.

It is not usefulness that contradicts the presence of aesthetic development, but the narrowness or immediacy of the useful result. The kind of utility which song has, especially in its more complex and refined forms, may be compatible with and indeed require something like an aesthetic sense in the animal. As a partial analogy, recall how it is largely useful objects, tools, that primitive peoples decorate and beautify. But in the case of song, the utility itself is enhanced and perhaps essentially constituted by the adornment.

D. Testing the Analogy

To recognize an analogy between bird song and human music is nothing new (B. Hoffman 1908; Fenis 1921; Saunders 1929: 125–31; Ingraham 1938; Herzog 1941; Craig 1943: 67–69, 144–77; Tiessen—a composer of music—1953; Thorpe 1961; and many others). But we now have new possibilities for testing the extent and validity of the analogy, the import of which is partly altered or enriched with every additional step in our exploration of bird behavior.

The scientific way to employ an analogy is to derive corollaries from it and compare these with observations. From the aesthetic analogy the following corollaries seem to follow.

(a) Bird songs will resemble human music *acoustically,* taking into account the simpler brains and other physiological features distinguishing birds from man (Chapters 2, 3). See also (e) below.

(b) There will be positive correlation between the extent of the biological *need* for singing (as shown by territoriality and other relevant behavioral-ecological variables) and the degree of development of *singing skill* (Chapters 6B, 8–11).

(c) In spite of (b) there will be a good deal of singing, especially in the more skillful singers, at times when there is *no pressing and immediate need,* most obviously in very immature birds, but also in adults (Chapters 2, 3).

(d) Birds with elaborate, refined, highly developed songs will tend to sing *more of the time,* in an hour, day, or year, than others, somewhat as intensely musical persons tend to devote more time and energy to music than less musical ones do (Chapters 6D, 8).

(e) Birds, like human musicians, will exhibit a tendency to *limit the monotony* of their singing, as compared to more purely utilitarian activities, such as walking or flying, in which motions may be reiterated immediately to an indefinite extent (Chapter 7).

(f) Birds with elaborate songs will *imitate* songs of other individuals and, at least in special circumstances (as in captivity), other species more than will those with primitive songs, showing that, like the more accomplished human musicians, their interest in sound patterns is more intense and catholic than that of musically insensitive creatures (Chapters 2D, 4).

Though the chapters mentioned are those which focus on the topics in question, they do not contain all that I have to say about them, and some supporting lines of evidence are omitted from the book. The foregoing (and still other) corollaries of the basic idea are well supported by observations, both my own and those of others. In assembling this evidence I believe that I have not indulged in unfair sampling—or neglect of unfavorable instances—to anything like the extent which would be necessary if my basic results were to be attributed to such methodological faults. I have tried to play fair with the facts and the reader, and I am confident that I have not egregiously failed in this. The failure would have to be egregious indeed to explain the theoretical outcome.

At any rate these are the issues with which this work is concerned. To establish the appropriate context for the discussion it seems necessary, in the next four chapters, to outline facts and methods which experts in the subject of animal music—and communication through sound—will find in part, but I trust not entirely, familiar. Chapter 4 and, still more, Chapters 6 and 8, move farther beyond precedent, asking questions scarcely put before and presenting factual evidence relevant to their answers. Chapter 7 is a somewhat extended and revised version of a previously published essay, which was a radical novelty in its time, and which makes a point central to the whole inquiry. Chapters 6–11 constitute an attempt to find and make use of parameters of singing by which we may be able to measure, at least in rough fashion, the extent and limitations of the aesthetic analogy between the various animals that can be said to sing.

2

Animal Music in General

❧

A. Why Animals Sing

Far more than the visual appearances of nature, the auditory aspects depend upon the actions of animals. Trees and grass, with blue sky or clouds above, and the background of plains or hills, rivers, lakes, or mountains make up the main features of visible natural landscapes. Moreover, the colors and shapes of the animals themselves are largely fixed and unalterable. By their movements they may change the locations of their bodies; but their colors and their approximate shapes are, with minor exceptions, generally outside their control.

Sounds are quite different. The voluntary production of a single sound may change the entire audible situation. Turning the head does not cut off the effect, as it does the sight of whatever one had been looking at. A few singing birds, or even insects, frogs, or toads, thus suffice to transform an auditory emptiness into a world of meaningful sounds. Above all, sound waves can be directly controlled by organs at the disposal of voluntary muscles, whereas light waves cannot be produced or altered directly and instantly through bodily movements. An animal can pass in an instant from silence to sound, from high pitch to low, from harsh noise to pure sweet tones, from loud notes to soft ones; and it can produce such changes in all sorts of different sequences or patterns. Thus sounds are fitted, as colors are not, for use in signaling rapidly, subtly, and in an infinite variety of ways. Also, whereas a mere intervening leaf or a little mist cuts off the reception of a visual signal, a sound goes through or around such obstacles, with only a slight loss in intensity.

That sound waves are peculiarly open to animal control does not, of itself, tell us to what extent this control will be exercised, by what species, and in what circumstances. First, there must be a need to communicate. The need may be to show the signaler's location (contact notes), his awareness of danger (alarm calls), or his readiness to mate (courtship songs) or defend a breeding or foraging territory (territorial song). These purposes and still others can sometimes be accomplished by visual means, provided the signaler is adequately visible to the signalee. So we come to the second obvious condition favoring the development of sound production: inconspicuousness. Singing insects, frogs or toads, and most of the land birds are small and, for various other reasons, difficult to see. As Armstrong (1963) remarks of highly vocal birds, they are weak in means of defense; moreover, he says, they tend to be palatable; hence they must be protectively colored and keep rather well hidden. Habits favoring inconspicuousness include foraging near the ground in forest where light is dim, or in open but grassy country, or on uneven or rocky ground where obstacles tend to restrict vision. Even prevailing clouds and fog may be important, and various other factors to be dealt with later. These include sexual isomorphism, making the sexes visually indistinguishable. For, although song in the full sense is by no means exclusively male, it is largely so, and it probably always serves in one way or another to distinguish the sexes, as when the male takes the initiative in avian duetting.

Note that conditions (such as ground feeding in vegetation) which make the animal depend upon sound for communication may also make it depend upon sound to betray the approach of enemies. Thus these conditions doubly favor its concentration upon acoustical indications of what other animals are doing.

A third factor in the development of sound production appears to be that the animal is unable to communicate by smell, as some butterflies and mammals do. Indeed, I think we may go further; if acoustical ability, including hearing as well as producing sounds, is to develop very far, the animal must not find its food and friends or enemies by smell to nearly the extent that most if not all land mammals other than man do. This condition is fulfilled, so far as I know, in all three classes of animal musicians. Living on vegetable matter or insects, they hunt food and avoid danger chiefly by sight, and least of all by smell. Birds actually go beyond civilized human beings in the relative importance of auditory and visual neural areas compared to the olfactory. Not long ago it was still disputed whether smell plays any role in avian life (Thorpe 1963: 344).

A dog or cat is chiefly engaged in investigating the smells in its neighborhood; but these smells do not fall into precisely controlled temporal sequences or patterns to which the animal itself can deliberately make equally patterned contributions. A dog (though it sees well) is above all a sort of chemist, unwittingly analyzing the molecular constitutions of things; but its own voluntary additions to these constitutions are crude and inartistic indeed compared even to the additions it makes to visible nature through tail-wagging and other movements. The typical Songbird, even the singing insect, on the contrary, lives primarily in a world of patterned sounds to which its own deliberate and delicately controlled contributions are substantial.

A fourth factor favoring song is that the animal's prey lacks the intelligence or adequate organs of hearing to take warning from the song. Nor can it be itself hunted by animals who would be likely to locate it by sound—unless it has always at hand a means of quick and almost effortless escape. Singing animals seem to meet these conditions rather generally. The insect or vegetable food will not take warning, and if a predator approaches, the animal is equipped to find safety with a leap into water or to another branch, or a quick flight into a bush, or simply into air. (Yet the largely nocturnal performance of amphibians and many insects suggests that without darkness to hide in their singing would be unsafe.) It would be different if rabbits were to go about singing; foxes could hunt them by ear. Or if foxes were to go about singing, rabbits could avoid them by ear.

Fifth, although sound production uses little muscular energy, it does take time, and hence if it is to be highly developed, foraging methods must be efficient so that not all the animal's waking hours go to seeking food. Some forms of animal food, such as worms, large insects, or lizards, which provide protein in sizable bits, may meet this requirement better than seeds, berries, or small insects. Flycatchers, seed-eating finches, and still other forms may forage less efficiently than thrushes, larks, wrens, shrikes, and other species living mostly on animal food and finding it on the ground. This may be part of the reason why ground-foraging favors song-development, as it very definitely seems to do (Chapters 9, 11).

Sixth, the greatest single factor favoring elaborate use of sound, at least in birds, is "territory." It is wonderful that, although a few individuals had realized this long before, the general biological community had little suspicion of it until Eliot Howard published his *Territory in Bird Life* in 1920. After that everyone had to put the idea in the center of his thinking about song. "Territory" means *spatial isolation* deliberately sought and maintained, in part at least by resisting the approach of others. Typically, a breeding pair actively discourages trespassing by a third individual of the same species and if necessary violently attacks the trespasser. But actual attack is a last resort, and the first line of defense is the territorial song. A good indication of the power of this defense was given by the English Robin (*Erithacus rubecula*) that left his territory because a caged Robin deposited in it kept singing and could not be reached to be silenced or driven away. The typical singing bird cannot endure to share his concert hall with another male of the species. As a poetic former student of mine, Carol Combs Hole, wrote, "There is a wall around the thrush and song creates his solitude."

It is important to realize that what the singer seems to dislike is not that another conspecific male is audible in the distance. The unsharable "concert hall" is not the entire area over which the animal's voice can be heard. Rather, so long as the singing neighbors keep their proper distance, there is some reason to think their audible presence is positively appreciated. In birds, though perhaps not in the more primitive types, the neighbors' songs come to be recognized individually, as is shown by the excitement produced if an individually different song is played on a tape recorder. Playing back the familiar songs is less stimulating. Also, migrating males are attracted to a region rather than deterred from it by the presence of singing conspecific individuals. This seems to be true also of insects and frogs. The question is only whether proper spacing will be available. Mere silence is not a desideratum.

Singing insects and frogs, which I believe are more or less territorial (Lanyon and Tavolga 1960: 47–48, 186ff.; Capranica 1968; Sebeok 1968: 293–96), make no effort to be out of earshot of their fellows. Normally others are well within hearing.

The most strongly territorial species live separated not only as pairs but even individually. Each feeds more or less apart. With many species this means being out of sight of each other, as well as of neighboring pairs, much of the time. This greatly increases the need for nonvisual communication. Thus complete absence of gregariousness is a factor favoring sound production. Bulbuls (Pycnonotidae) are more or less territorial, but in some species at least are very "chummy" by pairs, and this may be one reason why their songs are mostly not highly developed. The same seems to be true of the Common Indian Myna (*Acridotheres tristis*) as I observed it in Hawaii.

An important effect of separation is that if signals are to be interpreted from a distance they must be more distinctive than if they can take effect near by. Within a few meters only a few individuals and species will be present; with a much larger distance the number will increase as the square, or almost as the cube, of the distance, at least in a forest of tall trees where the third dimension counts heavily. Thus the listener to distant sounds has a much harder task of identification, whether of individuals or of species. And he will have much less frequent glimpses of the signaler to help him out. Joan Hall-Craggs has brilliantly shown how the need to signal to distant listeners has probably been important in the origins of human as well as avian music (Hinde, 1969: 367–81).

The necessity to be heard afar favors song-development also because it increases the need for low-pitched sounds, which are effective over greater distances (Ficken and Ficken 1962: 112; Oring, 1968: 398, 416). Not only do these lower sounds seem more satisfying to the human ear but they also mean greater musical possibilities for the bird, since ability to produce deep tones is, within wide limits, compatible with ability to produce shrill ones as well. Birds compelled to employ the former are likely to make some use of the latter in addition, thus achieving greater musical contrasts. From this point of view, dense growth has some of the effect of distance, as the deeper sounds are less damped by obstructions. Tropical wrens, living in dense thickets, tend to have amazingly low-pitched voices (in comparison, say, with the Winter Wren [*Troglodytes t. hiemalis*], not to mention many wood warblers). But these wrens also have rather wide pitch ranges. Dense growth has the effect of distance in another way, by decreasing visibility.

B. Songs and "Calls"

Let us consider more carefully the distinction touched on above between acoustical signaling in general and "song." Nearly all higher animals make noises, but only some make music, or in the normal sense sing. In spite of many borderline cases, the distinction is significant, especially in the higher types of birds.

First, animal music sounds to the human ear like music. Even insect songs, or those of frogs and toads, seem at least slightly musical. The word "beauty," as well as the word "song," occurs in works dealing with these utterances. And there is objective reason for this. The basic elements of music are rhythm, tones (pitch-definite sounds) as contrasted to noises, harmony, and melody. Insect songs are extremely simple but clear-cut cases of rhythm, and in some frogs there seem to be also the barest beginnings of melody. But snarls, growls, whines, meows, squeals, grunts, chirps, and squeaks are, by comparison, non-musical, i.e., noisy and with little complexity and organization, even rhythmical. Most birds, including many of the famous singers, have some quite unmusical call notes, for example, the harsh "scold" of the Mockingbird (*Mimus polyglottos*), or the "croak" of the Nightingale (*Erithacus megarhynchos*). These sounds are short, almost patternless, and the opposite of pure tones. (Students of some insects and frogs note a somewhat similar difference.)

Second, the less musical calls are used in a different way. They are tied much more directly to the immediately practical. The growl or snarl shows anger or hostility, occasioned by the momentary situation. (Cf. Stadler 1929: 347.) The other animal threatens to attack or to snatch away food. When the meat is eaten or the other animal departs the growl or scold ceases.

By contrast, insects or frogs may sing nearly all night, and birds nearly all day. This is a different kind of activity. Also, young birds "practice" or play at singing for many minutes at a time, as kittens play at fighting. They are not defending territory or seeking a mate; they are just singing. But they do not play at making alarm notes (although alarm notes are incorporated into some birds' subsongs). And puppies or kittens do not play at growling (unless as part of play-fighting). Song does not exhibit a narrowly defined or violent emotional state, but may express almost the animal's whole life for hours or weeks at a time. True, the song will warn territorial rivals, if they exist, but it is absurd to infer from the hours of daily morning singing that the animal awakens in a rage and begins each day with a long bout of passionate hostility. Moreover, song is concerned with at least a potential mate. There is no rage against her. It is chiefly the instinct or habit of the rival which makes the song a warning, and the instinct or habit of the mate which makes it an invitation or reassurance. In itself it is none of these. The song conveys no single crude emotion, but —especially in highly developed styles of singing—something like what life is to that bird at that season.

Song thus serves its functions in a different way from "scolds" or growls. The growl conveys momentary anger, and to others this means danger. In another way, a cry of alarm communicates a sense of danger. The presence of danger is what matters to the hearers. Sex, individuality, even species, are here more or less secondary. Danger is rather nonspecific. (On alarm and distress sounds see Boudreau 1968.) But with song it is the identity and seasonal condition or situation (e.g., lack of a mate) of the singer that is conveyed: its species, sex, breeding state, perhaps individuality, territoriality. Blanchard (1941: 21) found more than six ways in which songs of White-crowned Sparrows (*Zonotrichia leucophrys*) were used. "Song," as Armstrong (1963) says so well, is normally "the most complex and informative of a bird's utterances." It must stand apart, not only from sounds made by other species, but from sounds made by the same species at other times of year or in a different phase of the breeding cycle or by the opposite sex. And it must be a rewarding activity for long periods when nothing much is happening of interest to the bird. This implies highly differentiated, appealing, and memorable patterns. What else is music?

Recently, lying in bed, I listened to a frog (*Rana pipiens?*) making a sound like "crouch, crouch" at intervals. I counted the seconds between utterances (by saying "a hundred and one, a hundred and two," etc.) and found the pauses to be of roughly comparable lengths, about ten seconds. On later nights it turned out that shorter or much longer pauses obtained at times. I also found that the number of "crouches" in each stanza varied from one to four, with two and three most common. This "number juggling" is precisely what many birds (e.g., Carolina Wren, *Thryothorus ludovicianus*, and Tufted Titmouse, *Parus bicolor*) and a few insects (e.g., Katydids, *Pseudophyllinae*) do in their singing. The birds, as we shall see, can "count" a bit higher, but the avoidance of rigid numerical repetition in an otherwise highly-repetitive song is the same. If singing is sustained, but not rigidly monotonous, sound production, the frog was singing. It was doing something rather different from giving vent to a momentary spasm of fear, anger, or desire. True, there was the barest minimum of "musical" quality, but a beginning of rhythmical patterning was unmistakable.

The difference between song and other utterances is not absolute, nor is the distinction always fruitfully applicable, but, taking the phenomena in the large, it is a valid and important distinction, and very often the application is quite clear. There are aspects of animal life and of evolution that we shall not understand if we ignore this distinction. Ornithologists who avoid "song" by using "call" for every sound are conveying less information than those who try to distinguish song from other utterances. They may also convey less misinformation, but not necessarily. It might be quite puzzling the first time one heard a Hermit Thrush (*Catharus* [*Hylocichla*] *guttatus*) sing, if one had been told only that it had a distinctive "call." In learning a new set of birds, it helps considerably to know what highly musical songs are to be expected, and which are simple, which complex, etc.

There is perhaps some ritualistic number juggling in the calmer *pro forma* barking of dogs, in comparison to their snarling or growling when really angry or yelping when hurt. Howling is again closer to song, not only rhythmically but in its approach to tonelike sounds. The howling of wolves seems essentially song, both in sound and in function. It has no single narrow immediate emotional-practical meaning, but rather expresses the sense of rapport of the often widely dispersed pack and the individual's identity in that pack. It is communicative over great distances, as barking or snarling are not, and has territorial aspects. It spans well over two octaves (perhaps only one for an individual). The slow pace and upward, still more downward, slurs give it overall unity. It is sad that this fine music is gone from nearly all the original range of the animal and seems destined to disappear from what remains of it.

C. Singing Ability and Size

Small size favors song-development in two ways: It diminishes visibility and recognizability at a distance; and it increases the number of species to be distinguished from one another, since a given area can support many more small than large creatures (and this holds whether we count species or individuals). A large species is likely to sound different from a small one, no matter what each does with its voice, because of the lower pitch that larger organs tend to produce; but when many species of similar small size are to be discriminated, mere chirps, squeaks, or shrieks are not enough. There would be mere confusion, as there often is in bird houses.

Puzzlingly enough, in certain respects large size (within limits) also may favor song. For one thing, the size of the necessary foraging territory is increased. It also makes lower pitches and, in principle, greater pitch ranges possible, thus enhancing musical and imitative potentialities. In any case highly developed song does appear in some rather large birds, and seems to be proportionately most common in birds of medium size. (See Chapters 9–11.)

Greenewalt's denial (1968: 34) that pitch correlates "consistently" with size is perhaps true according to a reasonable interpretation of "consistently." But it might easily mislead. Thus, take his own list (p. 145) of 21 frequencies from 19 birds of widely varying types and sizes: The five lowest frequencies, averaging 240 c/s, are from species averaging 20 inches in length; the five highest, averaging 3 octaves higher, are from species averaging less than 6 inches! The eleven intermediate frequencies are from birds averaging 11 inches. Thus there is a definite correlation. Also the "Mourning Dove, several small owls, or the Brown-headed Cowbird," which Greenewalt cites as small birds with deep voices, are really medium-sized, as most species go. (See below, Chapter 10C.) Moreover, if small owls have deeper voices than some larger birds, large owls (except the Barn Owl, *Tyto alba*, "which does not hoot"—i.e., sing) have still deeper ones. Owls, like nearly all genuinely singing birds, tend to take advantage of the possibilities for low pitch which their size affords them. Hawks and eagles, with shrill voices for their size, are scarcely singers.

Small toads and frogs have higher pitches than large ones, small dogs than large, spider monkeys than Howlers. The deepest animal sounds I know come from a large hornbill, Emus, hogs, wolves, hippopotamuses, and lions. Coyotes (*Canis latrans*) have higher voices than the larger wolves. The trumpeting of an elephant may not be low-pitched, but I dare say (see Huxley 1964: 54) that it is not high compared to the squeaking of mice and the like.

There is a good reason, in addition to any anatomical ones, for large singers to have low pitches. With larger territories, they need lower-pitched voices, since, as we have seen, these carry the farthest. The

lowest-pitched wood warbler voice is probably that of the Yellow-
breasted Chat (*Icteria virens*), and it is the largest. Swainson's Warbler (*Limnothlypis swainsonii*), down in dense cover (which makes
the territory large from the standpoint of auditory communication),
also has a low voice and is larger than most in this family. Similarly
with the waterthrushes (*Seiurus* spp.) and the Ovenbird (*Seiurus
aurocapillus*). Is it possible that these species are larger partly because
they need deeper voices? The largest North American sparrow, *Pas-
serella iliaca*, Fox Sparrow, has about the deepest voice and lives down
in dense cover. One of the largest of the true larks, the Bifasciated
(*Alaemon alaudipes*), probably has as deep a voice as any; true, the
territory is extremely open and barren, but for that very reason it presumably must be large. The Calandra Lark (*Melanocorypha calandra*)
is large, with a deep voice and arid habitat. About the highest voiced
of our sparrows are those that live in open grassland and are extra
small: LeConte's, Henslow's, and Grasshopper (*Passerherbulus caudacutus, P. henslowii, Ammodramus savannarum*). Their territories are
moist and probably small.

D. Song and Imitation

An important feature of song is the extent to which it is learned.
Mere call notes or cries are more largely innate, and are not imitated
(yet see Lanyon 1960: 327–29; Hinde 1966: 333), except by other
(highly imitative) species as portions of their own song, when they do
not serve their functions as mere calls. It has yet to be shown that a
cat has copied the meow of another cat. But several species of singing
insects have been induced to change their rhythm in response to an
eccentric song produced for their benefit. (See, e.g., Peirce 1949: 188.)
(Even synchronizing fireflies [Lampyridae]—see Zahl 1971: 46, 50—
altered their rhythms when given distorted copies of them.) A subsequent investigator, perhaps unaware of the work with insects, put
grasshoppers (Orthoptera) of diverse species together, expecting to
prove that hearing the alien songs would have no influence upon the
way in which each species sang. On the contrary, at least ten species
imitated the singing of other species (Broughton 1965a, b). It remains
to be seen if batrachians can be induced to alter their songs. Patient
cultivation of the animal's interest and confidence is probably the pre-

condition, as we know from parrots and insects, and human infants learning to speak.

In addition, singing insects frequently sing in chorus, synchronously, and this too is a sort of imitation (Alexander 1960: 82–87). Howling wolves (*Canis lupus*) do something of the sort. Growling, whining, or scolding are not done in synchronized chorus; they are not voluntary enough for that.

A few cases are known of mammals below the primate level learning to reproduce sounds. A pet fox (*Vulpes* sp.) learned from his owner to hum something like scales (Schmid 1937: 138–40—orally confirmed to me by Konrad Lorenz); and a Boston Bulldog in Utah learned to pronounce 20 words (reported in *The Chicago Sun-Times* Sunday Magazine, 30 August 1953—confirmed in a letter to me from W. H. Perkins, professor of speech at the University of Southern California, who made a recording of the dog's utterances). Professor Perkins has heard of two other individuals of the same breed of dog "talking"; in all three cases, as also (in his opinion) in that of birds who have learned to utter words, the animal has been made "far more dependent on its master for its affectional needs than is normally the case with domesticated animals." But these rare mammalian cases— and to my mind their rarity is harder to believe than their occurrence —are to be set against a virtual infinity of avian and human auditory imitations.

Some students of the tiger (*Panthera* spp.) (Perry 1964) think that this animal imitates the calls of species of deer (different in different regions) on which it preys. However, according to Schaller (1967: 256–57) and Lewis (1940) this is a mistake.

It is significant that the only group of apes which have repeatedly impressed observers as somewhat musical, the gibbons (Huxley 1964: 59; Boulenger 1936: 94; Benchley 1942: 8–9, 18, 23–24, 30–31), also furnish the only reported case among the nonhuman primates of spontaneous vocal imitations: that of a Siamang (*Symphalangus syndactylus*), which, according to Mott, copied the barks of a dog and the squeaks of a Guinea Pig (*Cavia porcellus*) (Yerkes and Yerkes 1929: 74; Mott 1924: 1168). But all efforts to induce Chimpanzees (*Pan troglodytes*) and an Orangutan (*Pongo pygmaeus*) to imitate sounds have had meager or doubtful results (Yerkes and Yerkes 1929: 164–65, 305, 307). Chimpanzees are said to be much less voluntary in their vocalizations than in their gestures. They make various sounds, but usually involuntarily and in moments of excitement. In their calmer moments they are silent. Their deliberate activities are visually, not acoustically, guided. (Yet see Sanderson 1957: 158.)

Most apes can communicate by gestures (Yerkes and Yerkes 1929: 308–309) with much greater ease than by sound because of their plastic bodily and facial forms and their greater visibility to one another, resulting from their size and their tendency to live gregariously. The relative smallness of the gibbons and the density of their forest habitats must have favored their auditory concentration (Meyer-Holzapfel 1950; 1956: 447). Carpenter (1940: 172) speaks of the impossibility of seeing them in the forest. On the other hand, even the highly vocal Howler Monkeys (*Alouatta* spp.) seem to live in a world of gestures far more than songbirds could (Carpenter 1934: 82–89, 105–107). It is true that these monkeys defend group territories against other groups, which they often cannot see, but the territories are large, and the emphasis must be upon volume rather than fine distinctions of sound pattern. Their "howls" are very low-pitched and this alone distinguishes them from nearly all the bird sounds. And there are no roaring lions in their forests.

Gibbons (*Hylobates* spp., *Symphalangus syndactylus*) are "purely territorial" and, like most Songbirds, associate in monogamous families rather than tribes. They can be heard "literally for miles." However, like the Howlers, they do not have the same need for elaborate distinctive patterns that birds do.

Even the assumption that the larger apes have the proper bony-muscular structure for making speechlike sounds has recently been challenged by competent experts. The vain attempt to teach Chimpanzees to talk was recently followed by the more promising project to teach them a gesture language, enlarging upon their own natural system of significant gestures (Gardner and Gardner 1969). At almost the same time, in what promises to be an epoch-making experiment, a seven-year-old Chimpanzee at the University of California at Santa Barbara has learned, it is claimed, to understand 130 visual symbols and even something like sentences constructed with them (Premack 1970a, b; Calder 1970: 203–208). The considerable success of these efforts, compared to the failure of the other, well illustrates the difference between animals that favor visible and those that favor audible means of communication. Some birds fall more into one class, the rest, perhaps a majority, into the other. It has been said, perhaps with some exaggeration, that pigeons (Columbidae) behave similarly to Chimpanzees in that they produce involuntary sounds when they are excited but are normally silent. Thus sound with them has narrowly defined, instinctive emotional meanings. Song, and also "chatter" (Chapter 4), is something else. The more specialized for singing birds are the more their making sounds is deliberate and intentional, so far as they are capable of acting intentionally at all. One sign of this ability is their imitation of sounds. Those great imitators, the parrots (Psittacidae) (Chapters 4, 11), are not, with perhaps a few exceptions, to be termed singers. Still, the two great groups of known sound copiers are the singing birds and, to a vastly smaller degree, the singing insects. And I am inclined to believe that all singers have at least some slight tendency to imitate.

E. Male and Female Singing

Song is primarily a male activity. In insects the "male calling songs" are louder, more distinctive, more rhythmical, more complex, and continued longer than other insect sounds (Alexander 1960: 60). This is attributed to the great distances over which they must carry (we have seen how distance magnifies the need for distinctiveness) and to the fact that they are the initial link between adult males and females. With creatures as hard to see as insects this must be so. In some insect species females take part in sound production, and a clear case of duetting has been observed (Alexander 1960: 51–52). In birds there are hundreds, perhaps nearly a thousand, of such cases. They are mostly tropical, but a Palearctic example, noted by Stadler (1929: 348), is the Wryneck (*Jynx torquilla*). Curiously, some fireflies practice visual duetting (Evans 1968: 42)! This is one of the few cases in which light is controlled almost as directly and immediately as sound can be. Even so there is but one "pitch"; there is rhythm, but not melody. And the rhythm is less definite and sharp than in songs.

With the virtually complete lack of family life in insects and amphibians it is inevitable that duetting should not be a prominent feature with them. It also seems natural that territory should be less prominent, since their territories are in any case small, and indeed the distance function is here more one of attracting than of repelling. Mates must be attracted from a distance, but territorial rivals need be warned only from near by, and in many cases they can see as well as hear. In these animals also it is initially almost as important to attract males as females, since an aggregation of males singing more or less synchronously is a much more powerful sexual attraction than a lone male. Also, males may stimulate each other in this way, as happens in many birds.

F. Song and Visual Display

It has been said that visual display has an equal right with song to be considered a subhuman approach to human aesthetic attitudes, and that hence, if we distinguish "song" as more or less beautiful animal sounds, we should invent a word for beautiful visual display. I grant that, for example, the courtship antics of American manakins (Pipridae) are something like a visual analogue of song. Dance and music are in fact the two aesthetic arts which the lower animals most definitely anticipate. (Should we add architecture—nests, bower birds' bowers?) Music, however, seems more pervasive and highly developed. Since the dancing is viewed from nearby, it is usually not needed to identify the species out of many, and hence no such array of distinctive patterns is likely to result. (For an encyclopedic survey of display see Armstrong 1965. Also Andrew 1961 for a penetrating analysis of what was then known about the functions and presumptive origins of calls and songs in Oscines.)

It is clear from the functional standpoint that the more effective an animal's visual display is the less need there is for song. It used to be said that nature distributed her favors fairly, giving the visually undistinguished species beautiful song and the musically ungifted visual beauty. In terms of evolutionary theory this becomes a partial truth, somewhat oddly put. Visual and auditory conspicuousness or distinctiveness are, in general, negatively correlated. A qualification is that many species, e.g., California Brown Towhees (*Pipilo fuscus crissalis*), have neither striking visual nor auditory distinctiveness. However, there are then special features in the life style of the species which make it as conspicuous and distinctive as it needs to be—for example, foraging in the open in rather bare country, or the mated pair keeping rather close together. Also a few species that sing well are richly colored, e.g., Cardinals (*Pyrrhuloxia* [*Richmondena*] *cardinalis*), but they tend to keep rather well hidden in vegetation, especially apart from the effects of human actions, such as clearing out underbrush, cutting grass, or putting up feeders.

G. Nonvocal Song

We have not, so far, made any distinction between avian (or human) songs of the usual "vocal" kind and utterances produced by other than vocal means (e.g., the wings) which in some species function as songs. Though a Ruffed Grouse (*Bonasa umbellus*) on a log or a lark in the air (e.g., the Flappet Lark, *Mirafra rufocinnamomea*) or a woodpecker tapping on wood or on a metal gutter may seem more like a person beating a drum or some other percussion instrument than a person singing, I think the more significant analogy runs the other way. For the human being is using a tool constructed for the very purpose, while the bird is using built-in organic means, plus perhaps some feature of the environment which may be selected, but not constructed, for this purpose. I take "song" in the broadest sense to be the production of music by organic rather than truly instrumental means. Hence Orthoptera can be said to sing ("stridulate" if you insist) though the musical quality is minimal. Hence, also, birds and people sing, even though in the one case with syrinxes, in the other with vocal cords.

Whether or not wing music, or woodpecker tapping, or bill rattling, besides being deliberate and a form of signaling, is ever imitative seems not to be known. I assume this to be probable, as in my opinion should be assumed with all song. Kilham (1959) reports two woodpeckers drumming together in a duet. This is perhaps not far from imitation.

H. Song and Geologic Time: Insects, Fish, and Amphibians

Presumably the oldest forms of anything resembling music on this planet are produced by the insects and the amphibians. The former in general cannot accurately, if at all, discriminate pitches, but they sense amplitude changes and have unmistakable rhythm, which is enough to constitute a kind of music, as in human drumming. The temporal span of the patterns is often very short, even as compared to birds;

however, in some cicadas there are songs lasting about thirty seconds, or even ninety. These cases perhaps do not upset the rule; for in them the patterns are somewhat indefinite. There may be a vague division into two or three parts, say a soft beginning, a loud climax, and a diminuendo ending, or a first part with one indefinitely repeated phrase and a second part with a different repeated phrase, but otherwise no determinate overall pattern.

Fish have something like song (Tavolga 1966), but it appears to be confined to a few species and to be extremely primitive, with little or no use of pitch contrast, and to be slight or crude even in its rhythmical patterns.

Amphibians seem to have the beginnings of pitch and hence of melody, though I do not know if they have been tested for pitch discrimination. They do have suitable ears for it. Among the reptiles, some of the larger geckos (Gekkonidae) one of which I heard on Mount Makiling, Luzon, have definite patterns, though their voices are crude in the extreme. No cold-blooded animal can compare with birds as musicians.

I. Marine Mammals (Cetacea)

To judge from the few dolphin (*Delphinus* spp.) utterances I have heard, dolphins are not musical. Perhaps too few other comparable animal sounds are heard with them for the pressure toward distinctiveness and elaborate patterns to operate. However, though porpoises (*Phocaena* spp.) and dolphins are perhaps not singers, they may come under the classification of social chatterers (at least the Harbor Porpoise, *Phocaena phocaena*), since they sometimes herd together in groups containing scores of members. This suggests that they probably imitate to some extent, and there seems to be some evidence for this.

Recent recordings of "song" by the Humpback Whale (*Megaptera novaeangliae*) suggest that the larger Cetacea present a somewhat different problem. This singing, according to an advertisement of the book and recordings by Robert Payne and Frank Watlington (1970; see also Payne and McVay 1971), has been called "the most beautiful" of natural sounds. As a test of what we know about the conditions of animal musicality I wrote the following paragraphs while awaiting the receipt of the ordered book and records:

Whales are among the most auditory of all animals (Kleinenberg et al. 1969: 284–87; Kellogg 1961: 88; Slijper 1962:
223). They lack a developed sense of smell in the usual
sense, though they probably have some sort of chemorecep-
tors (Kleinenberg: 182, 287). The medium in which they
live severely restricts the distance they can see, but that
same medium, which is a far better conductor of vibrations
than air, enables them to hear at great distances. Their hearing is superb and they use sonar, but they are also sensitive
to very low frequencies, which travel farther than high
pitches.

Whales' brains, though not large in proportion to their
size, are large as brains go, and the auditory area is ample.
Because of the size of these creatures they may need considerable foraging and breeding space around them, and this
may have an effect upon musical development similar to that
of territory in some other types of animals. Whales have
parental as well as mating needs which doubtless require
signaling at considerable distances. Whether or not they imitate sounds is one of the significant questions. Lilly (1962)
claims to have observed such imitation in dolphins (*Tur-
siops truncatus*), and though his evidence is scarcely defini-
tive I incline to accept it as having some truth. Skepticism
on this point by Wood (see Alpers 1961: 101) may possibly
arise from the fact that Wood and his associates did not
have the same intimacy of relationship with their animals as
Lilly and his wife had, and we know from parrots and other
birds that this is sometimes crucial. That large size is not, as
such, hostile to song is suggested by evidence to be given in
Chapter 10. Only its connection with invisibility, or with
territoriality, seems to associate smallness with song. Whales
may be sufficiently invisible and spaced out to be in this
sense small enough for developed song. So I am not pre-
pared to reject Payne's claim in advance.

After receiving and studying the Payne recordings and accompanying spectrograms I wrote as follows:

The Humpback Whale songs—they seem surely songs—
in one respect at least surpass by a whole order of magni-

tude all other known subhuman utterances. Scientists who have studied the spectrograms agree that these animals utter contrasting "themes" in a definite sequence individual to the particular animal and lasting six or more minutes. This is quite beyond the brain of a bird, and it does not appear that gibbons do anything like it. The themes consist of phrases repeated an indefinite number of times, and thus they are variable in length, and with them the entire song, which may occupy as much as thirty minutes. Thus, though the order of themes is fixed, the performance is far from mechanical.

The voice of this animal varies over a wide range of pitches. Sometimes it is flute- or soprano-like, sometimes like a basso profundo, but also like a cow mooing, or again like a violin or cello, rather out of tune. There are no bell-like (clear yet staccato) sounds; rather the notes are prevailingly prolonged and slurred. Perhaps the medium of water is partly responsible for this. Many of the sounds have a grunting or wailing quality that is not to everyone's taste. Some are bird-like, high pure whistles.

Thomas Poulter has most kindly sent me a number of recordings of marine animals, including the Humpback Whale and the Gray Whale (which seems to signal but not to sing), and also a fine tape of the Siamang (gibbons). A tape of the Bearded Seal (*Erignathus barbatus*) shows that this animal, too, has a patterned utterance which also is clearly a piece of music, again with persistent use of slurred sounds, and a general tendency downward in pitch. Like most avian singers, the Bearded Seal is nongregarious. The song reminds one of the Potoo's much admired utterance (*Nyctibius griseus*, see Chapter 11); but it is much longer. Another of Poulter's marine recordings reminds me of a vireo's song, e.g., *Vireo solitarius*. However, none of these other animals have anything like the Humpback's majestic expanse of song pattern; in this respect the Humpback may be far closer to man as musician than is anything else on this planet. Like the most imitative birds (and I have little doubt that this whale imitates), it does not limit itself to the musically exquisite, as the Olive Whistler (*Pachycephala olivacea macphersoniana*) or the Hermit Thrush do, but works various sorts of acoustical gestures into a sufficiently (but not exquisitely) organized sequence.

We are told that the long sequence is begun again with almost no pause, thus seemingly violating my anti-monotony principle (Chapter 7). However, a lapse of 6+ minutes between a given element of the sequence and its rendering in the next round is a long time. We shall meet a somewhat analogous problem with birds having unusually long songs. Moreover, as indicated above, the reiteration of the whole sequence is only approximate. This is a much looser, less precise pattern than a single bird song lasting a few seconds. Monotony, in the sense in which some birds (mostly with primitive singing organs) exhibit it, is a very different thing. Without instruments even a man can hardly know that the whale is repeating his sequence, so how should a more limited brain be troubled by this repetitiveness? Payne is to be applauded for his efforts, perhaps not too late, to save this magnificent animal from extinction.

J. Singing and Brain Development

For singing to develop very far, not only must there be specialized organs for producing and hearing sound but brain development also must be adequate. Compared to birds, insects and frogs have only crude equipment for making sounds, and their capacity to grasp complex sound patterns must be far less. Only with birds and mammals are the basic resources of music opened up. A bird can copy a short human tune quite correctly, and human beings can derive considerable pleasure from whistling the more tuneful bird songs.

We know that birds have a capacity for grasping complex patterns far beyond that of their insect, reptilian, and batrachian "competitors." The most sophisticated tests of intelligence, behavioral "plasticity," ability to deal with novel situations, make numerical distinctions, apply principles to cases, or what you will, have repeatedly shown birds to compare rather well with some mammals. The bird brain functions so differently from the mammalian that simple comparisons of cortex development are misleading. (See Thorpe 1963: 336.) Perhaps bird migration and complex family life should have warned us of this. The fact is that, apart from the Cetacea, *birds are by far the closest of all creatures to man in their interest in sound patterns and skill in their production.* Not even the larger apes can compare in this respect! Chimpanzees have become abstract painters of sorts, but not musicians and not speakers of words. A great gulf yawns here. Only birds (not all birds, but many) are our companions in the sense for melodious sounds, and in the feeling that life touches life chiefly through organic means of sound production.

K. Summary

(A.) Sound, the stimulus most subject to animal control, is uniquely adapted to animal communication, especially communication from a distance, to meet the requirements of mating, territorial nesting and feeding, reception of warnings, or maintaining contact with other members of a flock. Skill in sound production tends to correlate with inconspicuousness (depending upon size, coloration, habits, and habitat), unavailability of smell as a signal, territoriality or wide spacing of pairs or individuals.

(B.) Song is the most informative or distinctive, complex, and sustained mode of sound production, and tends to be more akin to human music than mere alarm cries and the like. Its function is also different, less closely related to momentary emotional attitudes, such as fear or rage, and hence more favorable to the presence of aesthetic pleasure in the sounds and in sound production.

(C.) Small size favors song by decreasing visibility and increasing the number of individuals and species which must distinguish themselves in an area; but large size may favor it by increasing pitch range and the extent of territories, and possibly by furnishing brain capacity necessary for the most complex types of singing.

(D.) Song is more subject to learning, partly by imitation, than mere cries. By this criterion even insects have been, and frogs perhaps could be, shown to sing. In a few cases mammals other than man— including dogs, a fox, and a gibbon ape—have been known to imitate sounds. Most apes are practically without this capacity.

(E.) Song is primarily male, but regular female singing by birds (and gibbon apes) is common in the tropics. Fireflies have visual duets.

(F.) Song, as it tends to take on aesthetic characteristics, is analogous to visual display, including primitive antecedents of dancing, but it is more highly developed, in part because the communication is over greater distances.

(G.) Nonvocal song occurs in some species.

(H.) Song began on the earth in insects and amphibians, but reached its peak of development (in land animals other than man) in birds, who alone of the large groups have adequate sense organs, brains, and habits to make them even remote competitors with man as musicians.

(I.) However, certain whales in some respects surpass the birds in sound production.

(J.) Song development depends partly upon brain capacity.

CHAPTER

3

Bird Song Compared
to Human Music

They [birds] are the true masters.
—Dvořák

❧

A. Birds as Primitive Musicians

A great naturalist once guided me to a spot where we could hear a pair of Black-throated Wrens (*Thryothorus atrogularis*) of restricted geographical range whose lovely song duet few seem to have commented upon. As we left the spot, having heard two neighboring pairs sing animated musical duets, he addressed the birds, saying, "Thank you for the concert." Then he muttered, "Those who say bird song is not music are fools of the first water." A fairer judgment might be that such persons are either not well acquainted with bird songs or have not learned to distinguish between objective and subjective factors in aesthetic matters or between primitive, largely instinctive, and sophisticated forms of music.

Music, objectively regarded, is to be characterized in two ways, according as we take into account only the patterns of sound that are produced or also the behavior-setting of this production (Herzog 1941). Let us first consider the sounds alone, and taken singly. Birds utter both "noises" and musical "tones," and it is the latter which are more conspicuous in their songs, especially the more "melodious" songs. The tones can be as pure as in human music, though often they are between noises and tones. There are flute-like, truly chime- or bell-like, violin- or guitar-like, even organ-like, tones to be heard from birds. Some are almost as tender as a boy soprano, e.g., those of nightingale-thrushes (*Catharus* spp.) or the Olive Whistler of southern Queensland.

It may be that statistically birds use noises more and tones less in their singing than man does. Another relative difference is that avian singers, being mostly rather small, favor high pitches, which often sound thin and rather unsatisfying to man. However, there is some evidence that small Songbirds, singing in this way, have slightly higher upper limits of hearing (Schwarzkopf 1955), so that what to us are shrill sounds may be more "mellow" to the birds. This is supported by the fact that in general birds sing mostly near the middle of their pitch ranges, the lower limits of which are often much higher than in man.

Birds tend to use very brief sounds and may crowd several times as many distinct notes into a second of singing as a human singer can. Here, too, the biological significance of the difference is uncertain, since we have every reason to think that birds live at a faster tempo altogether than man does, and have a far higher, perhaps ten times as high (Thorpe 1961: 125), or even higher (Greenewalt 1968: 142), temporal resolving power for sounds. Thus what are excessively brief and hence insignificant elements of auditory experience for us need not be so for birds. The markedly higher temperatures, the faster heartbeat and other reactions, and perhaps the shorter and simpler neural paths point to the same conclusion. Thus in both pitch and tempo, especially the latter, we are more likely to under- than overestimate avian music.

In both respects also there are numerous exceptions to the stated differences between birds and man. I cannot think of any human music with a slower pace than that of the Varied Thrush (*Zoothera naevius*) of the Pacific coast of North America. One race (or species?) of the Nightingale Wren (*Microcerculus marginatus*) sings one note every 3–4 or more seconds (Chapter 7C). And as to pitch, many birds, for example, the Bifasciated Lark, have what is for us a comfortable pitch range.

Another only partly true statement about avian song is that bird notes tend to be slurred (as shown by slanting lines in audiospectrograms), sliding continuously up or down. However, many are not slurred appreciably. In one case Borror and Halafoff (1969) showed that an apparent slur in the singing of the Townsend's Solitaire

(*Myadestes townsendi*) is really a "glissando," a descending series of very brief notes. With birds' faster tempo this may often be true. But some bird notes seem well sustained on one pitch, e.g., the opening notes (½ second) of most Hermit Thrush patterns and most notes in the singing of the Andean Solitaire (*Myadestes ralloides*) and of the Desert or Bifasciated Lark. The Pileated Tinamou (*Crypturellus soui*) has some unslurred notes a second and a half in duration. Some human music, especially in Turkey and the Near East generally, favors slurs and quavers.

It is suspected that birds react somewhat to features of sound waves (besides those of frequency and amplitude) to which human response is limited. However, this difference between us and birds cannot be very great, because, for physical reasons, sensitivity to the aspects of sound waves which we cannot experience conflicts in principle with sensitivity to small pitch differences, and we know that birds discriminate pitches very well (Thorpe 1961: 127). Here, too, we are not hopelessly ill equipped to appreciate bird song.

Now we turn to the order or pattern of the sounds. "Order is the vast realm lying between the deadly extremes of chaos and mechanization" (Sachs 1953). This dictum of a great musicologist applies to bird song. Very few songs even tempt one to think of them as mere random handfuls of notes, and equally few seem wholly mechanical in their regularity. (See Chapter 7.)

Let us take the least favorable examples, a monotonic song, or a mere trill (the alternation of two notes over and over). This comes very close to mechanism; however, in such songs the length (the number of repetitions) is not fixed. The bird seems to exercise no freedom as to which notes to sing next, but it has options as to the number of repetitions to include in a given rendition of the song.

I accept Sachs's hint that aesthetic value requires an element of "chaos" or randomness. (See also Meyer 1956: 96, 195, 200). The fact is that randomness, quite as much as law, is a key operative concept in all our knowledge, from quantum mechanics and Mendel's laws to the aesthetic principle of the value of surprise and novelty. The bird songs which most of us rate highest are, among other things, those in which the aspect of unpredictability—at least apparent chance—is pronounced. If the bird has a repertoire of phrases or songs, you cannot tell at a given moment which one will be rendered next, and the larger the repertoire the greater the uncertainty. Thus a Wood Thrush (*Hy-*

locichla [*Turdus*] *mustelina*) has, say, nine songs, which can follow one another in 72 binary combinations such as AB, BA, EF, CF, etc. Two songs are sung within the timespan which the bird grasps as a whole, the proof being that, whereas by mere chance it would, one time in nine, sing the same song twice in succession (AA or BB or CC . . .), I estimate that this happens less often than once in a hundred times, perhaps a thousand. Thus the bird itself is experiencing scores of different contrast effects in the course of a few minutes' singing. Yet all the phrases are musically related and are in some appreciable sense similar. The European Song Thrush (*Turdus philomelos*) has a larger repertoire, also sung in something like random order, although there is a rather marked tendency to sing the same phrases two or three times in succession. Here the phrases are more varied, but less melodic. This is a looser form of music, less pure and concentrated, though freer and farther from possible monotony for our ears. It seems that the bird brain can achieve only a few musical effects, and a gain in one direction is likely to be paid for by a loss in another.

In some species the only element of freedom is in the number of repetitions of a note or phrase, or in the length of pauses between songs. Usually, there is something else to mitigate any impression of a mere mechanism. The Carolina Wren has many songs, each consisting of a different phrase exactly repeated a number of times. However, the song may begin or end unpredictably in the middle of a phrase, thus: kettle, teakettle, teakettle, teakettle; or, teakettle, teakettle, teakettle, tea. Moreover, although each song is usually sung a good many times before another song is introduced, the number of repetitions of the phrase on which the song is based varies about once in five times, being decreased or increased by one, thus: 33343323333343332. In this way the bird seems, from time to time, to make fresh decisions not dictated by the song pattern. There is experimental evidence (Hassman 1952, Koehler 1953, Lögler 1959, Thorpe 1963: 423, 1966b) that birds can count, i.e., distinguish between 2, 3, 4, 5, 6, sometimes even 7 successive sounds.

The evolution of bird song toward music can be seen in part as a progress from extremely limited types of free variety, within a broad unity of pattern, to cases in which the blend of randomness and predictability is much more striking. While in human music an entire composition lasting an hour may be "fixed" in advance by the notes, this apparent predictability is in part illusory, because human beings are freer in their rendering of a given musical pattern than an individual bird, which (apart from immature singing and "subsong") is rather precise in its reiterations (Thorpe 1963:423f.)—except where the bird widely deviates, that is, employs a different pattern. In the singing of an individual bird, departures from a fixed pattern are generally either so slight as to be scarcely detectable even by delicate instruments, including the human ear, or they are well over the threshold of the detectable. It is almost as if the execution of a pattern were indeed mechanical, and the variations were merely other pieces of mechanism. The freedom of choice is limited in most cases (apart from very young singers) to the decision as to which record to play next. Human freedom is much more pervasive and insistent than this, as we should expect from the fact that we, and not the birds, are "conscious," in a sense which is probably not possible without something like language.

Compared with human music, there seems but one radical inferiority in the best bird songs, the best of the subhuman music of nature: their ultrasimplicity, as shown above all in the extremely brief temporal span of the motifs, or musical units. A bird, it seems, cannot follow a fully definite musical pattern occupying much more than fifteen seconds (so far as species known to me are concerned), and only a few manage patterns of even six seconds' duration. This probably illustrates the "extremely short-run purposes" which Thorpe (1963: 45) believes we must postulate in animals. The average for all singing birds is probably a unit of less than three seconds. Most speech phrases learned by parrots appear to be about this length. Some Budgerigars (*Melopsittacus undulatus*) and other parrots do better, but their limit seems not much beyond 15 seconds. Gibbon singing, being a rather loose, protracted duet or chorale, is not easy to assess in this connection. The only timing of it which I know of, 12–22 seconds (Carpenter 1940: 17) suggests a longer span than in birds. Coyotes have a somewhat patterned howl, which is not, as I recall it, much longer than the usual bird song. As for vocalizing animals in general, thus horses, donkeys, moose, elk, seal, wolves, lions—so far as one can find definite repetitive patterns in their utterances—there is one law for them all, that they be short. The Humpback Whale, in solitary grandeur, is the sole known exception. Frogs and toads, geckos (whose songs are the longest in this list, except for those of a few cicadas), and the insects (Alexander 1957a, 1957b) have similarly brief temporal spans.

Man alone has well-defined (precisely repeatable), timed, and or-

ganized sequences of acts extending beyond a few seconds, to a minute
—or an hour. This, with the closely connected gift of language, is the
psychological uniqueness of man, who is indeed "the time-binding
animal." Of what use would language be if, before a sentence, not to
mention a paragraph, could be ended, the pattern was lost, and only
vague connections were felt between the early and late portions of the
utterance? One of Mrs. Kohts's conclusions from her important work
on the Chimpanzee was that, though this animal "can form ideas, these
last in memory but a few seconds" (Yerkes and Yerkes 1929: 375;
Yerkes and Petrunkevitch 1925: 106–107). White (1949) only slightly
overstates the case when he says that the other animals (at least below
the large apes) have no capacity to form true symbols.

It is to be understood that "memory" is not a single function; in a
certain sense birds remember for years, but this is "recall" (or the
exhibition of conditioning) after intervening forgetting; whereas, to
grasp a musical pattern, some sense of the early portions of the pattern
must persist throughout. It is such "retention" that is always extremely
short-run, save in man; and even in man, there is reason to believe
that it is a different function physiologically after a few seconds. (See
Thorpe 1963: 148, 155ff.) Within the very short run there may well be
no great difference between the function in man and in birds; beyond
that, man has something that is lacking in all the rest of the animal
kingdom, something not quite retention nor yet mere recall, but with
aspects of both; and it is this which makes him the rational animal.
One proof that the short-run function is somewhat similar in man and
birds is that as birds reiterate a phrase or song, their pauses seem fairly
satisfying even to us, although in the few seconds less happens for us
than for them, since they live faster. A man can listen to most repetitive
birds reiterating a song scores of times, with pauses typically several
times the length of the songs, without feeling any very annoying degree
of monotony. But cut the pauses to one-half or one-third on a recording, and the song does become irritating.

In one of the very best discussions of the subject of this chapter,
Craig (1943: 50–54, 144–47) uses a phrase which he might perhaps
better have avoided: "continuous musical composition." As he makes
quite clear and emphasizes, the species he studied shows no sign of
grasping more than three phrases (taking 2 seconds each, or 6 for the
set) at once or as a whole.

It is true that some birds have a single song lasting nearly a minute

or longer, but this—like some insect songs—is usually a relatively patternless prolongation, arbitrarily variable in length, of a single sound,
trill, tremolo, or buzz, like the song of the Grasshopper Warbler of
Europe (*Locustella naevia*) or of Fuertes's "Noonwhistle" (*Chamaeza
ruficauda turdina*), an antthrush (Fuertes 1914 (3): 3; Chapman 1936:
391). In some few cases a long song has greater internal differentiation,
for instance, the Plain-brown Woodcreeper's (*Dendrocincla fuliginosa*), considered in Chapter 11. However, the pattern is then not
sharply defined. We shall see examples in later chapters. "Long-
continued songs" (Saunders 1951: 35), which may last many minutes,
always consist of elements each lasting a few seconds at most, and
with no fixed order of sequence. Consequently there is no definite ending. That superb musician, the Solitaire of the Rocky Mountains, often
sings continuously for 20 seconds, but not in a fixed, repeatable pattern
(Borror, personal communication). The music of the neotropical *Myadestes unicolor,* or Slate-colored Solitaire ("the most beautiful song of
all"—Chapman 1936), is a repertoire of songs each lasting 2–5 seconds,
and usually repeated, with judicious pauses, about five times. (See
Appendix C.) (Because of the complexity of the songs, often containing 15 or more notes, with many distinct pitch intervals, this amount of
repetition does not seem monotonous.)

I incline to think that if a human composer were to subject himself
to the same drastic limitation in the time span of his patterns, he could
not greatly surpass the birds and he might easily do less well. True,
he could achieve a higher proportion of pure tones than most birds do
(but this would perhaps only accentuate the meagerness of the result,
since the mixture of tones and semi-noises is one way of securing rich-
ness of contrast from a few sounds), and he might luxuriate in simultaneous chords. Although birds can, and many do, sound two more or
less harmonious notes at once (Borror and Reese 1956; Saunders 1951:
274; Greenewalt 1968: 55–78), and there is some choral singing and a
good deal of duetting, still, simultaneous harmony or polyphony, other
than random (which is sometimes delightful, as when various species
or independent individuals sing more or less at once), is a minor element in bird music. But so is it in much human music outside Europe
and the modern world. Accordingly, if very simple musical designs can
be unfolded in a few seconds, and if pervasively musical effects can
be achieved by random alternations of related designs (and the Wood
Thrush and many other birds show how this can be done), there is no

reason to deny that bird songs are, as patterns of sound, and even by our standards, primitive forms of music.

Take any really simple element of musical form. It can probably be shown that it is clearly illustrated in the singing of birds. (See Mathews 1921; Garstang 1923; Cheney 1891; Koehler 1951.) Thus we have every elementary rhythmic effect: accelerando (Wood Warbler, *Phylloscopus sibilatrix*—Garstang 1923: 252; Field Sparrow, *Spizella pusilla*—Saunders 1951: 264); ritardando (Yellow-billed Cuckoo, *Coccyzus americanus*—Saunders 1951: 52); and other effects not too far from these in simplicity (e.g., Black-billed Cuckoo, *Coccyzus erythrophthalmus*—ibid.). We have crescendo (tenfold graduated increase in volume, applied in turn to each unit in a large sophisticated repertoire, by the Heuglin's Robin-chat of Africa, *Cossypha heuglini*); diminuendo (South American Misto Seed-finch or Grassland Yellow-finch, *Sicalis* or *Sycalis luteola*—Hudson 1920, I: 67–68); interval inversion; simple harmonic relations (thirds, fourths, fifths, octaves); retention of melody with change of key (Crested Bellbird of Australia, *Oreoica gutturalis;* Fijian Warbler, *Vitia ruficapilla* [I may have misidentified the species, of which I had but a glimpse]). Koehler (1954: 332) speaks of the "widely-distributed ability to transpose" and gives a fine example from a parrot. He also gives a supporting citation from Stadler (1934). See also Knecht (1940). From time to time, one simple musical procedure or another has been denied of birds, but always by someone with inexact or narrow knowledge of the phenomenon in its global extent. (The Songbirds in all Europe constitute but 5% of those of the world. Some European observers have felt that certain songs in Borneo, New Zealand, Australia, Africa, or tropical North America come closer to human music than those at home.)

Clear examples of theme and variations are found in bird songs. No musician could listen to a Bachman's or Pine-woods Sparrow (*Aimophila aestivalis*) for a minute and not see its song in this light. The theme is a sustained note followed by a trill (in some individuals a true musician's trill) on a lower pitch. The variations double or halve the tempo of the trill, put the trill higher in pitch instead of lower (invert the interval), break the trill into two parts on different pitches, vary the degree of pitch contrast between the long note and the trill, vary the location of the whole song up or down in pitch, break the trill into two parts, on the same pitch but with the tempo of one part much faster than the other, or change the trill to a quaver. The foregoing are all taken from a record by Saunders of one individual bird in a single performance, nor do they exhaust the variations, which ran to twelve. But the theme was never lost.

Comparing our emotional experiences with those of other animals is not easy, and aesthetic aspects of experience may be especially difficult. However, song is the extreme exception, the outstanding case in which the analogies become most accessible to objective (acoustical) study. We have audiospectrograms, oscillograms, notations in standard musical symbols (whose merely partial or limited accuracy must be admitted, but for whose complete irrelevance no valid argument has been given), and we have several other, perhaps even better, methods of visual representation. (See Chapter 5.) We can play songs at greatly reduced speeds to bring out details. The precision with which a Hill Myna (*Gracula religiosa*), for example, can reproduce our speech sounds and also a human melody ("The Farmer in the Dell," e.g.) shows that these other animals are not living in an entirely different auditory world from ours. (We know rather definitely that the gap is vastly greater with insects.)

Nicholson's analogy (1929) of beauty in song with the visual beauty of some animals is misleading in that the animals do not produce visual beauty by using their voluntary muscles to anything like the extent to which they use them to produce beautiful song. I suspect that song as music is primarily enjoyed by the singer himself. Whether or not it pleases his potential or actual mate (or—if properly distant—perhaps even his rivals), it tends to please *him* and thus to encourage him to devote much time and energy to it, as the functions of song may require. Beauty is a "reinforcer." It is not the only reinforcer, and this may be the reason why some of the generalizations I shall propose hold only broadly, or in a merely statistical manner.

Nicholson and others have contended that in some species of birds "subsong" is more varied and beautiful than territorial song, although the latter is presumably the more functional. However, Thorpe and Pilcher (1958) seem to show that while subsong has greater pitch range and is more long-continuing, it is inferior not only in volume (by definition) but also in tone quality and organization. In my evaluation of songs I consider territorial song as the norm, and take loudness, tone, and organization as dimensions of value (Chapter 6 E). In this and other ways I try to reckon with the necessity that natural selection of song must be for its effectiveness in producing certain biological results. But I find evidence that musical exquisiteness is in many species a major contributor to this effectiveness. Probably none of us quite knows how to strike the proper balance here, just as Nicholson himself wonders how far it is territory and how far it is mates for which males are competing. It is of course both, in some subtle ever-varying combination. Somewhat similarly efficiency and musicality (taken in its broadest reasonable meaning) may be interrelated.

In singing, birds tend to maintain a rapid, even (by our standards) fantastically rapid, tempo. Yet I have heard from New Zealand Tuis (*Prosthemadera novaeseelandiae*) slow, rather low-pitched songs (two notes a second, or less) which a musician, using so few elements (four to eight notes), might be at a loss to surpass as complete and satisfying compositions. A Rufous and White Wren (*Thryothorus rufalbus*) gives six or eight leisurely variations in pure flute tones on a simple theme— several slightly sustained (quarter?) notes followed by a series of much shorter ones (32nds?) perhaps a minor third lower in pitch, thus: −−− . . . . The variations (key change, interval inversion, dropping one of the opening notes, accelerando in place of the abrupt tempo change, etc.) could be surpassed, it seems to me, only on a level of complexity higher than the theme itself warrants. (See Appendix C.) The Little Grass Bird of Australia (*Megalurus gramineus*), by subtle use of rhythm, achieves eloquent though plaintive music out of a reiterated three-note phrase entirely on one pitch. And finally, what better music could be made out of two notes than is furnished by the European Cuckoo (*Cuculus canorus*) or (octaves higher in pitch) the North American Black-capped Chickadee (*Parus atricapillus*)? But perhaps better music could be made out of a pair of notes—by employing the octave, and this is just what the Queensland subspecies of Olive Whistler does in its famous "peeee-poooo" song, one of a half-dozen items in an individual's repertoire. (A subtle slur or grace note enriches the two-note contrast.)

The "best singers" reach higher levels than the others in complexity or free variety and exhibit a more coherent use of tone, interval, and rhythm. "Complexity" refers, first of all, to the internal variety of a single song or pattern. It refers also to variety between one song and another within an individual repertoire. Here again birds are drastically limited: a hundred notes, or at most three hundred, will fully define a good individual repertoire, compared to millions for a human musician. Some birds may seem not to have fixed repertoires; but except for young birds, and perhaps a few exceptionally flexible species, the constituent units are generally fairly stable throughout a season, if not a lifetime.

There are some fine songsters with a few rather complex songs, and some with many simple ones. An individual Winter Wren in northeastern America has a long, rather complex song, little varied from one utterance to another, but perhaps enough longer (by at least a second more) than the song of the European subspecies to barely justify calling the former, but not the latter, an outstanding singer. However, in most species that have been regarded as superior singers an individual has a repertoire of several patterns and there seem to be as many as a score, or even fifty or more, for each individual in some species, e.g., the Eastern Meadowlark (*Sturnella magna*). (See Saunders 1951: 224.) Each European Blackbird (*Turdus merula*) has, from my experience, perhaps six or seven rather complex songs, and each Hermit Thrush has a similar number of still more complex (but in part very rapid) songs. In these two cases the same song is very seldom sung twice in succession. The next utterance follows rather quickly, so that the contrasts between songs become musical elements also; in this way even five songs can yield twenty diverse contrasts in addition to those within each song.

I have not discussed the question of conventional Western musical scales because human music itself exhibits a considerable range of scales over space and time (Herzog 1941), not to mention that our modern Western scale is opposed by some musicologists (Redfield 1935: 185–95; Fokker 1955). Since birds often use harmonic relations and very often achieve melody and other musical effects, the gist of the matter is in them (Wing 1951; Borror and Reese 1956).

There is, of course, an element of conscious convention, artificiality, or intellectuality that is not to be expected of birds, in the way human musicians feel and think in terms of universal systems of pitch division, and also of time division (the "beat"). But since I have not been able to master these systems (though music is central to my life), I am naturally cool to the idea that this prevents bird song from passing as music. (Primitive man might not be musical either by such a standard.) There is nearly always an appreciable aspect of rhythm or melody in bird song, which in some cases gives a sense of musical perfection. Examples will be found in Chapter 10 in those species in which the second part of the numerical rating profiles begins with 99, indicating that tone and organization are maximal. The song of the Andean Solitaire is an example of this, and several writers, largely independently, have spoken of it in these terms. Another example is the Mountain Tailorbird (*Orthotomus cucullatus*) (Chapter 5D), which has been admired by writers who did not even have the benefit of a recording and the slow playing without which the structure of this fast, high-pitched, but almost unbelievably musical song is scarcely perceptible.

If some songs give us a sense of musical competence, others seem blundering, halting, or incompetent. Of one bird it has been said, "His voice is fine, if only he could find a tune," and of another, the "Whistling Schoolboy" or Malabar Whistling Thrush (*Myiophoneus horsfieldii*), that it "has forgotten its tune, but it whistles on" (Nichols 1937). However, considering the enormous gap between the anatomies and lives of man and bird, it remains astonishing how much musical intelligibility the utterances of the latter have for the former.

Knecht (1940) tested the abilities of some species of birds to discriminate and remember differences of pitch and simple melodic pattern. He concluded that birds have the basic requirements for musicality, although they seem not to distinguish harmonious from discordant intervals (thirds and seconds) as we do. They do have a sense for fifths and the octave and thus for octave quality. (It may or may not be relevant that his test subjects were not especially musical species: Budgerigar; Crossbill, *Loxia curvirostra;* Starling, *Sturnus vulgaris;* and two cardueline finches.) Reinert and Reinert-Reetz (1962) tested Budgerigars for melody discrimination and reached similar results. They say, however, that an elephant similarly tested did somewhat better! Neither kind of animal is a noted performer among animal musicians.

B. Song and Behavior

Musical sounds, in the psychological sense, are those which, to some extent, are appreciated for their own sake. Not that music may not serve a practical purpose; on the contrary, it often does so. There are war songs, magic-charm songs, etc. But there is a tendency for aesthetic enjoyment to free itself somewhat from the practical, as when war songs are sung even though no battle is to be fought. When a dog

whines because it is on a leash and wishes to scamper about, the re-
moval of the leash ends the whining, which was not indulged in for
its own sake. Similarly, a bird's alarm cries will cease when the danger
has passed. Now consider a bird which, by singing and threat displays,
has succeeded in bringing about the retreat of an intruding male from
his territory. Does he cease to sing? Far from it. One hears resounding
song, as though in proud triumph over the victory. Or again, the same
bird may sing vigorously for days before a mate appears. The mate
comes; for several days there is little time for singing as the mate is
being wooed and "shown about" the territory, and the pair bond is
being firmly established; but then (in most species) singing breaks
out again, especially if rivals appear conspicuous in the area. In all
this there is without doubt a good deal of utility. But its results are not
usually to be brought about the next moment, but only in the course
of hours or days (a long time for a bird); they are not limited to a
single outcome, but to several very different ones (securing a mate,
warning rivals off the territory, maintaining the pair bond).

Defending a territory—and still more, attracting a mate—is only
intermittently a desperate all-or-none affair like keeping possession of
a meat bone or escaping a hawk. There is seldom an extreme emer-
gency, when anything terrible can happen quickly. It is not to be
imagined that a bird engaged in territorial singing for hours is reacting
exclusively to the possibility of a successful invasion. There is ample
room, and some probable need, for its activity to be sustained by the
interest of the activity itself, both as a muscular exercise and as the
production of a pattern of sound which the bird itself is well aware of.
The more striking cases of imitation and of synchronized male-female
duets, which may be musically good joint productions, reinforce the
point. Here I know of nothing comparable to birds and man in the
rest of the animal world—admitting that male insects can synchronize
their monotones and that gibbons duet rather nicely.

It may seem odd that attractive sounds (to our ears, at least) should
serve as a warning to keep off. But since the sounds must also attract
a mate and make her feel welcome, they could not very well have the
sharply hostile, unhappy, or ugly sound of scolds or crude threat notes.
Moreover, no animal will make such unhappy sounds for long except
under the stress of actual unhappiness. They issue from a strained and
abnormal, emotionally somewhat costly, state of the organism. Terri-
tory-holding is too protracted and constant an affair to be accomplished

at such a price. Finally, since the rival bird is also a singer, he has to find the song patterns of his species attractive, i.e., "beautiful" not "ugly," the more so since to some extent they are learned imitatively— or at least reinforced—in the bird's first half year or so. What the rival finds unattractive is not the basic song pattern, but a rendering of it that is slightly different from his own ringing all too loudly in his ears. There is evidence that he likes to hear it in the distance, for there is some indication that males try to keep within hearing of one another (Gannon 1953; Darling 1952: 188).

It is agreed that songs must be more distinctive than mere threat or alarm notes (Marler 1955; 1959: 180ff.), but a musical interest is an interest in the distinctiveness of sounds, so far as this depends upon all the principal aspects of the sound pattern. A lion's roar can almost be recognized by its mere volume and low pitch, without any very special regard to particular pattern elements of rhythm or pitch interval. But with numerous closely intermingled species of small birds, nearly the same in size and hence in pitch- and volume-capacity, attention must be paid to much finer details if identification of species, sex, and breeding attitude is to be efficient. Would it not be a miracle if all this could be done, and yet no pleasure in sound-pattern as such developed?

C. Birds' Innately Limited Aesthetic Interest

If the singing bird has an aesthetic sense, why does it not enjoy the songs of other species as well as its own? If so, should we not expect all the birds in an area to gather around one or a few of the finest singers? My answer is: This is the opposite extreme to the former idea of *no* aesthetic sense, since what we are now asked to consider is a universal, highly flexible musical appreciation, without narrow innate preference or bias, and stronger than other impulses or feelings in the bird. What I am trying to defend is something more moderate or relative than either of these extremes. Birds have an innate preference for their own species' sound pattern, and for this we have some experimental evidence (Thorpe 1954). This preference is a relative, not an absolute force. The rather widespread incidence of obvious imitation under natural conditions, and its much more common appearance under sufficiently favorable artificial ones, demonstrates that a tendency to find songs of other species attractive, or at least interesting, does exist, though it is usually much weaker than various other impulses.

The preferential interest of a bird for the song of its species is strikingly shown when a recorded song is played in the presence of wild birds. It produces emphatic responses from one species and no particular sign of attention from the others (Koehler 1951). But yet, in case after case, involving many species, birds artificially reared away from adults of their kind have learned quite the "wrong" songs. I have heard a Western Meadowlark (*Sturnella neglecta*), reared by Wesley Lanyon in a trailer where adult larks could not be heard, sing songs of the Baltimore Oriole (*Icterus galbula*) and other species occurring in the vicinity. Yet wild meadowlarks have not, so far as I know, been reported to imitate. And were there no innate influences limiting or guiding imitation, how could we possibly account for the relative stability of territorial song patterns throughout a species, generation after generation? (That this stability obtains—naturally, with some exceptions here and there—we now know from recordings, whether or not we knew it before from memory or verbal and musical descriptions.) Thus birds, apart from highly imitative species (and to some extent, even these), are innately limited in the flexibility or catholicity of any "aesthetic taste" which they may be presumed to have. Since, however, even a human individual's appreciation of musical patterns is subject to limitations which are often puzzling to others whose taste is wider, or whose incidence of insensitivity is elsewhere, it is not necessary to deny that birds do have something like taste merely because their aesthetic narrowness, compared to ours, must be drastic.

D. Protomusic or Protospeech?

We need not argue about mere words. I am entirely happy to have it said (Koehler 1951; Sauer 1954: 83) that bird song is only a *Vorstufe* or pre-stage of music, just as bird calls of warning, assembly, and the like may be termed a pre-stage of speech (Koehler 1954). The question whether birds approach human music or speech more closely is perhaps unanswerable. But if we had to choose, I think we should say music. That a deafened Blackbird sang at an abnormally high pitch with "ugly," harsh tone quality (Messmer and Messmer 1956: 362, 377) may be evidence of musical taste in the normal bird.

Many good observers credit birds with some capacity, however slight, for musical "composition" (Koehler 1954: 333–34; Messmer and Messmer 1956: 374–75, 432, 433, 437; L. Howard 1953: 177, 183, 186, 190). Indeed, with imitative birds, at least, this capacity (or a striking illusion of it) is scarcely deniable, since the imitations are generally interwoven in a rather effective sequence of sounds which cannot possibly be inherited. Of course the capacity for musical invention is very limited, even in these cases. But can any bird construct a meaningful sentence, put even two words together to describe a feature of its environment? This appears to surpass avian brain capacity. Nevertheless, it is exciting to learn on good authority that parrots do sometimes use (and even invent) single words to name things or to express a definite wish or demand (Koehler 1951: 17). Evidence is accumulating that mistaken physiological theories have long misled scientists concerning the differences in learning ability between birds and mammals (L. Howard 1953: 141–62; Thorpe 1963: 336ff.; Schmid 1937: 214–16).

The earliest learning of tunes in children comes rather later, as a rule, than the earliest learning of the uses of speech. My daughter, aged 2½, correctly replied to the query, "What bird is that?" (one having just sung): "That's a Meadowlark." This performance was far beyond the scope of any nonhuman creature on the globe. But neither she nor most children of that age could rival a Talking Myna or perhaps a Bellmagpie (*Gymnorhina tibicen*) in the accurate rendering of a human melody. The earliest human learning of a tune I have known about was that of a boy 12 months old, son of a psychologist in Germany: I was privileged to hear this child sing himself to sleep, as he did customarily, with a correct little slow tune. But such an ability is rare indeed, and even it is scarcely closer to musicianship than some children of that age are to developed speech. This suggests that the ability to learn musical patterns requires something like the same degree and kind of cortical development as the barest beginnings of speech—which, as animals in general go, is high development. So while it may be too much to attribute "musical intelligence" to birds, "musical feeling" seems appropriate.

The primitive mode of singing in an individual bird's life is not the utilitarian territory-advertisement form, but rather the "functionless" immature mode of singing (Sauer 1954), the somewhat random, soft, free-flowing "playful" utterance of young birds and of adults at times of sexual quiescence and in the absence of any special instinctive drive.

It is now known that the essential form or style of this youthful singing is, in many species at least, innate and unique to the species, but
this does not mean that it is a mere automatic exercise. In its details, it
is a spontaneous playlike activity, like the cooing of infants, and we
know from observations on wild and hand-reared individuals (Mills
1931: 21–23; L. Howard 1953: 109–12; Sauer 1956: 179–88; Nice 1943:
51–54; Thorpe 1963: 362, 401) that play is a prominent phenomenon in
birds, often much like the scampering, tussling, and curiosity-evincing
investigations of kittens, puppies, and other young mammals. (For an
odd case in grown turkey hens, see Schmid 1937: 39.) Invention and
discoveries in sound production are demonstrable in this avian play.
More than all creatures save man, birds play with sounds, not only
sounds produced directly by their own organs, but even those resulting
from the handling of objects. Four instances have been reported, involving as many species and a larger number of individuals, of Songbirds playing at sound-making by dropping objects from their bills, or
pushing them off the top of a house or desk. The performances were
repeated over and over, and the birds gave signs of listening for the
sounds as "reward" (Mills 1931: 22–23; Sauer 1956: 179–82, 186–88;
Jaeger 1951; Marshall 1954: 80). It is also exciting to learn that young
Blackbirds apparently utter the most primitive form of their youthful
singing only in response to some sound or other (Messmer and Messmer 1956: 360).

Youthful singing, like other forms of play, is not (at least, after the
most primitive phase just mentioned, which in deafened individuals is
omitted) a response to fixed stimuli or releasers; rather, it is what
happens when there is no particular stimulus or urge, whether internal
(hunger, sex) or external (menacing objects or creatures, rivals,
mates) and the bird is "relaxed," "free," or "satiated." These conditions,
of course, are the very ones in which man is most likely to turn to music
or another of the fine arts. The activity tends toward no definite end-
results (after which it would subside, as eating does after the usual
amount of food has been taken), but rather, various forms of instinctive behavior, such as chasing, building a nest, courting, or catching
food, are simulated but carried only part way to their normal and
utilitarian outcomes, then begun over again from some point or other,
or dropped; and another form of behavior, often a normally antago-
nistic one, is initiated with no sign of frustration or anxiety (Sauer
1956: 183). This too is what happens in man's artistic activities (Og-

den, Richards, and Wood 1925; Pepper 1937: 45, 47, 63–78). Groos's
(1901) brilliant interpretation of art as a form of play—which, as Sauer
remarks, does not mean that it is trivial or lacking in intense interest—
still seems good sense, and it applies very nicely to birds. Activities
are enjoyed for their own sakes, the practical upshot being, for the
time, not to the point. Avian singing in this fashion has some analogy
to human musical performances in which the performer amuses himself. (On animal play see Thorpe 1966b; 1963: 22, 94ff., 362ff.)

It is significant that neither sound-imitation nor vocal play, such as
birds and infants indulge in, is found in Chimpanzees, which are evidently very deficient in musical sensibility or interest in sounds for
their own sake. (For the nearest they seem to come to it, see Huxley
1964: 45.) Their vocalizations are tied to definite momentary situations
with specific instinctive responses (Jacobsen, Jacobsen, and Yoshioka
1932: 61).

Out of the relaxed or playful mode of singing, the more functional
advertisement and courtship songs develop by a process of simplification, restriction, or stereotyping—but in some species also by elabora-
tion (L. Howard 1953: 178–79, 182–86, 196; Messmer and Messmer
1956; Sauer 1954), issuing in more sharply defined, usually relatively
brief, standardized patterns, fixed perhaps for years.

The highly imitative songs are, of course, somewhat different, being
in part creations, so far as the innate patterns of the singer are concerned. For this reason, and it is a cogent one, Sauer regards such
songs as on a higher level, more akin to human music. Yet there is a
modest but genuine aesthetic creativity in the development of clear-
cut, sharply demarcated and self-complete themes from somewhat rambling, free-flowing sequences of notes in immature singing, and in the
musically judicious alternation and spacing of these themes. Simplification and limitation, after all, are important means to aesthetic en-
hancement. "*In der Beschränkung* [limitation] *zeigt sich erst der Meis-
ter.*" I confess to a bias in favor of clarity of musical structure, and it
seems to me that the functional territorial songs tend to excel in this
respect, especially the less imitative ones. The imitative songs tend
toward a certain overall looseness, as it were, carelessness, of structure
which impresses one somewhat as do medleys in human music. The
prevailing preference in Europe for the not obviously imitative singing
of the Blackbird, the Nightingales (*Erithacus luscinia* and *E. megarhynchos*), and the Woodlark (*Lullula arborea*), in comparison to the

medley singing of the Sedge and Marsh Warblers (*Acrocephalus schoenobaenus* and *A. palustris*), may have a certain validity.

Sauer maintains, and others support him here, that wherever singing becomes sharply functional, where territorial rivalry passes over rather constantly into approaches to actual combat, or where courtship passes into a plea for copulation, song tends to degenerate (Sauer 1955; Lorenz 1943: 394; L. Howard 1953: 178, 187, 193, 199). This is what we should expect if there be an aesthetic factor in the evolution of song; for to say "aesthetic" is to say "not merely or too directly utilitarian." But we must be careful to balance this consideration against the seemingly contradictory one that unless an aesthetic activity has some connection with utility it will be unlikely to survive evolutionary change. Thorpe (1963: 425f.), apropos of some remarks of Craig and Lorenz (for both, see Craig 1943: 161–62), has correctly pointed out that purity of tone may sometimes give a competitive advantage, since purity means definiteness of pitch, and there must be some competition among sympatric species for the various possible frequencies in the few octaves available to small birds. Thus, considering evolutionary origins, musicality is utilitarian. Nevertheless, it flowers best in particular moments when the utility is not pressing or narrowly focused. For example, late-summer or autumn singing is sometimes particularly good. I recall an early September day in Georgia when a Yellow-throated Vireo (*Vireo flavifrons*) was singing at its very best, though it seemed unlikely that either courtship or territory holding were especially urgent at that time. There may be an optimum here between irrelevance to the survival needs of the species and too close or immediate a connection with such needs, as felt by the individual. Late-summer singing may be indirectly useful, for hearing it may help the young males to begin channeling their exploratory singing in the right grooves. There may also be a safety factor in having an agreeable outlet for extra energy such as singing provides, since in exigent circumstances the luxury activity can always be dropped, and thus there is a margin of power.

E. Song as Expressing Feeling

The appeal of music is, first of all, sensory and emotional, not intellectual. Far more than we do, birds live in a world of sensation, feeling, and impulse. When they are territorial they feel territorially; how far they think territorially is another matter. Territorial feelings, like many others, can be expressed through sounds.

How feelings are connected with the qualities of sounds is a topic that has been much discussed (Hartshorne 1934: 158–89, 225–34). Here it suffices to say that the connection exists, and that it does not derive essentially from man's special capacity to learn the use of arbitrary symbols. A newborn infant would be frightened or distressed by a tiger's growl. Everyone, and not solely human beings, feels the difference between a soft, sweet voice and a harsh one. There are built-in emotional meanings of sound that are responded to partly in common by the higher animals. The notion that birds are too primitive to participate in this response is, so far as I can see, without foundation. Then, too, all life is rhythmic, and the rhythms of music constitute, within limits, a universal language. (I have yet to hear exotic music that is as opaque to me as a language I have not learned. I delighted in Balinese music the first time I heard it, and enjoyed the much more primitive West African [Yoruba] songs a friend gave me a recording of.)

It has been said (Sibley 1952) that we cannot hope to understand what a song means to a bird, which sometimes mixes singing with fighting trespassers. But consider man's war songs and dances. He too combines music with many sorts of actions. And just as patriotism can have both harshly negative or hostile aspects and very positive and happy ones, as in the love of country, so perhaps can a bird combine vivid liking for his territory and his place in it with potential hostility toward trespassers. And here is a difference between birds and the two men fighting that Sibley mentions: The men may hate each other as individuals; not so two avian rivals for territory. So long as proper spacing with the recognized singing neighbors obtains, "God's in his heaven, all's right with the world." The animal feels that the entire situation, as it impinges on his life, is good. So the old cliché, birds sing to praise the Lord, like the other cliché, they sing to please their mates, has not been shown entirely devoid of truth or relevance. Why not sing when so much is going well? Surely a bird has happy feelings about its territory, which gives it food, shelter, and so much else.

Must not singing be enjoyable in itself? Other forms of skill are enjoyed, indeed all forms, I maintain, which are engaged in as freely and persistently as this one. And where is the line between all this and music? It is not thoughtful, sophisticated music, as ours can be. But neither was the singing of the one-year-old boy with his one little slow tune. There are many levels of musical feeling, as there are many levels of life, between insects, amphibians, or birds and man.

We know that songs are sometimes sexual stimuli, not only between mated birds but between rival males. This, too, is not absolutely unmatched in human life. The difficulty is not to find analogies but to know how to make them useful, rather than merely misleading. We shall develop an adequate science of behavior by controlling the analogies rather than by dismissing them.

More than fifty years before Howard, Bernard Altum (1868: 71–105) gave a masterly analysis (which is hard to surpass even today) of the functions of song in connection with mating and territory. But Altum argues that the "anthropomorphic" view of song as expressing the bird's "personal" feeling is therewith shown to be "without even an iota of truth." He speaks of the "infinite" difference between the "necessity" of song for specific practical purposes in the life of birds and our human singing "to express our feelings, to please ourselves and others, to put others into a certain mood." Altum is thinking of sophisticated civilized man, at one extreme, and of birds as mere "organisms," lacking even the most naive feelings, and compelled to reproduce their kind by certain actions, at the other. He has to admit that there is some song at every time of year, but explains its occurrence as connected with some slight resurgence of the reproductive urge. Today he would have to deal with the many cases we now know of birds singing daily throughout the year, particularly in male-female duets. He could still argue for the necessity of these activities. However, he fails to make Huxley's distinction, quoted at the beginning of this book, between the two types of valid answers to questions about behavior. And his account of the role of music in human life is also one-sided. Curiously, too, Altum's idea of the "harmony of nature" as conscious organism would seem anthropomorphic enough to scientists today, especially as it was proposed instead of natural selection to explain the origin of species.

To my mind Altum's strongest argument is the one dealt with in section C, that if birds have a musical sense they ought to be found gathering around the best singers to enjoy their performance. And this has never been observed. But where he sees only iron "necessity" in bird life I see minute degrees of freedom. The "limitations of avian musical taste" which prevent birds from ever going beyond some bits of imitation as signs of appreciation (not recognized as such by Altum, so far as I can see) of alien songs must be indeed severe. But perhaps the main point is that feeling for sounds is closely connected, even in man, but vastly more in birds, with feeling for the operation of producing sounds. Only a few species have much feeling for foreign sounds. They express this feeling by copying them, not by approaching to listen. Birds are activists, not meditative spectators. Very likely, if Altum were alive, he would fail to find that I had answered his argument. These are not easy matters to reach agreement upon. And there may be relevant considerations we both have overlooked.

F. Summary

(A.) Bird songs resemble human music both in the sound patterns and in the behavior setting. Songs illustrate the aesthetic mean between chaotic irregularity and monotonous regularity. When songs are reiterated many times in succession, pauses between reiterations are usually long enough to confirm the hypothesis that birds are sensitive to monotony (Chapter 7). One way of achieving variety in seemingly very repetitive ways of singing is "number juggling," e.g., changing back and forth somewhat irregularly between repeating a phrase 3, 4, or 5 times. Birds with repertoires of many contrasting songs sing them in no fixed order. Thus there is avoidance of mere mechanical regularity. But there is also some sort of unity by which specific and individual recognition is possible.

The essential difference from human music is in the brief temporal span of the bird's repeatable patterns, commonly three seconds or less, with an upper limit of about fifteen seconds. This limitation conforms to the concept of primitive musicality. Every simple musical device, even transposition and simultaneous harmony, occurs in bird music.

(B.) The behavior-setting of songs also favors the aesthetic hypothesis. Singing repels rival males, but only when nearby; and it attracts mates. It is persisted in without any obvious immediate result, and hence must be largely self-rewarding. It expresses no one limited emotional attitude and conveys more information than mere chirps or squeaks. In all these ways song functions like music.

(C.) The musical sense of birds is narrowly limited by inheritance, and has to compete with other—during part of the year, stronger—feelings or concerns.

(D.) Thus birds are primitive musicians, not advanced or sophisticated. Birds have a slight, but recognizable, capacity for "composition," chiefly during their first season.

Birds, like human beings, play with sounds in infancy, their immature utterances being more like music and ours more like speech. Bird utterances can be viewed as protospeech, but even more appropriately as protomusic. (Chimpanzees are farther from auditory speech than birds.) Playful, somewhat formless, immature singing develops into more definite patterns.

(E.) Song expresses feeling, according to principles partly common to the higher animals. That a bird sings "because it is happy" is not entirely foolish. Altum, the first clear-headed defender of the territorial function of song, argued passionately against the attribution of feeling to birds. But he failed to distinguish between evolutionary origins and present realities, or between the eventual functions of song and the bird's momentary feeling of what it is doing.

CHAPTER

4

Imitative Singing and Chatter

❦

A. *Three Kinds of Auditory Imitation*

The capacity to imitate sounds seems pervasive among birds, at least those of songbird type. Under natural conditions this capacity is not readily detected in most cases because it results only in the bird's learning to sing the standard song of his species somewhat better, or a little differently, than he otherwise would. But wherever conditions are made unnaturally and strongly favorable for imitation of songs of other species or of human utterances, rather than of the characteristic song-type of the species, unnatural song seems to result. Thus we have two types of imitation, that which copies normally singing males of the same species, and that which is more or less indiscriminate as to the species copied. In nature, the indiscriminate type is apparently very exceptional, but artificial situations show that the capacity is wide-spread.

A third form of imitation is of the male by the female or vice versa. We shall see that the assumption of male-female imitation explains certain otherwise puzzling facts. We now know that imitations vary greatly both in their functions and in their genesis. Some birds must learn from individuals they are somehow attached to, others need only to hear a song or sound to imitate it. Some can develop normal song without hearing it, but yet are influenced by normal songs if they do hear them.

But why, we may ask, is there any imitation at all?

B. *Why Animals Imitate Sounds*

Sound-copying must be regarded as a case of learning and indeed—in a broad sense of a vague term—intelligence. To do what the other is doing, where there is no complete inherited pattern for the deed, is to translate the form of the observed act into terms of one's own behavior. One must in some fashion "grasp" this form and sense those features of one's own habits which already fit it, compared to those which do not, rejecting the latter and receiving encouragement ("facilitation") to persist in or improve upon the former. It is thus that the prattle or babble of infants furnishes the foundation for the later learning of speech sounds (Mowrer 1952—a reference I owe to W. H. Perkins). Mowrer shows that the facilitation is based upon pleasant associations, and similarly that "birds learn to talk only when the human teacher becomes a love object for them." (This may help to explain why young birds normally do not copy songs of other species.) Almost from the outset human young are interested in the conventional meanings of the sounds they imitate. This tremendous difference between birds and human beings is the great dividing line (which may be closely connected with the avian limitation in temporal attention span spoken of in Chapter 3). But it does not, so far as has yet been shown, affect the mere aspect of sound-copying. (See Mead 1909; 1964: 100.)

It is important that, whereas an animal cannot see itself and its own movements as fully and distinctly as it sees the appearances and motions of others, it does hear its own voice quite well. This is one more way in which sound-signaling, especially as a bird practices it, is somewhat different in principle from visual signaling.

Compared to the enormous quantity of vocal imitation demonstrably found in birds, imitation of visual display is not, so far as I know, definitely documented at all. It requires more elaborate mental processes, since the similarity between what the bird itself is doing and what another is doing is less directly and adequately perceived in the visual case. A bird may imitate a man's whistling or even his talking, but what bird has ever imitated or tried to imitate a man's bodily motions? (An African Grey Parrot [*Psittacus erithacus*] has been anonymously reported to have imitated with its foot some motions of a man's hand. Even if this account is authentic, it may be a rare case.) For a bird to copy human movements is largely prohibited by anatomical differences; and here is still another difference between acoustical and visual imitation: Animals that are physically incapable of looking alike may sound very much alike. For birds to imitate man's physical motions as readily as apes do they would have to be much more manlike than they are in bones and muscles, as well as having more brain cells. (On apparent visual imitation by crows and parrots see Thorpe 1963: 398f.)

Imitation of sounds presupposes a flexible capacity for producing sounds, and an interest in sounds and sound production. Such capacity and interest is also what makes an animal sing. (It is not the evolutionary cause, but the immediate psychological aspect through which this ultimate cause produces its effect.) A striking example (out of many available) of the close connection between song and imitation is the following. A Malabar Whistling Thrush, a famous singer, which has never, so far as I know, been heard to imitate in the wild, was kept as a pet. It learned to imitate the song "For Me and My Girl," "all through and correctly," and also some bugle calls (McCann 1931). This species is rather large for a Songbird, and we shall see evidence that size favors imitative ability, although some very small birds imitate well.

A phenomenon akin to imitation is matched counter-singing, i.e., replying to songs of a rival with the most nearly equivalent songs from the bird's own repertoire (Hinde 1958; Lemon 1968, 1969; Lemon and Herzog 1969). I have observed this with Cardinals and Carolina Wrens, but it is reported of several other species. Since a bird responds strongly to its own song coming from another, this form of counter-song must be mutually stimulating.

Song being a means to reproductive isolation, it is necessary that imitation should usually stop short of extensive and conspicuous borrowings from alien species. For such borrowing, as a general tendency, would produce confusion and nullify the functions of song. We must therefore suppose an inherited narrowness in the interest which most birds usually feel in the sounds they hear. A young Wood Thrush is evidently not much impressed by the songs it hears unless they are Wood Thrush songs. Its musical taste or preference, you might say, is sharply limited. Hearing alien songs, it feels, as it were, "Yes, and so what?" Hearing a Wood Thrush song, it may on the contrary feel, "Ah, that's the stuff that's worthwhile." Yet make the conditions of life for the young bird sufficiently strange, and it will probably copy something unrecognizable as a Wood Thrush song. Thus it is not as though there were no capacity for interest in alien songs; there is only so much less interest that, in normal competition with the right songs, these alone are copied.

There is clear evidence that species which, even under natural conditions, copy all sorts of species—and not only their songs, but cries, alarm notes, or what not—have a less sharply defined inherited direction of musical taste. In no case known to me is the song of an imitative bird as distinctively musical as that, say, of a Wood Thrush. Always, also, the singing is loosely organized. What the imitative bird has as its innately assigned musical possession is more a general style than a definite pattern of singing. Into this style all sorts of elements can be fitted, as they could not be fitted into the Wood Thrush design for singing.

Why should evolution produce both types of birds, those with a narrowly defined, and those with a vaguer, more flexible or catholic, musical taste? Partly, no doubt, this is a matter of chance. But I think we can see ecological factors which might in some cases favor the trend toward miscellaneous imitation. Suppose, for instance, a bird is competing for territory with individuals of many species, not merely one; it will then be interested, even though in an unfriendly sense, in the voices of these various species. Imitation is a proof of interest; and the territorial rivalry of at least some highly imitative species (including the Mockingbird, the Chloropsis [*Chloropsis* spp.], and some Drongos [*Dicrurus* spp.]) is remarkably miscellaneous or generalized. (I fear this can hardly be true of Lyrebirds [*Menura* spp.].) Duplicating the songs of other species may help somewhat to discourage them from approaching. Not that they will necessarily be deceived into thinking that the mocker is of their own species; perhaps they will scarcely think about it at all, but if the species song has a tendency to inhibit invasion, similar sounds may also have something of this tendency, not by way of thought but of feeling.

There are other ways, perhaps more plausible, in which imitation may have survival value. If territorial proclamation through song is unusually important for a species, it may also be important that the proclamation should be continuous, or without marked pauses, for many minutes at a time. To avoid intolerable monotony in such continuous singing (Chapter 7), a plentiful supply of contrasting phrases or sounds is necessary. These sounds might perhaps be largely determined by the bird's genes, or by individual invention, or finally by imitation. Invention requires brain power; imitation is perhaps more within the reach of the bird brain. Since perhaps only simple song patterns can be determined by genes alone, imitation may, under some conditions, be the most efficient way to acquire the variety needed for continuous singing.

Marshall (1954) argues that continuity of singing is valuable and imitation one way of acquiring it. But he fails to make explicit the dependence of his reasoning upon the anti-monotony principle. Mere continuousness requires complexity and variety in singing only if that principle is valid. Otherwise a simple inherited pattern plus monotonous reiteration would suffice. Thus Marshall was using a principle he failed to formulate. What imitativeness does is to enable inheritance of a certain loosely determined style of singing, plus attention to sounds in the environment, to make a continuous stream of sound possible for an animal that would not be satisfied or stimulated by excessive repetition.

Another value in a complex song, such as imitation helps to produce, is that it can better express individual differences. (I owe this idea to E. A. Armstrong.) We have considerable evidence that song is not merely an announcement of the species but also an individual's identity tag. Not only the mate but also rivals need to recognize the singer individually, for otherwise they would never know whether adjoining territories were occupied by the same neighbors, with whom boundaries had already been settled in previous boundary disputes, or by mere strangers with whom understanding was still to be reached.

A question difficult to answer is this: Have the characteristic songs of any species been partly acquired by imitation of human beings? The robin-chats (*Cossypha* spp.) of Africa and the Indian Shama (*Copsychus malabaricus*) sometimes whistle what sound exceedingly like snatches of human tunes. Have these been picked up from man? Or is it a chance coincidence? North (personal communication) inclined to the former view. Since reading Tretzel's work (1967) on the development of local dialects (in two European species) derived from human whistling, I have come to agree with him. Conversely, and here I agree with Szöke and others, man has without doubt learned musically from birds.

Nicholson, in an imaginative passage (1929: 100f.), suggests that birds imitate partly for the appeal of the sounds themselves or for the mere pleasure of imitating, and partly for the pleasant feelings that in their past have become associated with the sounds. This leads me to the following: Some birds respond to the miscellaneous medley of sounds around them with a selective medley more congruent with their own unique sensory-emotional experiences. Thus they aesthetically assimilate their auditory environments and in this way find reinforcing satisfaction in performing certain functions which evolutionary processes have given them. Any attempt to imagine what life is to a bird is bound to be more or less fanciful. Still, Nicholson, influenced, as he hints, by Hudson, is wise to make the attempt.

Among the puzzling facts concerning imitation are the following: Why is it that imitativeness in Mockingbirds seems to increase as one goes northward from Florida to New England or Ohio? And why have so many parrots shown themselves such splendid mimics in cages, although not one has been observed to imitate in the wild?

The first puzzle is easy. R. T. Peterson suggested this solution to me (Hartshorne 1961). Going northward in this case means going toward the extreme limit of the range of the species (the southernmost limit, far down in Mexico, has simply not been studied in this respect). Near such a limit one finds but a few widely scattered pairs, whereas in Florida, say, many individuals and pairs may be crowded into a small area. A Mockingbird in a Miami park hears a dozen neighboring Mockingbirds, and not too much else; a Mockingbird in New England probably hears no other of its kind, but alien songs ring in its ears in abundance. Mockingbirds do not rule out other Mockingbirds as subjects to be imitated, and so, where the birds are closely packed together, their imitations of Wood Thrushes, Cardinals, or wrens are not taken exclusively from Wood Thrushes, Cardinals, or wrens, but are also taken at second, fourth, or tenth hand from other Mockingbirds. The northern individuals' copies are more accurate since they are made more largely at first hand and alien species constitute almost the entirety of what they hear.

The parrot problem is more subtle. To deal with it requires a new category.

C. Imitative Chatter

Parrots are among the most chummy, by pairs, of all birds. Yet the pairs often fly in flocks. Now how do the pairs preserve their identity in the flocks? Sight is hardly the sufficient answer, because birds are often hidden or well separated. But suppose the two birds had a tendency to copy each other. The result would be that each pair would develop a style of chatter, a dialect, slightly different from that of the others in the flock. If this be the case it would naturally follow that parrots in the wild would not be observed to imitate in the striking, easily noticed manner in which they imitate in cages. Especially where there is no mate, and human sounds are what it chiefly hears, the poor bird has to be chummy with and imitate a human being. And this imitation is of course detected. But who would be subtle and patient enough to notice the slight eccentricities of sound common to members of a pair, as contrasted with the general style of chatter of the species?

In arriving at the foregoing theory, published in 1961, I was influenced by Thorpe's discovery (1954: 467) that if groups of Chaffinches (*Fringilla coelebs*) are isolated from the outset in soundproof chambers each group develops its own somewhat abnormal type of song. Perhaps, I thought, a parrot pair is such a group, even though its acoustic isolation is not very great. Later, Gwinner and Kneutgen (1962) and Thorpe and North (1966) found that some *territorial* tropical species illustrate the same principle of pair imitations as a way of preserving the pair bond. In many nongregarious species the phenomenon takes the form of duetting, either partner being able to sing the entire song but each normally singing only one part of it, the male usually taking the first and the female the second and final part. Each pair has its own repertoire of duets. Most tropical American wrens (e.g., *Thryothorus* and *Henicorhina*) sing in this way. In such cases, pairs are year-round affairs.

Another example of imitation which is not song but, like some song, serves as pair bond, is found in the American Goldfinch (*Carduelis tristis*) and the related Pine Siskin (*Carduelis pinus*). It has been demonstrated (Mundinger 1970) that these finches keep in touch by pairs through imitatively determined flight calls. Either sex may imitate the other. This is precisely the use of imitation which first occurred to me while reflecting on the old mystery, why do parrots imitate only in captivity? My conviction was that the "only" was false, and that the pair relation, together with the somewhat gregarious habits of parrots, was the answer. Goldfinches are not highly territorial. They do sing, but they also chatter, and the two modes are quite distinct in their case. On the other hand, Boubou Shrikes (*Laniarius ferrugineus*), which furnished much of the data that led Thorpe and North to the pair-imitation view, are territorial. For reasons set forth in the two previous chapters, the chatter of territorial species is more musical, as a rule, and is more properly termed song.

Chattering is like song in that it is strongly subject to learning, in contrast to alarm cries, scolds, or immature begging calls. Goldfinches and some other related species can imitate flight calls after full maturity, as Mockingbirds can pick up new phrases.

Another feature common to chatter and song is the absence of a sharply defined emotional attitude, such as hostility or fear. The meaning is not "get out," or "look out," but "here I am." Any recognizable individual or pair identifying pattern will do. What, in many species, turns this limited need into the more exacting one met by song in the full sense is the necessity of being distinctive at a distance (see Hall-Craggs's masterly discussion, in Hinde 1969) and from a more or less invisible position. This immensely fruitful necessity is the gift of territory, plus foraging habits and plumage tending to conceal the bird. American Goldfinches are neither strongly territorial nor highly invisible. They sing, but only moderately well.

Gwinner studied a Raven pair (*Corvus corax*) and found that the female responded to the absence of the male by using imitations she had previously uttered only in her youth, but which the male had been using right along. Ravens seem to be mildly gregarious (or mildly territorial), and to have a conversational sort of "song" (Bent 1946). They pair for life. Kneutgen had a pair of Shamas, the female of which had at most three song motives in the male's presence, but in his absence sang his entire repertoire—with this species that is saying a great deal.

I have argued that imitation and musical sense tend to go together. Yet on the one hand we have exquisitely musical birds which seem to imitate only their own kind at most, and on the other, harsh chatterers like parrots and Budgerigars which imitate amazingly. And even Hill Mynas only occasionally produce a bit of music; in the only case I have encountered, it was a human tune. These birds are not singers but chatterers. Their utterances are not territorial but are elaborate contact notes for keeping a pair or flock in touch with each other. With parrots, at least, the birds will either be in sight of each other or not far apart much of the time, even though they may be far enough away to make visual identification difficult. Thus the species will not have to be identifiable from a distance out of a great many inhabiting a considerable area. The birds are in a manner conversing. It is often amusing to see and hear a pair of parrots flying across the sky, gabbing back and forth to each other. "Budgies" sitting together in a cage are similarly sociable, and far indeed from the typical songbird. A normal territorial song is addressed to isolated and often invisible individuals—indeed sometimes to an area empty of conspecific birds—but chatter occurs between members of a close-knit pair or flock. The chief stimulus for chatter is in the other bird (or human substitute). It need not be in the appeal of the pattern the performer is actualizing.

In her *Philosophy in a New Key* Susanne Langer denied that bird song is music. She was thinking of music as necessarily "conscious," involving thought. Even Szöke, who insists that avian song is music, says it is not "art." This is partly a mere question of words. I think it important to realize the analogy between conscious art and extremely naive approaches toward art. But Langer, as she told me, was also influenced by experience with her Budgerigars, ignoring the fact that birds of this order have only moderately good apparatus for sound production (3 pairs of syringial muscles), which is perhaps why even their enunciation of words is mediocre compared to a Hill Myna's. Above all they are chatterers, and do not sing except marginally. If the sounds produced by nongregarious birds are closer to human music, those of the gregarious and chummy ones are perhaps a little closer to human speech. Only parrots have been observed to use a word or wordlike noninstinctive sound to express a request of human beings.

Parrots do sometimes pick up a musical bit; the King Parrot (*Aprosmictus* [*Alisterus*] *scapularis*) in Australia, a rather ungregarious forest species, has a simple musical call in the wild. But essentially their interest is in companions, not in sound patterns; hence, whatever sounds a companion makes are also interesting. Human speech sounds may substitute for ordinary parrot chatter, provided there is no natural companion and some human being gives the impression of being sociable and helpful. (Hill Mynas will learn a tune, also the title of a song, or a harsh "Ah, shut up!" Or "Why don't you say something?" In Japan a pet Hill Myna called out, "Konnichi wa" [Good morning], from his perch in the garden to passersby.)

Close observation of Orange-winged Amazons (*Amazona amazonica*) has begun to turn up evidence that parrots do imitate in the wild, but imitate other members of the species (Nottebohm and Nottebohm 1969). In a later article Nottebohm (1970) says he has evidence that these birds engage in antiphonal duets (see also Power 1966), and like the writer, he sees a parallel with the Boubou Shrikes studied by Thorpe and North and mentions the Shama as another similar case. He also holds that local groups of parrots develop group dialects and that this can be an aid to evolutionary adaptation. Thus imitation in the wild by parrots can have two functions. Significantly, female Grey Parrots imitate very well (Jackson and Sclater 1938).

We are probably safe in dismissing the never very astute idea that parrots make no use in the wild of their unique facility in imitating. Nottebohm (1970) develops fascinating generalizations about the shift from "self-centered" (nonimitative) to "environmentally dependent" or "plastic" vocalizing, a shift which, he says, has occurred at least three times: in parrots, perching birds, and man—but apparently not in the larger apes or in monkeys! In all three cases there occurs in immaturity a stage of functionless playing with sounds influenced by sounds in the environment. The babble of babies is the human version. In all three cases also the plasticity, including the tendency to take on new forms from sounds made by other creatures, continues into maturity. Nottebohm tells of his Grey Parrot which, at the age of 20, was still adding to its repertoire of 100 imitated sounds. Many passerines also retain considerable plasticity in full maturity. Finally, in all three cases the imitative use of sounds has social functions, helping to unite individuals in pairs and give some cohesion to flocks, but at the same time to some extent isolating flock from flock and inhibiting interbreeding between them (as human dialects presumably do between human groups). In some situations this may have helped to produce new species.

D. Hill Mynas

In some ways the peak of the development of chatter is found in the Hill Myna. As I had guessed from experience with caged individuals, this species can hardly be said to sing in the wild. Brian Bertram (1970), in a model study, says it is "scarcely territorial," and his analysis shows that while one of the bird's four chief types of utterance (the "call") has "some" of the attributes of song, it has more of those of chatter. It is completely acquired by copying other individuals, curiously only those of the same sex (yet females call nearly as much as males); it functions to keep mated birds, and also members of flocks, in touch; and though there are individual repertoires of calls, each utterance is brief and, in spite of a good deal of immediate variety, there is marked discontinuity. Nor is there much resemblance to music. The reason is not far to seek. The bird is more concerned with immediate responses by the mate or flock member than with his or their utterances as sound patterns in themselves. The performance is much more conversational than the typical territorial song. That Mynas in the wild imitate only or chiefly other members of the flock also indicates that the interest in sounds is tied more closely to interest in inducing response than it is with many singers. This species has a matchless ability to reproduce sounds in general, and the reinforcement for its vocalizings comes mainly from interest in companions rather than in sound patterns as intrinsically pleasing. It furnishes a fine test case for the principles argued for in this book. This Myna may be the world's most gifted nonsinging chatterer. Its future is somewhat threatened by the export trade. Moreover, many birds are taken too late in life, after "imprinting" is about over, to fulfill the expectations of the purchasers.

E. Cries, Chatter, and Song

The division between mere calls and song with which we have been operating in previous chapters is insufficient. Utterances are of at least three kinds: (1) unlearned emotional outcries and contact sounds, (2) partly learned contact sounds, and (3) partly learned territorial songs. (There are also special courtship songs and still other forms of musical utterance, but in this book I am avoiding their consideration.) "Chatter" is my label for (2) insofar as the utterances are nonterritorial and largely unmusical. As we have seen, it often takes the form of imitation between members of a mated pair. In some duets (2) and (3) are merged into far-carrying, musical, territorially efficacious imitations between mated birds. The greater the distance that contact signaling must span and the lower the visibility the higher in general the probability that the utterances will be musical.

The element of "learning" common to (2) and (3) takes two chief forms: (a) imitation and (b) experimentation (especially by immature birds) with utterances and selection of those falling within inherited "limits of taste" (Chapter 3C) or agreeing with an inherited "template," as some call it. This is the only way that many mediocre singers, pigeons, for instance, seem to learn their songs. But they do learn them (Craig 1909: 62; 1911a: 404) and this, as well as the more musical quality stressed by Craig, distinguishes them from the mere cries of these birds. True, as Mr. Luis Baptista reminds me, Konishi and Nottebohm (Hinde 1969) give evidence that the Ring-dove (*Turtur risorius*) does not even need to hear itself or any other bird sing (in some experiments it is deafened from the start) in order to develop normal song. This suggests that the template and feedback, in some cases at least, are purely kinesthetic rather than auditory. Alexander (Sebeok 1968: 182–87) made a similar experiment on an insect, with similar outcome. These to me rather disconcerting results seem to negate my hypothesis that all that strikes us (and functions) as song involves some auditory aesthetic feeling. But it remains true that pigeon songs are "formless at first" (Craig) and only gradually take on proper form. Song Sparrows (*Melospiza melodia*) reared from the eggs by canaries in soundproof rooms sang normal songs in the end (Mulligan 1966). Yet in this species imitative ability has also been shown, whereas Craig found no evidence that Ring-doves can imitate. A member of this species, reared from the egg by foster parents of another species, adopts many habits of the other species, associates exclusively with it, tries to mate with it, but yet courts, bows, and coos in the manner of its own species only. It recognizes and responds to sounds of its foster nurses but does not copy them. (For a good summary of experiments on various ways and life stages in which birds learn songs see Hooker in Sebeok 1968: 311–37.)

Surprisingly Craig thought that the Ring-dove's "perch-coo" was sung out of mere good spirits and that the song was functionless, or appeared "to be enjoyed purely for its own sake." He also notes that it was often sung responsively, stimulated by another bird singing in the distance. Otherwise it was not subject to stimulation by passing events as other calls were. This seems a startlingly clear case of pre-

Howardian failure (by a great observer) to detect the role of "territory in bird life." Craig's pigeons, it seems obvious, were counter-singing territorially.

Even in Orthoptera some slight learning by practice is involved in singing, and imitation is not entirely absent (Sebeok 1968: 182–87), although Alexander, in an impressive summary, argues that the genetic determination of insect songs is virtually complete. He does not refer to Broughton's results (1965b), which suggest that insects (grasshoppers) are more capable of imitation than most students have thought.

Perhaps it is a question of degree. Insect songs are primitive musically, and so are most pigeon songs (but see Chapter 11A), compared to the territorial announcements of many Oscines. There does seem to have been an evolution of acoustical learning ability (including imitativeness) and musical ability, with significant interrelations between these capacities.

F. The Limits of Imitative Ability

Are (miscellaneously) imitative singers superior to nonimitative ones? Yes—and no. Imitative facility is a positive power, but so is the ability to achieve a higher degree of musical coherence than a medley represents. I take both into account in rating songs (Chapters 6E, 10).

Sauer (1954) is careful to say that an imitative song is superior to one which is innate rather than to one which, at least for all that we yet know, is perhaps partly learned through imitation of adults of the same species. And it may well be that the almost purely innate or genotypic songs, such as he showed that of the Whitethroat (*Sylvia communis*) to be, are never on a very high musical level. However, the Messmers' work (1956) on the Blackbird seems to indicate that the innate element is nearly as decisive in its case (yet cf. L. Howard 1953: 183–89 and Hall-Craggs 1962).

The imitative type of genuine singer, e.g., the Mockingbird, is often overpraised, not in the sense of being liked too much, for liking is a free privilege, but in the sense of being liked for partly fictitious reasons. It is not true, whatever some have said, that birds of this group, such as the lyrebirds of Australia or the North American Mockingbird, simply duplicate the music of all other birds. No species is a superbird, as one capable of such feats would be. The law of specialization, or of species limitation, as I call it (Hartshorne 1958a), is a fundamental principle which cannot be evaded: the law according to which a species of animal can do this, but not that, while another species can do that but not this—the law that achievement is always more or less exclusive. Each imitative species and individual specializes in the sort of thing it copies, and in the sort of stylization or distortion (to put it frankly) by which the accuracy of the copy is restricted.

A highly imitative species must be one with no very strong fondness for any one musical pattern; and hence it must have a rather loose sense of overall musical form. It cannot care too much whether a sound be harsh, a sprawling handful of notes, a mediocre or brief tune, or an elaborate musical structure; except—and this is a notable exception—that it will somewhat disfavor the last. For even an imitative species has to have some style, some unity of pattern, of its own; hence, like all medleyists, it must utilize other compositions (of any length) only in snatches. This is true of the Mockingbird (Nice and Nice 1931) and the lyrebirds (Hartshorne 1953): They prefer to copy brief, often unmusical songs or mere call notes; or to take bits, torn out of their musical context, from the more elaborate and highly organized songs.

A Mockingbird takes a phrase out of the variable sequence of the Wood Thrush, simplifies even this phrase (in all cases which I have heard), and either repeats it immediately two or more times (which is quite contrary to Wood Thrush practice and musical spirit) or passes immediately to something different and musically rather irrelevant. In either case he misses the main musical point of the song, which is the eliciting of exquisitely harmonic contrasts between the successive phrases in the sequence, these phrases being both deeply contrasting and musically related. Far more adequate is the Mockingbird's rendering of the Carolina Wren; somewhat more adequate, his version of the Cardinal.

Considering the amazing variety which they give us, the medleyists are wonderful performers and deserve our enthusiasm; but they can never substitute for those fine performers who excel in musically unified, clear-cut patterns or sets of variations on a single pattern type. Not that the better imitative species lack unity—no good medleyist does. But the unity is of a looser kind, and not a substitute for the more integrated or more "classical" style. Besides, the imitative birds do not attain the highest degree of purity of musical tone. Even a Chickadee can exhibit such purity to a degree probably beyond the reach of the Mocker.

I once asked a veteran observer of Southern birds what he thought of the Mockingbird's imitations of the thrush. "Poor," was his reply. To the same query regarding imitations of the Eastern Meadowlark (I have yet to note even an attempt at this), he answered, "Not very good." In Australia (Hartshorne 1953: 116f.) I spent many hours listening to the stunning performances of both species of lyrebirds, and to the several forms they were imitating. I never once heard what seemed to me a full duplication of any of the most musical of Australia's other species. I conclude that vague or suspiciously absolute statements by enthusiasts, though acceptable as expressions of feeling, should not convince us that the principle of exclusive specialization can be transcended. Imitative species have their own remarkable skill, entirely deserving of admiration, but it is *their* skill, not quite that of the other highly developed songsters around them.

Sometimes we are told both that the imitations are perfect and that they improve upon the originals. If "perfect" means exact, there is inconsistency. What actually happens is that extremely simple songs seem glorified when put into the context of an impressive medley, or when uttered in a louder or deeper voice. There are all degrees of faithfulness in the reproductions. The poorer ones will often go unrecognized and so will not be counted against the bird's abilities! But sometimes even a poor copy is unmistakable if the bird copied has a highly distinctive song for the area and if one hears even such poor echoes of the song only in regions where the imitated bird is found. Thus in Georgia I used to hear poor *Mimus* versions of the Wood Thrush, but in Austin I never heard such a thing, though I still live with Mockingbirds. I also never hear Towhees (*Pipilo erythrophthalmus*) imitated, whereas this happened now and then in Atlanta. (The Towhee's mediocre song was nicely done.)

As already remarked, a very good reason for the inexactitude of some imitations is that they are not firsthand. One bird, say, has picked up a Towhee song, perhaps before he moved into an area; his neighbor, who may not have heard the original or may not have noticed it, copies the copy. And so the faithfulness is diluted. It cannot be that Mockingbirds imitate only alien species or Mockingbirds not imitating alien species. From this, and the admission that copying is not absolutely exact, innumerable degrees of inexactitude follow with logical necessity. The only alternative is to take imitation as a magic power, able to do anything.

I grant that the foregoing reasoning has much less (but still some) force when applied to lyrebirds. They have large territories, richly inhabited by other singing or vociferous species. Their imitations average much more faithful than the Mocker's, with the qualification, however, that their muscles for voice control are inferior, and I do not believe they could come even as close as *Mimus* does to the tone quality of a Wood Thrush, for example. The famous recording of an isolated Massachusetts *Mimus* establishes that species as capable, in exceptional circumstances, where he does not hear others of his species, of equalling, perhaps surpassing, the lyrebirds in faithful duplications of sounds. But in the average case, there is no doubt at all, the lyrebirds are the greater mimics. They can of course reach lower pitches.

G. The Distribution of Imitative Ability: Imitation and Size

There is some reason to think that imitativeness correlates with size. Make a list of large Oscine birds which could be said to sing, and another list of small singing Oscines. I think it will be clear that the proportion of good imitators is larger in the first list. The two lyrebirds, several Drongos (*Dicrurus* spp.), and several species of bowerbirds (Ptilonorhynchidae) are among the rather few large singing Oscines. All are noted for their skill as imitators. In captivity, Bellmagpies, Common Crows (*Corvus brachyrhynchos*), and Ravens imitate remarkably. The list of small singing Oscines would be huge, but the intensive imitators would be a mere handful by comparison. In the United States, indeed in the Americas generally, not one out of hundreds of small singers is known as an habitual imitator; whereas out of the much smaller number of singers the size of a Catbird (*Dumetella carolinensis*) or larger there are about a dozen. Jays (*Cyanocitta* spp., *Aphelocoma* spp.) are imitators in subsong. And the only wood warbler (Parulidae) credited with this habit is the largest one in the family, the Chat. Parrots are mostly large and even Budgerigars not really very small.

One explanation may be the greater pitch range of medium or large birds. The only other explanation I can think of is that, according to some authorities (e.g., Rensch 1954), large size, other things being anything like equal, is generally correlated with more intelligence (thus rats compared to mice, etc.). In spite of some individual small birds that open bottles and some small species that use tools (see Thorpe 1963: 374ff.), Rensch's arguments and experiments seem cogent. Imitation, I have argued, shows a kind of intelligence; hence, on Rensch's principle, we should expect the imitators to be large rather than small. And so, it seems, most of them are.

Imitative singing is worldwide, from the far North (Bluethroat, *Erithacus svecicus*), through the deep tropics to Patagonia, South Africa, Australia, and New Zealand (Tui). In England only the Skylark (*Alauda arvensis*), Song Thrush, Starling, and Marsh Warbler seem outstanding, and none of these seems to equal the best medleyists in various other areas. In North America, besides *Mimus* and the introduced Starling, there seem to be only the Catbird, the California Thrasher (*Toxostoma redivivum*), perhaps a few other thrashers, and the Chat. Thus nearly all are in one family, the *Mimidae*. Only the first two species seem very impressive in this respect.

The Carolina Wren was once credited with imitation, but no careful observations whatsoever bear this out, and much contradicts it. Any species, especially in subsong, may imitate occasionally, but if there is a song not of the normal medley type it is the song of this wren. It is far too meticulously organized, too neat and tight in design, and somewhat too discontinuous and lacking in immediate variety to fit. Mockingbirds love to imitate this species, so perhaps someone read the relationship backward! There is also a faint resemblance between some Cardinal songs and some Carolina Wren songs, and between the songs of the Kentucky Warbler (*Oporornis formosus*) and some of the Wren's songs, but there is no reason in either case to see more than resemblance. The Wren is found in many places where the Warbler does not occur, but the song does not vary correspondingly. I consider this attribution a blunder, or at least an exaggeration. Bewick's Wren (*Thryomanes bewickii*) has also been said to imitate other species. Perhaps it occasionally does, but not as a major factor in its style of singing. Wrens are not medleyists.

Australia claims the largest proportion of highly imitative species, perhaps with justice. But South America has half a dozen members of the *Mimus* genus, several claimed to imitate very well, and Middle

America has the Black Ouzel (*Turdus serranus*), which sounds a good deal like a Mockingbird and imitates. India has the Shama, the Racket-tailed Drongos, and several *Chloropsis* species said to give good or even "perfect" imitations (Ali 1949, 1962, 1964). Africa has fine imitators in the robin-chat (*Cossypha*) genus, also the Capped Wheatear (*Oenanthe pileata*). The two Australian lyrebirds are indeed among the finest of all cases of combined singer and mimic, weaving all sorts of sounds into a splendid coherent recital. Several bowerbirds apparently are almost pure mimics, giving somewhat disconnected echoes rather than a coherent medley. As one Australian puts it, they are "nonsinging imitators." Most of the other Australian cases can be easily matched elsewhere. The largest number of imitators in a single genus seem to be in the American *Mimus,* the African *Cossypha,* and the worldwide *Turdus.* Perhaps *Acrocephalus* should be added, and the larks *Melanocorypha, Alauda,* and *Mirafra* (not *Lullula* or *Alaemon*).

Of course families in which there is no singing at all are likely to lack imitation, apart from the massive exception of the parrots, at least one or two species of which do sing. Imitation among the 1000+ species of Suboscine perching birds has not been reported, to my knowledge. Since these creatures are vociferous and in many cases songful, I expect that observations of imitation by them will be made, though undoubtedly their utterances are much more narrowly determined genetically than are those of parrots or Oscines. Many Suboscines duet, as readers of Skutch or Hudson know, and though the duets are mostly only crude forms of co-singing, much farther from developed imitation than the forms we have been considering, still there is scarcely an absolute distinction between duetting and imitation. If this is correct, then barbets (Capitonidae) (Payne and Skinner 1969) and woodpeckers (Picidae) (Kilham 1959) are not completely devoid of imitative ability.

The majority of good miscellaneous imitators are tropical or at least subtropical. Of course, the majority of birds of almost any kind are tropical. Yet if instead of tropical we say nonmigratory, I think it is true that such species are more usually good imitators than migrants are. The best migrant imitator, if Hudson is to be trusted, may be the White-banded Mockingbird (*Mimus triurus*). Possibly almost as good are the Bluethroat and the Marsh Warbler and Blythe's Reed Warbler (*Acrocephalus dumetorum*). Perhaps also the warblers *Sylvia nisoria* and *Hippolais icterina.* But the following residents, the two lyrebirds, the Spotted Bowerbird (*Chlamydera maculata*), the Australian Heath-wren (*Hylacola pyrrhopygia*), several *Cossypha* of Africa, half a dozen Indian species (of *Chloropsis, Dicrurus, Copsychus*), some larks, the now nearly worldwide Starling, and some other species seem as capable. It is clear, however, that the correlation between miscellane-ous imitation and the mild climate or food habits that make permanent residence possible is lower than the correlation between these factors and duetting. Duetting, especially in its more developed forms, is bound to correlate with residence, since it implies a high degree of cooperation between two individuals such as only year-round associa-tion makes possible, and this apparently does not occur with migrants.

Miscellaneous imitation has no such close connection with perma-nent pairing. Indeed, the Mockingbird, e.g., does not, at least con-sistently, practice the latter. (Chisholm and others believe that lyre-birds generally do mate permanently.) Yet, for whatever reason, migration and the resulting short song season somewhat disfavor imi-tation, which, after all, is rather a luxury, since specific and, to a con-siderable degree, individual distinctiveness are possible without it.

H. Summary

(A.) Imitation, which is of several kinds, is pervasive among Song-birds.

(B.) Imitation expresses interest in sounds (visual display seems not to be imitated) and, in pronounced cases (F.), a less sharply defined musical taste. Its utility is probably primarily that of increasing the individual distinctiveness, variety, and hence (Chapter 7), continuity of singing. Imitators imitate each other, which sometimes dilutes the accuracy of their copies of foreign sounds.

(C.) Parrots imitate in the wild in a way which gives pairs, perhaps also flocks, their own dialects. Some true Songbirds also have such dia-lects, either as pair duets, or as parrotlike chatter, which (D.) is most developed in Hill Mynas.

(E.) Bird utterances divide into (1) innate "cries," (2) learned and more or less imitative but nonmusical and nonterritorial "chatter," and (3) learned, more or less imitative musical and territorial songs. In some cases the latter, as pair duets, have also the function of chatter.

(F.) Imitativeness is always within limits, and (G.) is widely distributed among families and regions. It is not sharply distinguishable from duetting and some forms of male counter-singing, or synchronous singing, as in insects. It is more common among large than small birds, and in the tropics or subtropics than elsewhere.

The old dichotomy, calls and songs, may be retained, provided calls include nonmusical chatter as well as cries. The old distinction has some biological significance because of the association of the more musical utterances with territory; also because they constitute more nearly self-sustaining, self-reinforcing activities, independent of immediate environmental stimuli (Nicholson 1936: 7). The bird enjoys them more in and for themselves.

5

Describing Songs

❦

A. Proposed Methods

Rider Haggard was fond of the adjective "indescribable" to convey a sense of the wonderful beauty of his heroine. Writers about songs sometimes use the same paradoxical description. Scarcely less cryptic is "wild," used in more than one bird guide. "Ventriloquial" is to my mind not very helpful either. But perhaps, as is often said, all effort to describe songs is vain. It is also said that, thanks to the tape recorder and gramophone, there is no longer any need for descriptions. But, as Saunders points out, playing a recording has by no means the full value of a description. The record merely puts the hearer in the virtual presence of an identified singer, so that he may perhaps recognize the song on a subsequent occasion. Identification, however, is only one purpose of description. A description is an interpretation or analysis; it is the phenomenon illuminated by thought, put into a system of ideas. In addition a description using visual means (such as musical notation) has the general advantage of visual representation, that complex structures can be surveyed as wholes and relationships of parts studied at leisure. Also it will probably be many years before the majority of songs over the world have been adequately recorded. For these and other reasons, written and other visual representations of songs will remain necessary.

Recordings can be turned instrumentally into sound spectrograms (sometimes called sonagrams) or other visual translations, and these have important advantages. They are far from perfect and foolproof, however. A small vertical difference near the bottom of the 'gram may mean an octave, but near the top it may mean a very different musical interval. Thus octave relationships are not immediately apparent. Differences in loudness are also poorly represented. For them one needs oscillograms made by a quite different apparatus. In one way or another, in any translation, there are always distortions or the introduction of what experimental scientists call artifacts and information theorists, "noise." All description or analysis has its risks. There is always a margin of error, a probable degree of misrepresentation. (For a defense of the accuracy of spectrograms see Poulter in Sebeok 1968. But see also Hjorth 1970, who for some purposes prefers the "Melograph Mona," which gives both an outline of melody and indications of fluctuations of loudness.)

Spectrographs have serious limitations: great expense, restriction to a short temporal section of the utterance for each exposure, and a tendency to lose either temporal accuracy with narrow-band adjustment or frequency accuracy with wide-band adjustment. (See Appendix D.)

Some writers advocate musical notation, but it is obvious that birds are not bound by human musical conventions. (Neither are human musicians, in any absolute sense. And Asia has had different conventions from the Western world.) Szöke advocates the following method: playing recordings of bird song at 1/8, 1/16, 1/32, or in some cases even 1/64 their original speed, or in other words lowering the pitch by 3, 4, 5, or 6 octaves, then using the most exact known musical notation (Bartók's) to set down what one hears. The reason for the slowing down is presumably the slowness of human perception compared to that of birds. But do birds have even 16 times the temporal resolving power of human beings? Also is there no chance of distortion in the translation into musical notation? Impressive musical patterns emerge, but do they owe nothing to the human listener and his choice of musical symbols? This seems unlikely. Nevertheless, for some purposes this method may well prove to be the best of all.

Thorpe (1961) has sometimes used another method. He tries to correct for the admitted distortions of sonagrams by certain changes in the visual patterns. This method undoubtedly has merits.

It is worth noting that certain facts about songs can be correctly expressed in words by a careful listener. Thus, if a song lasts four seconds, this can be stated with approximate accuracy by using a stop watch. If it is habitually sung 4–6 times per minute; if it is all on one pitch, or if there are wide pitch contrasts; if there are many distinct notes (apparent to the human ear) per second, or only a few—these and other facts can be ascertained and set down. Furthermore, Saunders (1929, 1951), using a notation similar in some respects to spectrograms long before they existed, tells us with remarkable accuracy much about how the birds of New England and some others sing. Other writers, using standard musical notation, have also given valuable indications. Absolute faithfulness to the reality is lacking, for there is no perfect method here. But any sequence of sounds has some sort of structure, and this structure can be more or less closely outlined by suitable descriptive devices.

A favorite device is syllabication. With some songs this is certainly helpful, especially for remembering a song. We tend to recall things in words. And there are songs which do in fact strongly suggest certain human speech sounds. "Cuckoo" (German *Kuckuck*) has some resemblance to the bird's utterance. But the critics of this procedure can easily show how crude and relatively uninformative it is, especially for some songs. Vowels are very "impure" sounds, and consonants are even farther from pure or musical tones. Yet there are many musical tones in bird song. It is thus apparent that syllables are grotesque makeshifts where the more musical songs are concerned, just as musical notation is a makeshift for the noisier songs. When Beebe heard the "Organbird" [wren] (*Cyphorhinus aradus*), what came to his mind were not syllables but musical notes. And the bird does sing in musical tones, not in speechlike sounds (apart from the guttural accompaniment in some races which I take to come from the female). On the other hand the Chebec or Least Flycatcher (*Empidonax minimus*) sings something quite like "Chebec." A spectrogram could perhaps show this. The song has never been called musical, and few birds come as close as this to English speech.

There are other difficulties with syllabication. Different linguistic habits make trouble, and the foolproof symbols for the pronunciation of syllables are almost as technical as musical notation. North (1950) has devised a simplified musical system which some might find usable. I sometimes think that the chief objection to musical notation is just that most of us are not smart enough or sufficiently well trained to use it. It is also difficult to write rapidly.

Many songs are so rapid that, except by using something like Szöke's method, it is humanly impossible to set them down either in musical or in Saunders's notation. But then it is also impossible to give relevant syllables for them, even in the crude sense of "relevant" which is usually all that is possible with syllables. Such songs are in some respects, and to some extent, truly "indescribable" by noninstrumental methods.

Saunders, nearly always sensible, perhaps yielded a little to temptation in complaining that playing the musical scores of Cheney on a piano did not, with one exception, make it possible for Chapman to recognize the bird in question (Saunders 1929: 139). First of all, as Saunders himself remarks, musical scores fail to give timbre, and the piano, of all instruments, is the farthest from birds in this, and some other respects. Birds have been called violin-like, bell-like, bugle-like, organ-like, flute-like, but not, so far as I know, piano-like. One ought at least to play the scores on a piccolo or high flute. Or better, whistle them, ideally in the uniquely adequate way Saunders was capable of. (He could reach higher pitches than most of us.)

All the methods yet devised have their uses, and none renders the others simply superfluous. It is to Saunders's credit that he uses unusually careful syllabication in a subordinate role.

Certain rhythmical patterns and something of melodic structure, as well as certain vowel-like and sometimes consonantal sounds, can be conveyed by syllables, thus: "witchety-witchety-witchety," Maryland Yellowthroat (*Geothlypis trichas*), or "how-is-teaver-how-is-teaver-how-is-teaver," one song of the Carolina Wren. But the tinkling, sometimes flute-like musical beauty that the latter bird manages to blend with the apparent syllables is not expressed.

It must never be forgotten that there is no such thing as *the* song of a species, if this is taken to denote a fully definite structure common to all individuals. Moreover, probably most individuals have at least some versatility. The wren whose song I just tried to put into syllables had other, quite different songs. Dispute about which syllables are appropriate is futile unless it is known that the same sound sequence is being described. It is nothing against the syllabication of the Eastern Towhee's song as "Drink your teeee" that some individuals sing "drink teeee," lacking the drop in pitch suggested by "your." Some sing both forms. Others sing "drink, drink teeee." The name "Tow-hee" was presumably suggested by the shorter version. What we have here is not three descriptions of one phenomenon but three phenomena about equally well or ill described. The West Coast subspecies (*falcifer*) has dropped all but the "teeee," a striking case of a musically degenerate subspecies (unless it should, as some think, be taken as a distinct species). In this book I shall not often deal with regional or subspecific differences. But that they, as well as individual differences, exist is not to be forgotten.

Whatever method is used, I at least find it helpful to try to whistle songs to myself after the birds. This forces one to give heed to the structure. Imitation presupposes grasping the pattern of what is to be imitated. One of the basic arguments for viewing birds as musicians is that they do imitate patterns.

Since Songbirds are singers more than talkers, to rest content with mere syllables for their utterances is like trying to guess the tune of a folksong from its words. If musical training were more universal, this attitude could scarcely have arisen. Mendelssohn's "Songs without Words" could hardly be indicated by inventing words sounding like the music, omitting the musical scores. With many though not all bird songs this is what we have—musical rather than, or in addition to, speechlike sounds.

For those who are not musically trained, perhaps even for those who are, a notation like that of Saunders seems indispensable. Like spectrograms it is a graph of the sound patterns. Thus $-----$ stands for a somewhat sustained note sounded five times in slow tempo;

$$-$$

$$-$$

$$-$$

$$-$$

while $-$ means a more rapid series of such notes each higher than the last in pitch; again .... is a series of brief or staccato notes on the same pitch, forming, if rapid enough, a "trill" in the nonmusical sense common in ornithological writings, while ·.·.·.· is a true trill. As the reader can see, vertical distances stand for pitch intervals and horizontal ones for time intervals. Wavy lines indicate fluctuations in pitch with no break in the sound; slanting lines indicate slurs upward, /, or downward, \. Slurs are very common. Saunders was able to do all this to scale, so that ½ inch horizontally meant 1 second, and 1½ inches vertically meant an octave (or ⅛ inch for each semitone). Not many could duplicate this achievement with anything like his accuracy.

It is to be understood that straight lines, whether horizontal or sloping, are likely to oversimplify the song. For full accuracy, the lines must very often be curved or broken.

The Saunders method failed to do one thing which the spectrogram does, and that is distinguish between narrowly limited frequency spread, i.e., "purity" of tone, and broad spread, i.e., "noisiness." Thus he did not distinguish — from ∎. The first would sound musical, the second, harsh or unmusical. Both may appear in songs we think of as musical, but the thin lines assume greater prominence in such cases. Narrow vertical lines in a spectrogram mean "clicks," very brief noisy sounds. (Saunders uses such lines for a different purpose, unfortunately.) Slanting lines, as already stated, betray upward or downward slurs. If the lines are narrow, the slurs will sound musical. At what point the slant is to count as vertical, i.e., as denoting a lack of frequency definition, is a delicate question. Apparently a rather slight slope suffices to "redeem" the sound musically, /, or even much closer to the vertical, depending upon the resolving power of avian or human ears. (See Chapter 6C.) Note that "noise" has a negative meaning in information theory. Music is in a sense more informative than noise, a more sharply defined message. This is one of many ways in which aesthetics is relevant to science. Make a line thick enough and it stands, not for a sharply defined portion of the pitch possibilities, but for all the possibilities indiscriminately.

It is not entirely clear to me why one cannot use thick lines to indicate noisy sounds, thus duplicating the spectrograph. True, it is perhaps hard to do this in field notations. But one can make a box, □, compared to —.

Here is an example of the problem of description. The White-browed Warbler (*Basileuterus leucoblepharus*) in southeastern Brazil has the most musical of the sixty or so songs of the wood warbler family known to me. Mrs. Mitchell (1957) thinks it comparable in musical excellence to the Winter Wren's song. She describes it as descending the scale. I had no difficulty in recognizing the song from her account. (I did eventually see and hear the bird singing.) The song does, like a fair number of others, descend the scale; but there is a complication: It is the only song I know that *zigzags* downward. The first note is the highest, the second considerably lower, the third is between the first and second in pitch, the fourth lower than the second, and so on. The song ends on a final upward flourish (Figure 1). The total number of notes seemed to be at least 15 (3½ seconds). This

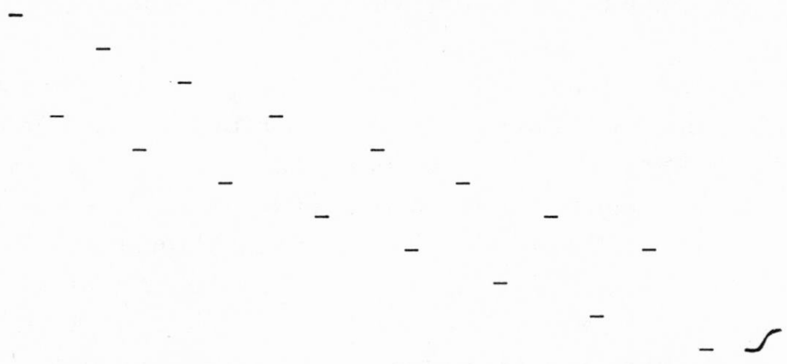

FIG. 1. *Song of the White-browed Warbler*

song seems to be unique in the world, yet it is so "logical" that one wonders that it is so rare. I might not have noticed the special feature of the song had I not attempted to whistle it.

Some songs are so easily described in unmistakable aspects that seeing the bird adds little to the certainty of the identification. Thus only one bird in North America, perhaps in the world, the Varied Thrush, sings a sustained note with a humming undertone and perhaps a slight break in it, then a second or two later another similar prolonged note *on a different pitch,* and so on, four or five different pitches altogether, in various orders, the tones having a quality "like escaping steam." This song is one of the slowest in the world, and the slowest in the United States. The habitat in this case helps, being highly distinctive, but it is not necessary to know that. It is interesting that this bird is now seen to be a ground thrush and that White's Ground Thrush (*Zoothera dauma*) in Japan sings rather like it (though I think with a simpler song). So does the Aztec Thrush (*Zoothera pinicola*) in Mexico. Although the plumages of the three birds are much less similar than their songs, a common origin and spread via Bering Strait seems reasonable.

There seems to be but one bird in North America, the Canyon Wren (*Catherpes mexicanus*), that, in ringing musical tones, descends the scale in at least seven steps, usually with a slight upward flourish as finale (Figure 2).

B. Hold's Notation

For those able to use it the best notation seems to be that of Hold (1970). His essay tends to supersede all previous work in the visual

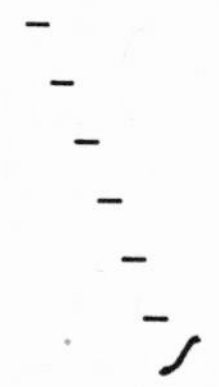

FIG. 2. *Song of the Canyon Wren*

representation of song. He reviews what has been done in this field, seeming to miss nothing (except a work in Japanese by Kawamura), and argues cogently that syllabication is at best only an adjunct, that standard musical or "staff" notation, whether in Cheney's, North's, or Szöke's (Bartók's) form, has both important advantages and important disadvantages. Also that, while the graphs by Saunders are the best of the hitherto available devices, they fail to show the difference between tones and noises, and can show loudness only by compromising the representation of pitch (by thickening horizontal lines and so seeming to imply a greater pitch spread instead of greater amplitude).

Hold's own striking proposal amounts to a combination of the Saunders graphs, plus modified staff elements, syllabic indication of timbre or phonetics (used also by Saunders), and verbal indices of dynamics (e.g., "cresc." for increasing loudness). The modified staff elements, taken partly from Schmitt and Stadler (1919), include the use of ♪ for "tones" with a strong mingling of nonmusical sounds, and ♪ for sounds that are essentially nonmusical (i.e., hopelessly impure or confused in frequency). The lower limits of figures like ♪♪♪ indicate the lower pitch limits of the noisy sounds in question. A central seven-line portion of a graph (see Figures 1 and 2) indicates the relevant octave (most songs staying largely within an octave). Octave limits are given in heavier lines. Only notes with definite pitch are to be represented by lines.

Figures 3 and 4 show Hold's system in operation, in comparison with spectrograms, graphs, staff notations, and three "compromise notations," the last being considered the most adequate, especially in Figure 4. (In Figure 3, (b) is also good.) The vertical lines show the very noisy character of the "chattering trill" or "gobble."

The notation brings out the limitation of the Nightingale's singing which Garstang and many others (especially non-Europeans) have

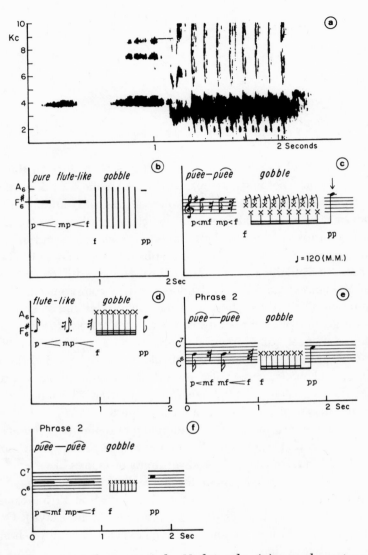

FIG. 3. *Phrase 2 of the song of the Nightingale: (a) sound spectrograph; (b) graph notation; (c) staff notation; (d) Compromise Notation 1; (e) Compromise Notation 2; (f) Compromise Notation 3.*

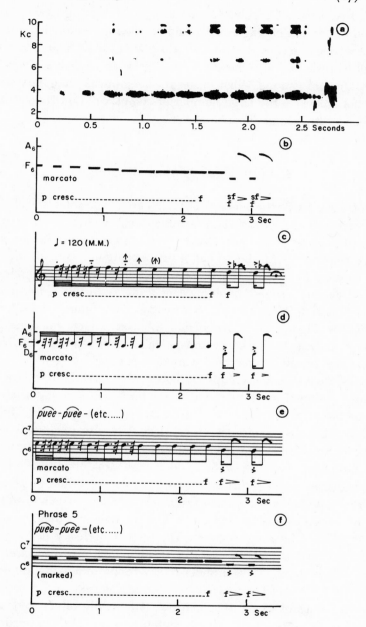

FIG. 4. *Phrase 5 of the song of the Nightingale: (a) sound spectrograph; (b) graph notation; (c) staff notation; (d) Compromise Notation 1; (e) Compromise Notation 2; (f) Compromise Notation 3.*

noted: that it is not highly melodic or tuneful, relying heavily as it does on reiteration of single notes, and employing some noisy sounds. An extreme contrast is the New World Slate-colored Solitaire or the Hermit Thrush, and also the Woodlark, Blackcap (*Sylvia atricapilla*), or Blackbird of Europe. What makes the song outstanding, in spite of these limitations, is the large number of complex phrases (up to 24), and their neatness and dynamic power.

C. The Basic Types of Song

Songs have parts, the simplest of which are single sounds, called by some writers "notes." However, in strict musical usage a *note* is a single pitch; I follow Bondesen and Davis (1966) in preferring this meaning for the word, and with them I call a single continuous sound, whether it remains on one pitch or is slurred between two or more pitches, a *figure*. I also use "sound" as equivalent to figure in this sense. It may help to think of "5" as *visually and spatially* one figure while "10" is two figures. Figures are grouped into "phrases" which, for some purposes of analysis, are taken as units, combined or repeated in diverse ways. I use the word "pattern," varied sometimes by "song," for the most *inclusive definite* groups of notes which the bird utters. By "definite" groups I mean those which the bird uses on many occasions and too often for the sequence within groups to be taken as random. Suppose a bird has phrases A, B, C, D, E. If it always sings them in this order, or does so many times in succession, ABCDE forms a pattern, a superphrase. (A phrase could be called a subpattern.) But if the phrases are sung in various orders, roughly at random (with some preference probably for certain fragmentary or approximate orders), then by chance the order ABCDE will occur now and then, in which case it will not be a superphrase. The longest perfectly definite patterns I can find last about 15 seconds, and these are very rare. The majority of patterns are well under four seconds, and many are under two seconds. One of the shortest patterns is ⅔ second, and constitutes the entire song of Henslow's Sparrow. Apparently all he can do is repeat his tiny set of notes after a suitable pause. Some approximate patterns last longer than 15 seconds. Thus *Chamaeza ruficauda* (Chapter 11B) ascends the scale in very small steps, and it may take 20 seconds or more to reach the upper limit of its pitch range, whereupon it may stop or simply reiterate the highest note several times. Or, there are songs in which the bird accelerates and then decelerates. In all such cases known to me the pattern is vaguer than a definite set of notes. Hence the time length is variable. In the vaguest case of all the pattern is just reiteration, either of a single note or of two notes on different pitches, the last being what musicians call a "trill." How many reiterations there are is left open by the pattern.

Apparently quite determinate musical forms are possible for birds within very narrow temporal limits only, much under ½ minute, probably under 20 seconds. "Long-continued" singing is a more or less random sequence of patterns, not governed by a single pattern.

Robert I. Bowman greatly surprised me by the information that members of a population of Fox Sparrows in the Sierra Nevada have repertoires, each unique to the individual birds, of 2, 3, 4, or even 5 songs, and a given bird sings his songs in an *order* which he seldom varies. The songs last about 2.4 seconds, so that the total pattern, neglecting pauses between songs, takes up approximately 5, 7, 9.6, or 12 seconds. Thus my denial of patterns of more than 15 seconds can still stand, in a fashion. However, if pauses (5 seconds each) are counted, the total performance occupies 10, 17, 24.6, or 32 seconds. Each individual's having its own largely fixed sequence of songs would facilitate individual recognition, but from the aesthetic point of view it means less variety, a more rigid repetitiveness. The songs themselves are notably musical. At present no other case like this seems to have been reported.

In speaking of a pattern as definite or fixed I refer to the individual bird, not the species. Probably no wholly definite pattern is fixed for an entire species. But the variability of singing in a species is one thing, in a single individual, quite another.

Perhaps the simplest phrase is that consisting of two figures, each a different pitch, as in "cuckoo." True "trills" are rapid reiterations of such phrases. (In the strictest musical sense of the word the two pitches are a half-tone apart, but it seems impractical for ornithologists to attempt this degree of precision.) Some writers use the term also to cover the rapid reiteration of a single note or pitch. With Davis I avoid this usage, or employ quotation marks to distinguish it from the proper meaning of a reiterated pitch contrast. Davis calls any quick reiteration of a figure a rattle, but one must remember that the quality may be beautifully bell- or flute-like. A true trill is different from a rattle because the repetition in the former is not of a single figure but of two discontinuous ones, whereas in a rattle it is a single continuous sound, whether one note or a slur, that is repeated.

The basic problem in music and in all aesthetic creation is to combine repetition with novelty, the expected with the unanticipated. In trills or monotones the only features not anticipated are when the song is to begin and the number of reiterations. This is a very rudimentary form of novelty. Most birds do better than that. With nearly all the better songs the complexity cannot be defined by a simple formula. Thus, for example, to say that the Crested Bellbird sings "pan-pan-panella" gives no idea of the ways in which an individual varies his theme from moment to moment. In this respect sonagrams, too, are misleading, unless many "shots" are presented of the same individual.

Among ways of singing we have the following not sharply distinguishable kinds:

(1) Simple repetition: Each individual has a single pattern which he reiterates, at intervals, with practically no variation, hundreds or thousands of times per day.

(2) Repetition with variations: An individual has basically only one song, but he treats it as a theme subject to variation. An extreme example is the Pine-woods (Bachman's) Sparrow, that wonderful songster of the southeastern United States, whose variations are so dramatic that it might be more natural to think of them as distinct songs.

(3) Repertoire of repeated songs: An individual has a number of distinct songs, each of which is generally sung over and over at suitable intervals, as in (1), before another is introduced. The order of patterns is largely unpredictable. The Song Sparrow is an outstanding example, except that it often has several slight variations for each song (Mulligan, personal communication) and so may belong under (4). A better example is the Chaffinch.

(4) Repertoire plus variations: The individual commands several songs, and in repeating each he now and then introduces several variations which do not alter its basic theme. The Carolina Wren and the Cardinal are fine examples. The chief mode of variation, especially with the Wren, consists simply in varying the number of elements in a song. If the theme is the rapid reiteration of a certain phrase, thus, "pillier, pillier, pillier," the number of reiterations will shift now and then to one fewer, or one more, than the number which is standard for that song. The Cardinal goes much farther in such number juggling,

for one of his songs may involve now a dozen, now only two or three, reiterations of a note or phrase. But both Carolina Wren and Cardinal possess repertoires of basically distinct songs. Only days of observation can give any idea of the complexity of their repertoires.

(5) Variable sequence: An individual sings a song once (or reiterates it several times in a rapid series), then without any marked pause introduces a different one, which is similarly quickly disposed of, and thus he goes on, from one pattern to another. The total number of patterns may be small, as in the Yellow-throated Vireo, or large, as in the Red-eyed Vireo (*V. olivaceus*). The sequence of patterns is not fixed (if it were, the whole song would constitute a single pattern), but is somewhat variable, free, or random. It is almost (but not quite) as though the bird were throwing dice to determine which unit to render next. An example, kindly furnished to me by D. Kroodsma, is a Rock Wren (*Salpinctes obsoletus*) sequence: ABDADBAEFBEAEFGEA-GHGHIEIHJIKJIKJKJL. Note the complete avoidance of immediate reiteration. Such singing is an exercise in contrasts. Some Rock Wrens have a hundred patterns (Kroodsma, personal communication) and they work through the repertoire in the irregular fashion indicated.

(6) Medley-sequence: An individual sings a variable sequence of patterns, some of which are or contain imitations of other species of birds. This type of song is likely to be showy and to attract popular attention and acclaim. Types 5 and 6 are what Saunders calls "long-continued songs," since there may be no substantial pauses during many minutes of performance.

The outstanding or "best" songsters of the world are divided among the foregoing types, with the possible exception of type 1. Only the most complex single songs repeated without variation or alternative can *perhaps* atone by their inner variety for the lack of relief inherent in this style of singing. The Winter Wren is the best example known to me. But probably his song should be classified as a case of repetition with variations, since there are small deviations from time to time in the rendering of the song, chiefly in slight omissions or abbreviations. The other five types all include songs of outstanding excellence. Indeed to exploit to the full the possibilities of any one of them taxes the resources of the bird brain. The law of "exclusive specialization" results in a plateau of excellence reached by some hundreds of songsters scattered about the world, each of which is near the limits of avian musical capacity in some respects or other, but none in all respects. What some birds gain beyond a certain point in musical integration, they tend to lose in variety, and vice versa. Again, some excellent singers have simple songs, but atone for this by the large number of distinct songs; others have more complex songs, but fewer of them.

It seems idle to argue as to which type is better or shows higher development in singing skill. Again, how can one prove that purity of tone and exquisiteness of harmonic contrasts do, or do not, make up for lack of variety? In extreme cases of the latter deficiency I personally rule out the classification "outstanding" (capacity for variety of actions is one measure of skill), but only in extreme cases; a moderate dose of variety quite reconciles me to a song if its musical perfection is striking. But vice versa, a mild approach to musical perfection, as in many imitative species, reconciles me to a song which excels in variety, complexity, and fluency. I believe this is the only way in which futile debate can be avoided. It is the same with human music and other art forms. We must not demand all the merits in high degree in each work of art, or we shall never be content with any. But neither should we set too high a value upon one isolated merit. In that case, a single chord could be accepted as a composition, or an ever-varied but never musically-integrated sequence might also pass muster.

It should be noted that there are two modes of variety as between songs or phrases: *immediate variety*, found in types 2, 4, and most of all in 5 and 6, and *eventual variety*, found in types 3 and 4. Immediate variety is in general correlated with continuousness of singing (Chapter 7), the longest pauses being found chiefly in types 1 and 3, the shortest in 2, 4, and above all in 5 and 6.

D. Some Descriptions of Songs

Saunders (1951) has said of the Lark Sparrow (*Chondestes grammacus*):

> [The] song is highly musical and attractive. It consists of a series of short notes, two-note phrases, trills, and cherrs, varying considerably up and down in pitch. The cherr-like notes seem to be the most characteristic. Variation in the same individual is very great. A bird sings one song after

another, no two of them alike. I recorded six songs from one bird, each sung only once, and while I was recording one, the bird would sing others that I was unable to get, so that the total number, all sung in a very few minutes, was decidedly more than six.

The bird often sings in flight, and the flight songs are sometimes prolonged [see Fig. 5, no. 3] to two or more times as long as the ordinary two- or three-second songs.

—Pp. 301–302.

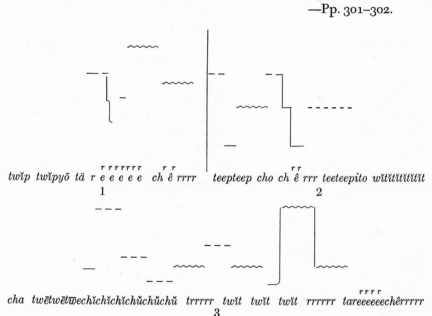

twĭp twĭpyō tä r e e e e e ch ê rrrr   teepteep cho ch ê rrr teeteepito wĭtĭtĭtĭtĭtĭt

1   2

cha twētwētwechĭchĭchĭchŭchŭchŭ trrrrr twĭt twĭt twĭt rrrrrr tareeeeeechêrrrrr

3

FIG. 5. *Songs of the Lark Sparrow*

In his diagrams Saunders shows only pitch and time, the one vertical, the other horizontal, and he allows only a single pitch to each sound no matter how great its frequency spread. Hence the unvarying thickness of the lines has no significance, and his vertical lines do not represent sound but only show that the end of one note and the beginning of another on a different pitch are simultaneous to the ear. If frequency spread were shown, the lines for the "cherrs" would be much thicker.

The Lark Sparrow's song is Type 5 (since there is no imitation). In spite of the variety of pitch arrangements, the singing is all in one style,

with trills and cherrs prominent in every song. Because of the total
scope (wide pitch contrasts, many contrasting songs) and the musical
quality, this is a superior songster, in the best 5% in the contiguous
states of the U.S. and, I think, in the best 5% in the world (see Chapter
10).

From the length of a repeated song (shown most accurately in sonagrams) and the normal rate of songs per minute, one can calculate
the lengths of pauses and the degree of continuity. For this reason, one
of the most useful, in some ways the most useful, of the regional books
is *Birds of North America* (Robbins et al., 1966) since it gives both
audiospectrograms (which are small and rather indistinct, it is true)
and the rate of songs per minute for many species. On pp. 308 and 316
of that book we learn that Henslow's Sparrow's song lasts less than ½
second, Cassin's Sparrow's (*Aimophila cassinii*), 2⅜ seconds, Bachman's
or Pine-woods Sparrow's, 4 seconds. Also, that the first song is noisy
rather than musical, which is shown both by the verticality of the lines
in the spectrogram (*pace* Irby Davis) and by "unmusical ssllick," while
the other two show a mixture of tones and slurs, confirmed by "musical" and "beautiful." Finally the third song (obviously much the most
complex and delicate of the three) is said to be varied and to be sung
4–10 times per minute, from which we can deduce high continuity and
guess that the bird has a repertoire of patterns or songs, not just a
single song. Thus it is not Type 1, and the form is too definite for
Type 6. Beyond this we are not given sufficient information to decide
among the remaining four types.

The three songs illustrate three gradations of singing skill: (a) primitive or crude, (b) refined but simple, and (c) refined and complex.
The biological significance of these by no means merely anthropomorphic distinctions will concern us throughout most of the rest of this
book. One hint or two here—the third song is sung in much the most
concealing habitat (small trees as well as tall grass) and the first in
probably the least concealing (grass only). A similar contrast is found
between the habitats of the North American thrushes with the least
highly developed songs (the Robin, *Turdus migratorius,* and the blue-
birds, *Sialia* spp.), and those of the truly forest thrushes, e.g., the
Catharus species (see Chapter 9E).

Spectrograms give but slight indications of variations in loudness.
To show these Greenewalt (1968) uses a form of oscillograph, as well
as a spectrograph. As he says, oscillograms bring out complicated pat-

terns of amplitude change which, and there is evidence of this, may serve birds as recognition marks, along with the timbre and the pitch contrasts.

Among the species which Greenewalt treats in this dual way are the Common Loon (*Gavia immer*), the Western Grebe (*Aechmophorus occidentalis*), and the Cardinal. Greenewalt remarks (p. 33) that the simple form of the songs of the Cardinal (p. 49, Figure 36b) and the Tufted Titmouse (Figure 28b) puts them "not far from loon and grebe." We are all in debt to this author for his original work on the physiology and physics of song, but I disagree with his remark as follows. (1) The Cardinal's pattern as shown (two sloping, somewhat curved figures repeated four times) occupies over 2½ seconds, while those of the other species are much shorter. (2) A normal Cardinal song has two and often three parts, of which the spectrogram shows but one. (3) A Cardinal has a repertoire, and it has not been shown that this is true of the Grebe and the Loon; also (4) a Cardinal sings each song in a number of ways, chiefly by fragmentation, dropping this or that part, or by number juggling. (5) The Cardinal has a greater pitch range than the Grebe or Titmouse. Finally, (6) the voice is sweeter than those of the other birds mentioned; though I admit this could hardly be told from the spectrograms. Titmice have repertoires and practice variations, but otherwise are mediocre singers. Saunders was not being merely sentimental when he termed the Cardinal a "great artist," and no careful person is likely to say this of loons, grebes, or titmice.

In the remainder of this chapter four songs, all of Type 5, will be dealt with.

Two North American songs have often been described with great care. It has been shown (Wing 1951) that the Hermit Thrush's song approximates a complete pentatonic scale, with all harmonic intervals in play, and this is a notable fact for subhuman music. Here is an old-fashioned but musically expert encomium (Cheney 1891):

> After striking his first low, long, and firm tone, startling the listener with an electric thrill, [he] bounds upwards by thirds, fourths, and fifths, and sometimes a whole octave, gurgling out his triplets with every upward movement. Occasionally, on reaching the height, the song bursts like a rocket, and the air is full of silver tones. A second flight, and the

key changes with a fresh, wild, and enchanting effect. . . .
Start from what point he may, it always proves the right one.
When he moves off with

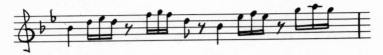

and then, returning, steps up a degree and follows it with
a similar strain

it is like listening to the opening of a grand overture.

The most recent study, and the most thorough of all, by Szöke's
slow-down method, shows that a song of this species, less than 2
seconds in length, may have 45–100 or more notes and 25–50 or more
pitch changes, not a few of the notes being sounded simultaneously,
as in the Wood Thrush (to be dealt with next). (Szöke, Gunn, and
Filip 1969.) Thus it is indeed, as Szöke says, a "musical microcosm."
He calls it "the highest summit in the evolution of animal music so
far known to us." He speaks of "its strongly human-like forms lasting
not more than 1–2 seconds and its pitch level ranging from b^3 to c^6
(1980–8448 cps)." Thus Cheney's poetry was not unrelated to the facts
of nature.

Szöke's collaborator Filip has devised a "fundamental-frequency
recorder" which is claimed (I am not sure rightly) to come closer
than the usual instrument to giving a clear picture of the musical
structure of the song and an objective check on the correctness of the
staff notations which Szöke makes of songs played at greatly reduced
speeds.

Here are two accounts of the song of the Wood Thrush.

In a moment one is oblivious to all else. . . . How is it
that a bird has that inimitable voice? . . . Whence the in-
spiration that, with the utmost refinement, selects and ar-
ranges the tones in this scrap of divine melody?

—Cheney (1891)

Mathews (1921) has this account.

His notes are usually in clusters of three, and these *are of equal value**; the commonest one of the clusters is an admirable rendering of the so-called tonic, the third, and the fifth tones, thus:

That is one of the best things the Thrush can do, and he does it splendidly too; there is no doubt about his intervals; they compose a perfect minor chord. After a pause of a second or two the bird supplements the minor with the major form a third lower, thus:

Then after that comes something like this, with the last note doubled:

which is immediately succeeded by a pretty relative phrase with a vibrating final note:

* The Hermit, on the contrary, sustains his first note and follows it with a series of rapid and brilliant ones.

Still the singer continues, and in a burst of feeling rapidly
reels off the following:

There is a harmonic overtone to nearly all the notes of the
song, and frequently a strange and vibrant if not harsh tone
succeeds the three-note group, thus:

It is difficult to explain the nature of a voice so peculiarly
musical; undoubtedly the Thrushes possess extremely short
and extremely long vocal cords, and probably the latter
are vibrated along with the former thus producing a singular
effect of harmony. The rapidly repeated resonant note which
frequently completes a phrase has a distinct metallic ring,
which strongly reminds one of the musical ripple of the
blacksmith's hammer as it bounces upon the anvil.

According to Deignan (1945), the White-tailed Blue Robin (*Cin-
clidium* [*Myiomela*] [*Muscisylvia*] *leucurum*) has a song which re-
calls the *Hylocichla*. When I heard it in Malaya it did remind me of
the Wood Thrush, in its refined quiet strength and beauty and in the
succession of contrasting phrases, each lasting about a second. (The
Malayan bird, however, does not equal the rich, partly simultaneous
harmony of the American one.) Note that in the diagram of the songs
(Figure 6) successive figures are rarely on the same pitch (except in
no. 12).

These pseudospectrograms are not nearly so accurate as Saunders
was in his work. The songs were sung in the order given except that,
after no. 12, the bird began repeating some of the earlier items. The
repertoire probably exceeded 15 items. As in the two thrushes considered above, no pattern is repeated until at least one contrasting pattern

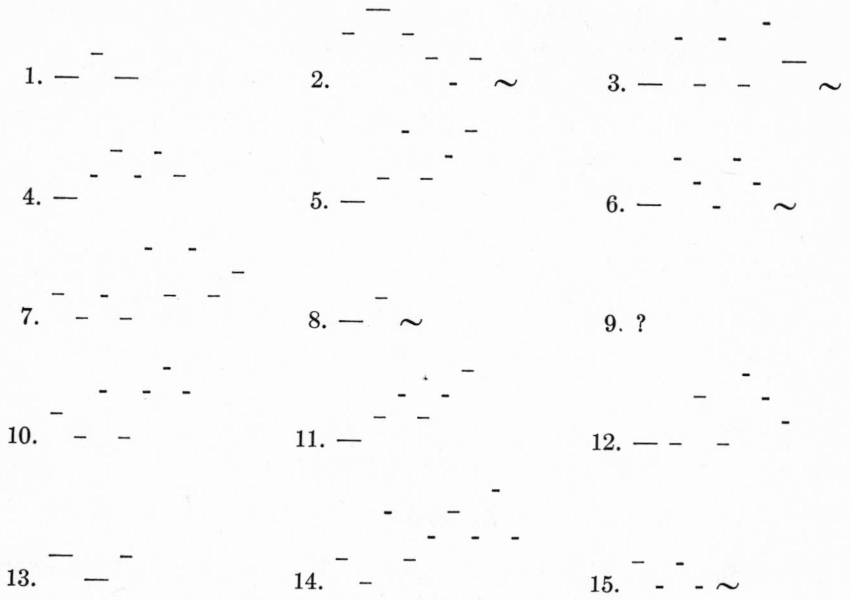

FIG. 6. *Songs of the White-tailed Blue Robin*

The symbol ∼ in nos. 2, 3, 6, 8, and 15 represents an unmusical rattle. The structure of no. 9 I found baffling.

has been sung. Long and short notes are frequently alternated, as in nos. 3, 7, and 11, but, unlike the species to be considered next, this bird does not begin songs with short notes. Although pauses averaged 5 seconds the singing is relatively continuous since each pattern was contrasted with its predecessor; thus the pauses count to some extent as parts of the music, as musical "rests."

In the field the full patterns cannot be detected and the songs seem to have scarcely half as many notes as they actually contain. The unaided ear catches the obvious contrasts only, but does receive an impression of musical beauty. Some of the songs (nos. 2, 3, 6, 8, and 15) end with a rather unmusical chuckle. But otherwise this bird is a flutist par excellence.

Several writers have praised this song but in indefinite terms. It is a montane species, like many other superior tropical singers, and is a highly typical case of extreme invisibility. As Deignan says, one scarcely sees it unless it happens to come out of the dense bushes onto a forest path. I saw nothing of it during two days of listening until I sat by such a path and waited. It sang from the ground. For the bird's size its voice is remarkably deep and mellow.

Another musical song which cannot be adequately judged without slow playing, that of the Mountain Tailorbird (Figure 7), can be heard

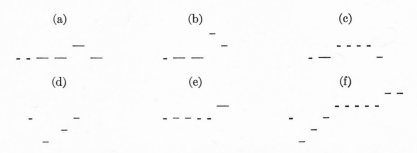

FIG. 7. *Song of the Mountain Tailorbird*

A sequence, e.g.: a c e f a b f a c b d a c b, lasts 63 seconds.

at the same spot (Fraser's Hill, Malaya). The song has received some attention but has not been definitely and correctly described. Contrary to Smythies (1953), the song is not a single pattern reiterated "in a remarkable number of keys." The general pitch level varies from song to song but the melody usually varies also. As with the Wood Thrush and the Robin discussed above, successive songs always present some contrast, so that, although the pauses are much longer than the songs, continuity is not to be considered low, the contrasts being part of the music. The singer is tiny and its voice is high-pitched, but slow playing reveals perfect tones. Nothing is squeaky, harsh, or merely chirpy. (The song is very unlike the mediocre ditty of the Common Tailorbird, *Orthotomus sutorius,* a bird living in much greater visibility.) Like so many superior singers, this species is hard to see in the dense, often cloud-bathed forest understory it inhabits. This is why in at least one book its very presence and its song are overlooked. But one observer (Ogburn 1953) waxes eloquent: "striving in tones of unutterable sweetness and rarity to reach and then exceed the upper ceiling of audibility, lost to all other concerns in the mists of his forest home on the high slope of a volcano." Playing the song at quarter speed brings out the structures.

The figure shows six patterns (the bird may have had more), three closing with falling pitch, three rising at the end. None, it seems, is ever immediately reiterated. Falling cadences (a), (b), and (c) are used 10 times in the sequence of 14 songs. Thus the suspense created by the "gothic" upward trend noted by Ogburn is adequately balanced. Some suspense is felt in (b), but the other two falling patterns, (a) and (c), occur half of the 14 times. Out of a possible 13 direct contrasts, 9 occur. None is directly repeated. All contrasts seem musically effective and the patterns attractive, even after many hearings. The lowest pitches are in (d) or the first part of (f) (which is the same). Except in (d) the bird repeats a note or two (but not perhaps a figure —see spectrogram IV., Appendix D) several times in each song. But (d) is a mere fragment of (f) used occasionally as a separate item. Achieving variety through fragmentation is a regular practice of many species.

If I am told that the bird feels nothing of all this, I ask: (1) How is this known or even knowable? (2) Why and how, in that case, does the bird avoid direct repetition? (I never noted repetition in any sequence, though there is a 3 to 1 probability for it in this sequence alone) and (3) Why does it exhibit the characteristic musical biases about rising and falling cadences and, within limits, maximizing contrast? This species (like the previous one) presents a superb example of song type 5 (variable or free, *partly* random sequence). If anyone thinks there are exact laws, other than statistical, determining such sequences I do not envy him the task of trying to conceive them. I think he would be pursuing a real will-o-the-wisp. But there are aesthetic principles limiting the randomness somewhat. Beauty (and freedom) is always a mean between the classical determinists' supposed world and chaos.

Philip Wildash (personal communication) thinks this song does not quite equal the Blackcap's. But (I assume) he has not heard it at slow speed. The unaided ear can do more justice to the lower-pitched European song. I find this song one of the most charming, just as Ogburn evidently did.

This species could be heard from the hotel—and also down the road a small distance—at the top of Fraser's Hill, Malaya. With it near the stream, besides the highly musical Robin, is the Lesser Shortwing (*Brachypteryx leucophrys*), which has a pretty song lacking in scope or variety. These three species have refined songs; all three birds are exceedingly hard to see, especially the Robin and the Shortwing. Only by sitting motionless beside a path did my wife and I see either. The Robin sang as we watched him in the path. The Shortwing we saw was the female, but the song came from the same spot always, and it fits descriptions as did no other song in the area not otherwise identified. I have no doubt whatever that I heard the Lesser Shortwing sing. It is a good but not a superior singer.

E. Summary

(A., B., D.) Available methods of describing or analyzing the phonetic features of songs are set forth and illustrated. The method of Saunders is preferred, especially for those who do not read musical notation, but for those who do, Hold's combination method, in part the same as that of Saunders, is recommended (B.). It is contended that recordings and spectrograms do not abolish the need for noninstrumental methods, and that all the proposed methods have some value.

(C.) Six basic song types are distinguished: simple repetition, repetition with variations, repertoire of repeated songs, repertoire with variations, variable sequence, medley sequence.

CHAPTER

6

Measuring Song

❦

A. Annual Amount of Singing

In this chapter I aim to show how some aspects of song behavior may be measured, at least precisely enough to yield relationships not attributable to chance. It will be no fatal objection that different observers do not in a given case assign exactly the same values to the variables. This often happens in science, but statistical analysis may make the differences harmless or unimportant.

Some relationships are objective and yet, even apart from vagaries of measurement, irreducibly approximate or statistical. Thus, for all its backward eddies, the flow of a stream does correlate with the slope of the landscape. Yet if only small bits of the stream are seen at a time this may not be apparent. Such are the problems we encounter in this chapter and those that follow.

The first variable to be considered is annual amount of singing. I take a year as the period of measurement in order to cover the entire cycle of activities. I shall confine myself to Oscines to avoid unmanageable complexity. Some species sing at most a few hours or days in the spring; others, during much of the year.

"Amount of singing" is ambiguous. Some species sing for many minutes with scarcely a pause; some sing a song of one or two seconds and then invariably pause for a period five, or even a dozen or more, times as long. The latter, or "discontinuous," type uses but a small fraction of the "performance" period in actual singing. Time and energy are thus freed for other activities. To measure continuity we need to know values for two of the four variables: song length, pause length, "cadence" (song plus pause, or the time between the beginning of a song

and the beginning of the next song—Reynard 1963), and number of
songs per minute. Five songs per minute gives a cadence of 12 seconds;
and if each song lasts 2 seconds, the bird sings 1/6 of the performance
time. Some sing even less than this. With others the performance time
is virtually all singing, giving a continuity fraction of 1.

There are two sorts of pauses: those (usually substantial) separating
merely reiterated songs or phrases, and those (usually slight, Chapter
7) between contrasting songs or phrases (as with many thrushes). Not
only are the pauses in general shorter in the second case, but the bird
is less free for other activities, since it must retain a sense of what
preceded the pause and select a different song to follow. Many birds,
even some with small repertoires, are almost infallible in avoiding repetition until at least one contrasting phrase has been used. Their pauses
are really part of their singing and are scarcely discontinuities. Still,
if they are unusually long for this kind of singing (never very long,
a bird's memory not sufficing for that), I take them to some extent into
account. If this is a mistake, then some of my higher continuity estimates should be considerably lower.

Annual amount of song is the number of hours of performance times
the continuity fraction, or it is the total number of songs times the
average length of the songs. Of course, the numbers in question are not
easily arrived at. I have found but one careful published estimate
(Rollin 1943a) of annual output of song—186 hours for the English
Skylark. From data supplied by Jared Verner (personal communication) it appears that Long-billed Marsh Wrens (*Cistothorus palustris*)
sing at least 150 hours a year. However, for purposes of comparing
species, we can employ probabilistic indices of comparative amounts
of singing, such as the "song season" (number of months or days in
which a species is reported by observers to be in "full song") plus
some fraction (I take 0.4) of the number of months or days in which
there is some but not abundant singing. The resulting number measures how much a species sings compared to others only insofar as further relevant factors, such as continuity, are equal. Comparing species
one by one, they may be very unequal; comparing large numbers, the
difference is in the same direction as the seasonal difference, i.e., the
birds with longer seasons also sing more in other respects.

It is conceivable that singers with very short pauses compensate for
this by extra large gaps (minutes or hours) between "performances."
Continuity and "persistence" may vary inversely. Rollin (1943b) compared the Willow Warbler (*Phylloscopus trochilus*), a mildly discon-

tinuous singer, with an extraordinarily continuous one, the Skylark, and found that the former sang just under ⅔ as much per day—62 compared to 99 minutes. (To his credit, Rollin did not count pauses as singing. See also Rollin 1945.) Since the continuity difference is still greater, the warbler "performed" more while singing less. It seems likely that a Mockingbird, to mention only one species, singing with high continuity and also sometimes at night, would often far surpass either of the above daily figures. It may be significant that the Skylark spends energy in flying during performances, and this may shorten the singing. Habitual flight-singers are a small minority of all singers.

There are some species, e.g., the Cactus Wren (*Campylorhynchus brunneicapillus*), which sing daily throughout the year. In these extreme cases, length of season means less than it normally does, for such singing is chiefly a contact device between pair members, as in many wrens, and a short burst of song every hour or so may suffice for this purpose. Such singing is also usually discontinuous in the sense explained above. Length of season may, in the opposite way, be somewhat misleading where there is intensive night-singing, unless there is correspondingly less singing by day. In general, night-singers seem to sing freely by day and to produce a greater amount of song per 24 hours than other species. The exceptions appear to favor the correlations we shall be concerned with.

With all qualifications (see Chapter 8A), song seasons are, statistically speaking, indicative of annual amounts of song. If we take continuity into account, this indication is strengthened; for on the whole the singers with short seasons sing discontinuously. Thus, nearly the entire wood warbler family, including its tropical portion, are discontinuous and have short seasons, while thrushes have somewhat longer seasons and are much more continuous. The Brown Thrasher (*Toxostoma rufum*) has a short season and is highly continuous, but this case is atypical.

B. Correspondence of Amount to Need

Song being functional, its amount must correspond to the intensity and duration of the needs which it serves. The need for song (Chapter 2) seems to arise chiefly from two factors: isolation or territoriality (separation from potential or actual rivals or even mates); and invisibility of the bird in its habitat.

That the annual amount of singing increases with need may be seen by comparing some of the large or more homogeneous families in the Americas. A number of species whose habits are rather well known (thanks partly to Skutch's tireless observations) and with which I have some acquaintance in many states and countries are listed in Table I. T stands for territoriality and all forms of isolation, I for invisibility, S for length of season, and C for continuity. Each variable ranges from a rating of 9, the highest rank, to 1, the lowest. Families may be rated according to the ratings of most of their species.

TABLE I

Family	$T \times I = Need$	$S \times C = Amount$
Troglodytidae	$9 \times 9 = 81$	$6 \times 7 = 42$
Mimidae	$9 \times 7 = 63$	$4.5 \times 9 = 40$
Turdidae	$9 \times 8 = 72$	$4 \times 8.5 = 34$
Vireonidae	$9 \times 6 = 54$	$3.5 \times 7 = 24$
Parulidae	$9 \times 4 = 36$	$2.5 \times 5 = 12$
Paridae	$4 \times 5 = 20$	$5 \times 4 \times 0.5 = 10$ (see below)
Tanagridae	$3 \times 3 = 9$	"Mostly sing little" (Skutch 1954)
Corvidae	$3 \times 2 = 6$	"Little at any time"

Of course the table is a rough sketch (some details are given in Chapters 8B-D, 9B-G, and 10B); but I think that careful observers with wide experience would not suppose that the last four groups deserve anything like the estimates of either need or amount which the first four do. (The Paridae, in general, are not only discontinuous but somewhat meager in their performance periods, even in spring. Their habits enhance their visual identifiability.)

The first correlation, then, is of need with annual amount. If the facts are at all as I have suggested, this correlation gives some support both to the theory of the functions of song and to the supposition that annual amount of singing is a significant variable.

C. Correspondence of Need to Song-Development or Skill

Birds that forage in flight fly "well," if this means swiftly, with efficient energy use, versatile control of direction, and so forth. Moreover, this skill in flying, an evolutionary achievement which must have been reached in numerous steps, is intuitively apparent to the human observer. Swallows, hummingbirds, and swifts give a sense of ease, versatility, and grace as one watches them fly. Is there anything analogous to this in song? I am sure that there is, but it is not without reason that some ornithologists are skeptical on this point. For one thing, we have had to react against the naiveté of our recent ancestors concerning the difference between human intuitive impressions of birds and objective facts of avian biology. That I, for instance, find the flight of swallows more graceful, more beautiful, than that of Chimney Swifts (*Chaetura pelagica*) or hummingbirds, is, as it stands, a fact about me—or perhaps about human beings—rather than about birds. What is a fact about these birds is that all three kinds fly with great skill, in terms of speed and efficiency (ability to spend most of their waking lives in the air, to change direction sharply, etc.). Moreover, this skill is apparent to us almost at a glance, as well as through instruments of measurement. This is the sort of distinction I am proposing about song, as measured intuitively and also, in whatever ways possible, objectively. I am not identifying the two approaches, but asserting a rough or partial correspondence. Nicholson (1936: 19) once suggested the same point. I claim that it can be supported by valid statistical evidence (Chapters 8–11, also below, D).

In one way the above analogy understates the case; for while flight is primarily a means of locomotion, not of display, song is essentially auditory display. Hence auditory impressions, as such, are entirely relevant. It is true but not decisive that human audition is not directly relevant. It may be a useful indirect indication, and, at least until we are immeasurably farther than we are now in the employment of instrumental means of recording and analyzing, it may be foolish not to take this indication into account. The main objection is probably the inferior temporal resolving power of the human ear. Spectrograms and slow playing of recordings can help us here. In this way Szöke (1962) reached the conclusion that from a musical point of view the Woodlark is the most skillful of European singers; but a number of us (e.g., Koch) have said this all along, and no one seems ever to have thought of this species as less than a very good singer. Nor do I know of a singer that was thought poor that seems to call for a high rating on the basis of slow replaying and spectrograms. In general, poor songs sound worse played slowly, while good songs sound as well or

better. I say this after considerable experimentation. Szöke's forth-
coming book will be of great interest in this regard.

Greenewalt (1968) points out the "beautiful" complexity which instrumental analysis exhibits in the Lapland Longspur (*Calcarius lap-
ponicus*). But its song has long been praised by those who are familiar
with it, and I have omitted it from my list of highly developed songs
only because there has been no evidence that the bird has a substantial repertoire of songs, as Meadowlarks, e.g., do, and because the song
seems somewhat less complex than the Bobolink's (*Dolichonyx oryziv-
orus*), for example. Greenewalt makes much of the pitch range of the
Brown-headed Cowbird (*Molothrus ater*). This is indeed remarkable,
but it is the only impressive aspect of song-development in this species!
The song lasts less than a second, and consists of 15 sounds. There
seems to be only a minimal repertoire (see Saunders) of two songs.

L. I. Davis, veteran recorder and observer of Neotropical birds,
shows that what appear to be mere noises to our ears and in spectrograms of the ordinary kind may, on slow playing and more careful
spectrographing, turn out to be definite frequencies altering extremely
rapidly, or two sound waves, one modulating the other. And so, for
example, the Chipping Sparrow's song (*Spizella passerina*) is not so
unmusical as it seems to be. Nevertheless, overall it is a poor song, for
the internal complexity of tones Davis (1964b) seems to reveal in it
are used in an extremely repetitive fashion. (See Spectrogram V., Appendix D.)

As another example, Borror has written me that he is not sure that
Henslow's Sparrow's song should be called "poor," and suggested that
I try it at quarter speed. I have done so, and have also tried one-eighth
speed. It is a neat little pattern of five figures:

Even at half speed the Song Sparrow exhibits a whole repertoire of
patterns, each with several times that number of figures. And at one-
eighth speed the Lapland Longspur's splendid pattern has 15 distinguishable figures, each slurred over two or more notes. I think that
Henslow's Sparrow commands a piece of music that as such escapes

the human ear; but it is still a very humble piece, and implies mild rather than strong ecological forces favoring song (medium rather than low visibility, not very large territories, not very many species within hearing that must be distinguished).

It is important to realize that terms like "good" or "poor" suffer not only from subjectivity but also, a quite different point, from vagueness. Does "poor" mean in the lowest one percent, or the lowest ten? Borror wrote me that LeConte's Sparrow is more clearly poor than the Henslow's. I agree. But both are in the bottom five or ten percent. And "poor" is a reasonable word for this. An old anonymous Chinese writer was sharper than most of us in this matter. Instead of simple adjectives, e.g., "jealous" or "drunk," he would write, "three parts jealous" (out of ten) or "five parts drunk," etc. Mere adjectives, even with adverbs like "very" or "slightly," are vague, whether or not they are evaluative. Without numbers there is little definiteness.

I do share with the four writers discussed above the conviction that we come closer to hearing what the birds hear in their songs if we play them at half or quarter speed. For any purpose other than that of aiding recognition in the field this is how they should be played. However, even if Greenewalt (1968: 142) is right that birds have much better than ten times our temporal resolving power, it does not follow that all the microdetail which we miss is biologically important. Some of it almost surely is, hence the value of instrumental aids, but a bird's power of reacting to a multiplicity of details must be limited, and the "high points" of organization which our ears pick up may be by far the most important features of most songs. I am not convinced, though I am open to conviction, that the evidences I shall offer in this and later chapters for the biological relevance of human impressions, critically and judiciously evaluated and employed, can be upset entirely by the argument from the radically diverse temporal resolving powers of avian and human ears.

In some matters only rough comparisons are possible, yet these comparisons may be useful. Since ability to sing is clearly a skill, it must have degrees. There must be causes for the various degrees; but we cannot find them unless we can measure the degrees.

One source of confusion here is that each species has the skills it needs, or it would not be there—at least not for long. So, as my only ornithological teacher (Sewall Pettingill) once said to me, the Least Flycatcher's crude and weak little song is "as functional as a thrush's."

Surely. But there is a difference between a skill that meets a slight need and one that meets a great one. Some birds seldom need to fly and then not far, so they fly slowly and in "labored" fashion. In one sense they fly perfectly well, in another not well. As an evolutionary achievement, fewer or smaller steps were presumably needed to reach their present level of flying ability than to reach that of a swallow. Flying ability, or singing skill, can be lost, but the first time the ancestors reached the present low level marked one end of the evolutionary ascent that we are measuring, the other being given by the more remote ancestors which could not fly or sing at all.

Many ornithologists are deeply convinced of the hopeless subjectivity of the idea of singing skill. However, (a) this skill is not the only important variable in bird study the estimation of which has subjective components; (b) while such expressions as "sings well," "highly developed song," even "beautiful song" are of course in some degree subjective or anthropomorphic, they are in some degree also objective and scientifically relevant; and (c) they can with care be made more so. Finally, (d) I shall present massive statistical evidence showing that, while the thesis of *unqualified* subjectivity ("the thesis of subjectivity," for short) throws light on detailed differences among observers or writers, it fails to explain the broad outlines in the incidence of singing skill as humanly judged, whereas the thesis of qualified objectivity, in conjunction with relevant ecological and other objective considerations, does explain these outlines.

The first bit of evidence for this view is now to be presented. Others follow in some of the later chapters.

D. Incidence of Highly Developed Song in Taxonomic Groups

During many years of studying songs in many countries, I have been drawing up and revising a list of approximately 200 of the world's outstanding singers (Chapter 10B). These are about 0.05 of the Oscines plus the two lyrebirds. In recent years I have used the personal rating system to be explained in the next section; but the species on the list (called for convenience, *singers or s.s.) have been praised by others and include the singers of a large majority of the most highly praised songs in the literature in several languages. If this list has only personal or humanistic import, the distribution of the *species over the bird families should be random, except as reflecting special relations of birds to man. In fact, the distribution is in close accord with known principles of avian anatomy and ecology:

(a) All are perching birds.

(b) Only two, the lyrebirds, are Suboscines.

From (a) and (b) we see that singers which man finds superior have more elaborate muscular equipment with which to sing (see Thorpe 1961: 107; Ames, 1971: 94, 106, 118, 133–36). Yet this equipment is not used as a criterion in comparing the complexity, etc., of songs. I have heard nonperching and nonoscine songsters in many lands. Some sing well (see Chapter 11), but—with the exception of the lyrebirds—they all fall short of the highest rank in several dimensions. And lyrebirds, like parrots, have three pairs of syringial muscle-attachments, compared to two or one for other nonoscines.

(c) In Table I (in section B) the first three families, with maximal needs and amounts of singing, have the only highly developed songs in the eight groups. By my reckoning the three families have about half of such songs in the world, although they are but one tenth of the Songbirds, far fewer than the other five groups.

(d) Three families (or subfamilies)—Turdidae, Troglodytidae, and Sylviidae—totaling 665 species (Austin 1961) have about 110 *singers; while the Hirundinidae, Campephagidae, Corvidae, Paradisaeidae, Grallinidae, Bombycillidae, Artamidae, Sturnidae, helmet-shrikes in the Laniidae, Estrildinae, and four subfamilies of weaverbirds, Ploceidae —914 species in all—have either none or at most 6. The reason for this extreme inequality is not in any personal or human trait but in known facts of bird life. Among the larger groups, wrens are the New World family, true warblers the Old World subfamily, and thrushes the worldwide family which in highest degree meet the conditions putting selective pressure upon song-development: territoriality and invisibility (given feeding habits, habitats, and plumage). By contrast the group with few or no first-class songsters are at the opposite extreme of gregariousness (polygamous habits in at least one case: the birds of paradise, Paradisaeidae) and visibility. A bit less extreme are 1558 species in 16 families or subfamilies, e.g., Nectariniidae and Muscicapidae (whose foraging habits automatically furnish some visual display), Pycnonotidae, Timaliidae, Parulidae. These birds are mostly nonterritorial or in some sense gregarious, or brightly plumaged, or live in well-lighted places, or in some way are able to exert influence visually, often through sexual dimorphism. In this group, 25 or fewer belong to the *singer list. The remaining Oscines (about 800) are intermediate both in need for song and in number (50 or fewer) of superior songsters. Here then is massive statistical evidence that the human organism is sensitive to the realities of song-development as a functional dimension of bird life.

In Table II the groups considered above are arranged in order of decreasing need for song. (It must be borne in mind that species that are somewhat conspicuous on modern lawns may have been less so in earlier times when grass was uncut and other wild vegetation was present.)

TABLE II

Number of species	*Habits, etc.*	*Need for song*	*High-ranking songsters*	
			NUMBER	PERCENTAGE OF SPECIES
665	Territorial, invisible	Intense	110	17
app. 800	Moderately territorial and invisible	Medium	50	6
1558	Gregarious (nonterritorial) or visible	Slight	20	1.3
914	Gregarious and visible	Very slight	5	0.5

E. Six Parameters of Song-Development

Although results can be obtained by more casual methods, better results should be achieved by making the criteria of "good singing" as definite as possible. In fact songs, like other aesthetic objects (as was explained in Chapter 1B), can be rated by relatively objective physical aspects. These, I suggest, are the aspects which measure the difference separating a particular manner of singing from not singing at all. Lower and lower degrees of song-development approach the zero of singing as a limit. Thus, suppose a bird's voice is weak; this is closer to making no sound, and so to not singing, than if the voice were strong. (1) *Loudness* then is our first measure of song-development. It must be related to the size of the bird—we do not expect a wren to be audible as far as a typical thrush is—but in principle a loud song is more of a song than a faint one.

Again, suppose a song is extremely simple. This, too, is closer to no song than if it is complex, since the series, fewer and fewer notes or sounds, ends in no sounds and thus no song; a single note is hardly to be distinguished from a mere call, such as an alarm note. And its distinctiveness is bound to be less if there are many species comparable in size and basic structure. Thus (2) complexity, which for brevity I term *scope,* is our second dimension, or subvariable, under the comprehensive variable, song-development. Next (3) is *continuity.* A Henslow's Sparrow sings a song lasting 0.3 second, but usually pauses about 14 times as long between repetitions of this song (information from Donald Borror). Here the discontinuity fraction is 1/15. The lower this ratio, the less the bird can be said to sing at all. (4) The fourth variable is *tone,* the musical quality of the single sounds in a song, where "musical" implies an approximately single frequency except for harmonic overtones. Birds which are thought of as radically songless, like the domestic hen Chicken (*Gallus gallus*), usually lack tones, and both avian and mammalian alarm or anger notes tend to be "noisy" or nonmusical. But in general "songs," whatever exceptions there may be, and even if singing is defined by its functions (such as territory advertisement), tend to be much more musical than mere calls. Song-development is thus in part a progress toward frequency control or sharp definition of pitch, as against miscellaneous, blurred frequencies. A small minority of functional songs seem close to the zero of this development.

(5) Certain pattern aspects which give impressions of unity-in-contrast, or what *Gestalt* psychologists call "closure," are common to human music and bird song, and are not found to the same extent in the cries of songless birds, or in mere calls of singing birds. Such aspects are rhythm, harmonic intervals, melody, key change, interval inversion, theme and variations, crescendo, accelerando. Many musicians have commented upon the occurrence of these in bird song. Let us call this subvariable *organization.* It is harder than the others to judge objectively; but the remedy for this difficulty is found, not in ignoring the factor, but in estimating it as objectively as possible. For it is clearly important. An unorganized sequence of sounds would not have the ready recognizability and memorability which the uses of song require. So this variable, too, approaches the zero of singing at its lower limit.

(6) The last dimension of song-development is *imitativeness,* the

tendency to reproduce sounds which the singer has heard, to learn songs by listening to them. There is evidence that not just some singers but probably all of them, especially among Oscines, have something of this tendency. Of this variable also the zero of singing is probably the lower limit. I am inclined to take all complex songs as proof of considerable imitative power.

When songs are called "melodious," "sweet," or "beautiful," it is chiefly the fourth and fifth subvariables, tone and organization, which are being appreciated. These variables do have biological significance, since tones yield more distinctive patterns than noises, and a good *Gestalt* is more readily recalled and recognized than a poor one. But for signaling at a distance loudness also is important, while continuity enhances the individual's power to dominate or hold the attention of mates or rivals, and scope increases the possibilities for individual distinctiveness, which we know to be important for many species. Also, scope (insofar as it consists of "immediate variety") makes the higher degrees of continuity possible (Chapter 7A). Imitativeness is perhaps not valuable in itself, but it is at least a means of achieving scope, and hence continuity, and it expresses a mental flexibility which may be useful in other applications.

Six measures of singing are now before us, but they are still unquantified. However—and here I am much indebted to Myles North (correspondence)—numbers from 1 to 9 may be assigned to each subvariable. Our formula then is: SD (song-development) = $L + S + C + T + O + I$ (the sum of the values for loudness, scope, continuity, tone, organization, and imitativeness). The highest rating, 9, in each dimension would give a total score of 54 points. No actual species exhibits this theoretical "perfection." Always there is weakness in one or more dimensions. But scores of 47 or 48 do, I find, occasionally occur.

In the assignment of numbers, elements of arbitrariness or caprice are bound to enter. How shall we determine just where, between maximal and minimal loudness (for the size of the bird) to place a species? Shall we measure the distance at which it can be heard? But this depends partly on many factors, including the keenness of the observer's hearing for the pitches occurring in the song. The sensitivity of some birds for high pitches is apparently greater than man's. For us the high-pitched song of the Golden-winged Warbler (*Vermivora chrysoptera*) is much weaker than most songs, but some physical measurements by an ornithological physicist (H. Mayfield 1966) yielded normal loudness in decibels. Possibly it would be better to ignore this variable, provided that we excluded obvious whisper songs and subsongs not functioning as distance communications. However, this simplification would not make a serious difference to the conclusions I wish to draw.

My practice of allowing each species some credit for imitativeness, up to 5 points if the song is complex, is certainly open to question. But at worst it results in giving more weight to differences of scope than they would otherwise have, and there is a case for this anyway. In measuring scope (or complexity and versatility), shall we consider only the number of notes needed to specify a normal individual repertoire of songs or phrases, or the number of musical intervals? Either way there are difficulties. Nevertheless, it is plain that some songs are vastly more complex than others.

Human judgment of song, in the absence of statistical evidence of its relevance, might be thought useless to ornithology. But statistical evidence must be met on its own ground, rather than by *a priori* pronouncement of invincible subjectivity, or unsystematic citing of seemingly unfavorable cases.

To show how the six-dimensional system works, I give some examples. Someone has said that the Bellmagpies (*perhaps* more than one species) do not sing, "as Europeans understand song." What did he have in mind? Unconsciously, I am quite sure, it was the low pitch of the singing of this very unusually large Oscine. The only other feature that could make its performance seem out of line is its tendency to engage in group singing. But this in itself is not necessarily a demerit, either musically or biologically (for the group singing has the function of proclaiming group territories). True, some of the notes are impure, and even "hoarse." Many notes in the European Blackbird's song are impure or nonmusical, but they are so high-pitched that one does not think of them as hoarse. But it is not a musical demerit to be lower-pitched than most bird songs. After all, human music is like the Bellmagpie's in pitch, rather than like the Nightingale's or the Skylark's. Thus our rating brings out the musically relevant features and ignores others which are musically and biologically neutral, and which would have bothered no one who had been used to birds of this size and consequent depth of voice.

How shall we rate this song? It is loud, mildly complex, semicontinuous, mostly musical in tone, nicely melodic in pattern. The ability shown to concatenate several voices to good effect is essentially the same as imitative ability. And we know that pet Bellmagpies imitate excellently. So we have 977.786:44; i.e., about 80% of "perfection." We have filtered out the irrelevant oddity (low pitch) of the song and focused on its musical and biologically pertinent features. And not surprisingly it is the Australians' admiration for the song, not the quoted visitor's refusal to admire, which is vindicated.

It has been debated which is the supreme North American songster: the Mockingbird, the Wood or Hermit Thrush, the Western Meadowlark. Let us see:

> Mockingbird 899.767:46
> Wood Thrush 978.994:46
> Hermit Thrush 988.985:47
> Western Meadowlark 986.985:45

The conclusion seems to be that the four are nearly equal. If our scheme is sound, any very strong preference among these species will be a largely personal matter. I rather prefer the Meadowlark and the Wood Thrush, but the former is somewhat discontinuous, and the latter somewhat lacks variety, as the 7 indicates. However, as compared to the Hermit Thrush, its musical form is slightly nearer perfection, as can be made apparent by playing a recording at half speed. (Yet see Szöke, Gunn, and Filip 1969.) Also it has more volume. The Mockingbird's song is superb in scope, but somewhat lacks musical tone and form.

One can of course argue that to make imitative ability only one of six dimensions is to underestimate its significance. One can say that a Mocker is many birds in one and so must be in a class superior to all except other Mockers. But then some unmusical bowerbirds are superior to the Hermit Thrush and the Nightingale. Some limits must be put to the force of this argument (already discussed in Chapter 4), or it will lead to biologically absurd conclusions. There seems no ecological reason (see Chapter 9B–G) for bowerbirds to excel to this extent, or for mimids either. It is claimed that Nightingales introduced into Florida (dying out soon after) were adequately reproduced by Mockingbirds. I am not aware of any record to prove this and I disbelieve it, even though the Mocker's style of singing resembles the famous European bird's more closely than it does the Wood Thrush's exquisite melodies.

A foreign ornithological visitor confessed himself unable to understand the reputation of the Wood Thrush. It seemed exquisite but ultrasimple to him. Slow playing is the remedy here. Combined with the superb musicianship (see Chapter 5D), the complexity is enough to make this one of the wonders of nature.

One American student scorned the "meretricious" virtuosity of the Mocker compared with the more "sincere" or genuine musical feeling of the Cardinal. But sincerity is indeed an anthropomorphic criterion. I rate the Cardinal 877.894:43. Thus I credit it with 4 more points under tone and pattern or unity, but 7 fewer points in other respects. It is a more elegant musician, but in a much more limited set of tasks. One Englishman compared the Cardinal favorably with the Nightingale, while another scolded him almost bitterly for such treachery. I give the European bird several more points, but take both to be superior singers.

Such attempts to escape irrelevant prejudices are no doubt doomed to incomplete success. I claim only that they are better than no attempts at all. The Cardinal is a fastidious musician in that he seldom does anything badly, in the sense in which Mockingbirds do many things badly, whether judged as imitators or as musicians. But he has fewer patterns in his repertoire than either the Mockingbird or the Nightingale. Both contrasts are there in nature, and both may have ethological relevance.

The difference between mere personal preference and sober judgment of song-development is nicely illustrated by the remark of Saunders that though the Carolina Wren is probably the better singer, the Winter Wren is more pleasing. He is right on the first point, and the second may only mean that the one is a New England bird which he has heard much more during his lifetime. Having lived more with the more southerly bird, I find it the more pleasing. But in objective fact of complexity and power, it is also superior.

F. Summary

In this chapter I have tried to quantify certain aspects of singing with the hope of eliciting significant correlations among them. Annual amount (A.) of singing is found (B.) to correlate with the degree of need for song, and this (C.) with song-development, a relationship confirmed (D.) by noting the distribution of accomplished songsters in taxonomic groups. Six dimensions according to which song-development can be measured are set forth (E.). It is argued that these variables of singing have biological significance, and yet are influential in human judgments of birds as "good" or not so good singers.

G. *Preview of Later Chapters*

In later chapters (9–11) we shall see additional evidence that, statistically speaking, if birds are to give maximal satisfaction to human ears they must be territorial and inconspicuous, not because man likes them so, but because only then is skill in singing of maximal biological importance. This skill, though not exercised for man, but for themselves, is detectable by man.

Since amount correlates with need and need with skill (degree of song-development) it seems that amount and skill must also be related. This will be shown in Chapter 8. Birds that sing better also sing more. In Chapter 7 the power of the aesthetic analogy to elicit and explain relations obtaining statistically between continuity and versatility will be exhibited.

Chapters 5–12 support the contention that it is the biology (or at least the ethology) of birds that suffers so long as we refuse to consider their animal music as just that—music, but of a kind that can be made by, and function in the lives of, creatures radically lacking in intellect, though with adequate organs for hearing and making sounds, and capacity for simple emotional responses to the sounds they produce.

The Monotony-Threshold and the Correlation of Continuity with Immediate Variety

❦

A. The Avoidance of Monotony in Oscines

What stimulates animal organisms is change; what deadens response is sameness, or persistent repetition (Barlow 1968). This is true especially of repetition at brief intervals; for with long intervals, the attention span is exceeded and there is fading of memory in the immediate or active sense. (Latent memory, conditioning with associative recall, is another matter; even in a bird it may span long periods; but we are speaking of what needs no recall, since it has yet to be forgotten.) With long intervals, brain cells perhaps revert approximately to their previous state, other activities intervene, and thus the tenth or hundredth occurrence of the repetitive factor is experienced in its contrast with these intervening events, or with a certain "freshness," and not as monotonously repetitive. If then there could be "intolerable monotony" for an animal, it would be produced by many repetitions unrelieved by substantial pauses. Applying this to bird song, we deduce that a bird which sings the same song over and over will probably have marked pauses between reiterations of the song, while birds without the tendency to such pauses will have at least several different songs and will avoid using any one of them over and over in direct succession. In other words, repetitious or "nonversatile" songsters tend to be "discontinuous," and continuous songsters to be versatile. (Exceptions will be considered below, especially in section D.) Let us now define these terms more closely.

First as to *versatile:* An individual may sing an identical song—neglecting seasonal changes and very slight or infrequent deviations—hundreds or thousands of times per day (or night); or, on the contrary, it may have a repertoire of several or many different songs or phrases sung in no fixed order, many or all of which are used in every performance lasting beyond a minute or two. The majority of the world's most famous songsters are examples of the second or versatile type. Species essentially repetitious we shall term "nonversatile," for example, the Prothonotary Warbler (*Protonotaria citrea*). Species intermediate in variety we term "semiversatile," for example, some of the wrens considered below.

In another way of singing, which we shall call the "eventually versatile" way, there is a repertoire of songs, but an individual sings each song a good many times before introducing another (Type 3 in Chapter 5C). In the short run—perhaps even for many minutes, or possibly a day—such a singer does not differ much if at all from a nonversatile singer. Thus the Eastern Meadowlark often repeats one song, at intervals, over and over; yet Saunders has noted 53 *different* songs from one individual within an hour and believes that the normal repertoire is 100! Probably most "nonversatile" species are, in mild degree, eventually versatile (two or three songs, taking a whole day and a whole season into account). For most of the purposes of this chapter eventual versatility is a species of nonversatility. This qualification is important.

Continuity concerns the extent to which singing is free from interruption, during a normal "performance period" of a minute or more, by "substantial pauses," silences longer than those separating notes within songs or phrases. There is no sharp line between pauses and musical "rests" such as those, slightly separating contrasting patterns, that are found in the singing of some thrushes of the genus *Catharus*; but if a bird habitually sings several or many notes a second for two or three seconds, and then is silent for eight or more seconds, this is highly discontinuous singing. With such a singer there is *much more silence than song* during any period longer than a few seconds. A Grasshopper Sparrow may seem to be singing "steadily" for several minutes; but the four to six brief songs per minute, possibly one or two more in the early morning, occupy only from 8 to 12 seconds, leaving about 50 of silence. Thus the bird sings less than 20 percent of the performance time; during the remaining 80 percent, it may be watching the surroundings, listening to the other birds, and the like. Now contrast this with the Brown Thrasher, which pours out an almost unbroken stream of sounds for minutes on end. During a normal performance such birds sing more than 50 percent of the time. These are the "continuous" songsters. Between the extremes are the "semicontinuous" ones, singing from 30 to 50 percent of the performance period.

At least a thousand Oscine species in the world, one may guess, are nonversatile, singing one song over and over dozens or hundreds of times in succession, and probably over three hundred species are continuous; yet these two large classes (with scores of each of which I am familiar) seem scarcely to overlap in a single instance among the true Songbirds. Where are the Oscine singers that are as repetitious as the Field Sparrow, Vesper Sparrow (*Pooecetes gramineus*), or the Corn Bunting (*Emberiza calandra*), and at the same time as continuous as the Brown Thrasher or the European Song Thrush? Yet it seems that it ought to be easier to repeat the same song over and over rapidly than to sing many different songs or phrases at an equal rate. Easier, except for the threat of monotony, at least to the listening bird, and to the singer if he is attending to what he is doing. Birds "adapt" quickly to continued stimulation of the same kind, that is, they turn their attention elsewhere. Only in two ways, it seems, can this "monotony-threshold" be avoided: either by varying the activity in question, here the singing; or by pausing long enough so that other activities and lapse of memory intervene.

It is to be borne in mind that singing is normally a deliberate or free performance. A bird can be driven by fear or a sense of urgency to fly faster or farther than it would otherwise fly, even to the point of great fatigue, as over a body of water. But singing is not so urgent in the immediate sense. Also, whereas flying serves primarily to transport the creature through space, the biological values of song are social and psychological, and thus the interestingness of the song, for performer and avian listener, is of its essence. Repetition carried so far as to inhibit attention and cause the activity to lapse into an automatism for the singer and a negligible stimulus for the listener (mate or rival) is scarcely compatible with the status of song in the bird's life.

When interest is maintained by pauses, rather than by versatility, how long must the pauses be? My reasoning—which may be least correct with respect to *very long or very short* songs or phrases—is as follows: Most of the set songs or phrases are between 1 and 3 seconds in duration; few are more than 5. The explanation seems to be that the span of attention, or of vivid memory, is about this length in most songbirds (Craig 1943: 166). There is then a presumption that a longer song than usual means a longer memory span, and hence the need for longer pauses if each rendition is to be equivalent to a fresh start. Continuity, accordingly, is properly taken as a ratio. But what ratio will define "discontinuity," that is, pauses suitable for repetitious singing?

It is clearly not enough that the pauses be slightly longer than the song, for this would mean that memory is only a little less than "vivid"; whereas a bird singing a unit a thousand times or more a day, as most of them do, must recover freshness virtually completely, must have almost *no* sense of what (from our point of view) it has just previously done. The pauses, then, must be much longer than the songs. Physiology or psychology will eventually tell us a good deal, no doubt, about the sort of proportion we should expect here; but it seems reasonable that somewhat over twice the duration that can be grasped as a whole, as songs must be to be recognized, should be required for freshness. This is provided for by our definition of discontinuous singing as less than 30 percent of the performance time, leaving at least 70 percent of silence, or 2⅓ times as much. This ratio was arrived at empirically, as an effort to make sense out of such facts as this: that many hundreds of repeated songs are between 1½ and 3 seconds, while the shortest pauses for them range, with rare exceptions, between 3½ and 7 seconds, respectively, which our 30–70 ratio calls for. Or again this fact: Craig (1943: 24, 25, 54, 62, 67, 72) showed that the Wood Pewee tends to sing his third, or special twilight, phrase an ever higher proportion of times as he changes from leisurely daylight singing to the many times faster rate of his "twilight" song; but this tendency is halted almost exactly at the proportion of 50 percent for the preferred phrase. Why? Because, beyond this proportion, the phrase must sometimes be repeated immediately without intervention of either of the others, and the bird avoids immediate repetition of any phrase, above all this one, when its pauses are short, though it has no hesitation about repeating either of its daytime phrases many times over when singing with the long pauses (8 seconds or more, instead of 1) of its leisurely singing. We shall meet other species that thus exhibit, through a dual mode of behavior, the difference between long pauses that make variety unnecessary and short ones that require it.

Consider the contrast between two species, the Ovenbird and the Brown Thrasher. The Ovenbird has a song with little internal variety in each utterance, and the only variation from one utterance to the next is in the number of times the "teacher" occurs. If this three-second song were to be sung every five seconds or so, we human listeners, at least, would find the monotony very trying. But the bird seldom pauses less than 10 seconds, usually more than 20 (Hann 1937; Nice 1931). Now observe the Thrasher. He hastens on from phrase to phrase, immediately repeating most of them once or twice only, until, after a minute or two, his repertoire has perhaps been exhausted and new items no longer appear, although the old ones may present themselves in new orders. Pauses are so short that one can seldom time them definitely. A bird performing in this fashion is doing almost nothing but sing. It is his life, for the time being; he therefore puts into it whatever sense of complexity he possesses. The sharp separation of song perch from feeding area on the ground is symptomatic of his concentration. The Ovenbird, on his lower perch, seems to give his much simpler song more incidentally, while largely intent on other things.

The tendency toward very short pauses in the "singing" of various insects suggests that in their case the simple repetitive patterns may come closer to being a measure of the creature's capacity. Katydids (*Pterophila camellifolia*) [Orthoptera], however, are somewhat versatile (Shaw 1968). Many of the lower orders of birds seem nearer to this level than the Songbirds are.

The monotony-threshold, or limit of tolerance for repetition, thus doubtless varies from species to species. We may also reasonably suppose that a creature which is satisfied by small or poorly defined contrasts within its basic song pattern will feel less need of variation in successive utterances of the pattern. Purer musical tones define more definite contrasts. A creature which nicely contrasts two or more relatively pure frequencies each time it sings will be more likely to feel the need for contrast between one utterance and the next, or for substantial pauses. We shall see that the striking cases of disproportionately low versatility relative to the continuity are furnished by species whose lack of sensitivity to the value of contrast is shown by the song they repeat as well as by the mode of repetition.

The anti-monotony principle inhibits birds from combining high continuity and low (immediate) variety. It does not, of itself, inhibit them from combining low continuity and high variety. Yet this form of singing is also rare. Presumably there is advantage in continuous singing, so that it will occur in the absence of the inhibiting factor spoken of. Also, if the pauses were long enough for the bird, a short-memoried creature, to have forgotten the previous phrases, the successive contrasts would lose their effectiveness and the bird might as well repeat. Indeed, unless the repertoire were very large, some direct repetition would be inevitable. Then, too, a bird which develops great variety is investing much of its capacity for complex behavior in singing, and so it is likely to have a stronger urge to sing and to be disinclined to punctuate its singing with pronounced pauses. These reasons taken together seem sufficient to explain the rarity of discontinuous but immediately varied song. And so anti-monotony and the urge to keep singing combine to maintain a strong positive correlation between continuity and immediate variety.

B. Some Hypothetical Statistics

If Oscines alone are considered, I take the statistical situation to be something like that symbolized by Table III. Let us consider nine logically possible types of singing produced by combining three degrees (from least to most) of immediate variety: V, VV, VVV, and of continuity: C, CC, CCC. Criteria for the threefold divisions are necessarily somewhat vague or arbitrary. Shall we say that a continuity ratio (length of song divided by the cadence) of less than 0.20 is C and a ratio of over 0.50 is CCC, while CC covers ratios of 0.20 to 0.50? And how many songs or phrases sung in contrasting rather than repetitive fashion will be V, VV, or VVV? Whatever the difficulties, there are several degrees of the two variables and there must be some possibility of making a reasonable division. Then, in a sizable random sample of Oscines, say the 135 in the Saunders *Guide* (1951), something like the percentages in Table III will emerge. In other words a large majority will be on the diagonal V/C, VV/CC, VVV/CCC. Above all, the upper left- and the lower right-hand classifications will be nearly empty.

Since great variety, VVV, is a supreme evolutionary achievement, minimal in the primitive singers (insects, frogs, nonoscine birds) and

TABLE III

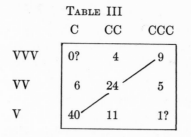

	C	CC	CCC
VVV	0?	4	9
VV	6	24	5
V	40	11	1?

maximal in man, small percentages are to be expected in the top row. For similar reasons, high continuity is also exceptional; hence the small percentages in the right-hand column. Most avian singers are neither highly continuous nor highly versatile. But this does not explain the concentration along the diagonal V/C, VV/CC, and VVV/CCC, or why percentages in the top row increase toward the right, in the right-hand column toward the top, and in the middle row toward the middle.

No doubt the needs of some species are better served by discontinuous than they would be by continuous singing. In the pauses a bird may forage, it may listen to a rival which it can then "answer" ("counter-singing"). But this does not explain why the discontinuous singers are mostly V/C, and the repetitive singers mostly in that group also. To explain the association of continuity with immediate variety the considerations urged above seem required.

Armstrong suggests (1963: 243) that the aesthetic explanation of the association is alternative to the explanation through "selective advantage." However, this advantage comes from the behavioral expressions and eventual consequences of the aesthetic feeling. It is not a case of either-or, but of both-and. To do the right things birds must have the right feelings. They are not mere machines. Or are they?

Some would say that it is the behavioral aspects alone that matter in science, and that any psychical "intervening variables" may be neglected. This is comparable to "black-box" theories in physics, the sufficiency of which has been much debated. I hold with those who regard such theories as incomplete. One should not cut off inquiry in this way. And the statistically strong evidence for the anti-monotony principle seems to give us a window into the box. I hit upon the correlation of continuity and variety while pursuing the aesthetic analogy. And no one has explained the facts in any radically different fashion from the one I adopted.

Dr. Pettingill has suggested to me that continuous singers are those which sing from song perches removed from foraging locations: for example, thrushes, which are often ground-feeders, but usually sing well up in trees; larks, which feed on the ground but sing from bushes or in flight; Mockingbirds and thrashers, which in this regard are like thrushes; lyrebirds, which sing from mounds but do not feed there. Warblers and wood warblers, flycatchers, whistlers, sunbirds, tits, honeyeaters, etc., are discontinuous singers, singing as they feed, or between mouthfuls. Reed warblers (*Acrocephalus* spp.), which are continuous, may perhaps fit the generalization if they feed mostly on or close to the ground or water and sing higher up in reeds or bushes. Armstrong (1965: 222–23) suggests that discontinuous singers may improve their safety from predators by moving between songs and that continuous singers are likely to be those out of reach or well-hidden from predators while they sing. These suggestions seem pertinent. But they do not explain why continuity tends to occur only with immediate variety. The explanation of that is the aesthetic sensitivity found especially in Oscines, but to some extent in singers generally.

Armstrong (1963) objects to my taking the Willow Warbler as example of low (immediate) variety and low continuity, V/C. He is right, it is not an example of that. However, it is a fairly good example of VV/CC, and thus confirms the correlation. (I am here indebted to correspondence with Dr. Michael Schubert; see also Schubert 1967). It has been remarked (Marler and Isaac 1960) that a somewhat more varied song does not always mean greater continuity. The correlation is not exact and invariant. Marler did not intend this as disproving the relation as at least statistically valid. Nor, in the example he gives, is it clear that the variety in question (of a Mexican population of the Brown Towhee) is immediate. Eventual variety is not to the point. Also, my generalization is statistical, allowing for combinations such as VV/C in some numbers, and possibly a very few V/CCC. With so many factors in biology and so much difficulty in measuring any of them, one cannot expect an analogue to the Newtonian laws of motion, and indeed I do not believe biological phenomena are as fully determined as that, even apart from obstacles to our knowledge. But they are subject to approximate generalities holding in most cases.

Several investigators have discovered a phenomenon that might seem in some conflict with the anti-monotony principle. The Chaffinch sings repetitively from a repertoire of several songs, and the intervals between repeats of the same song — A,A,A . . . — are shorter than between the last A and the first B in another series B,B,B ... (Hinde 1958). It is suggested that singing of a song inhibits for a time the singing of the same song, but then facilitates it. However, both within a sequence of repeats and between sequences, intervals are long enough to satisfy anti-monotony requirements (6–12 or more seconds). And clearly it is one thing to break off a series of repetitions and another to contrast songs systematically. In one case monotony is relieved chiefly by silence, in the other by musical contrasts. So long as a bird is content to reiterate, it has nothing to decide except when to sing again, but when it feels moved (by a kind of cumulative "boredom"?) to change the tune it must recover from the boredom and adopt a new "set" and a new choice from the repertoire. In contrast, a bird that changes the tune each time escapes boredom more radically, and its "set" is toward the enjoyment of musical contrast rather than the contrast between song and silence. A similarly exact study of Mistle Thrush singing (*Turdus viscivorus*) reached somewhat similar results, except that the intervals were much shorter and also the musical repetitiveness less egregious (Marler and Isaac 1963). This bird has vastly more immediate variety and much shorter pauses (about one-third the length, on the average) than the Chaffinch.

Another apparent but perhaps slight discrepancy is that White-throated Sparrows, which are repetitive-discontinuous singers, limit the rigidity of their repetitiveness by sometimes omitting part of the song, or by increasing the number of triplets with which the song usually ends, but do not employ this mild form of variety any more often when singing with their shortest than with their longest pauses (Falls, in Hinde 1969). However, since pauses in this species are usually at least 10 seconds and only occasionally as brief as 5 seconds, and the songs are generally less than 4 seconds, the bird may be classed as a case of V/C which occasionally deviates into V/CC, or perhaps VV/C, but hardly into V/CCC. Though I would not have predicted Falls's observation, 5+ seconds is a goodly time to mitigate monotony, at a bird's tempo of living.

Winter Wrens, whose songs in most parts of the U.S. average at least 5 seconds, often have pauses of no greater length (Armstrong 1955: 56), and now and then may omit the pause between two songs. At worst this is again a case of V/CC. Five- to eight-second pauses are substantial: during them much can happen for a bird. The Winter Wren's song is the longest definitely reiterated pattern I know of in

North American singing, and it is fast and complex. I have not been able to find out for certain how *exactly* it is reiterated, but in any case the internal structure of the song furnishes a good deal of immediate variety, and between any one part of the song (say in the first second or so) and the next reiteration of that part fully 9 seconds intervene. Also this bird, as Armstrong points out (1955: 78), often engages in counter-singing, so that while neither of the two rival birds perhaps enjoys any contrast between its own successive utterances, each does experience the contrast between its songs and its rival's. All this is a long way from the monotony found in some nightjars (*Caprimulgus* spp.) and barbets. (I discuss these really gross exceptions to anti-monotony in section E.)

Armstrong (1963: 267) interprets a phrase in an essay by Marler, Kreith, and Tamura (1962: 14) to imply an exception to the anti-monotony principle. However, that Oregon Juncos (*Junco oreganus*) often sing the same theme "for long periods without a break" means, according to the context, without changing to another theme. It does not mean "without normal pauses." Juncos are discontinuous singers.

Three families of North American birds are outstanding in continuity of singing: the mockingbird-thrasher family or Mimidae, the thrushes or Turdidae, and the vireos or Vireonidae. Scarcely a member of these is less than semicontinuous. (See Saunders 1951.) It is almost equally difficult to find one that is less than semiversatile. (Hutton's Vireo [*Vireo huttoni*] will be considered in section D.) The Mimidae are the most versatile and continuous singers in North America. (See Bent 1948.)

(See Hartshorne 1956a for many details relevant to the rest of this section.)

Two great American groups consist largely of highly repetitious singers which (cf. Chapter 8B), as our theory requires, are also highly discontinuous: the "sparrows," finches of the subfamily Emberizinae, and the wood warblers or Parulidae. In most cases they have short set songs which are merely reiterated, at least in any one usual perform-ance of a few minutes. Rates are as a rule between 5 and 7 per minute, with a maximum of 9 or 10, which, with the brevity of the songs, means a usual continuity of about 20 percent and a rarely exceeded maximum of 30 percent. Exceptions are instructive. Thus the Lark Sparrow is in my experience the most continuous singer in either of the two groups, and it is the most versatile. Saunders (1951: 301) says: "A bird sings one song after another, no two of them alike." He recorded 6 different songs from an individual, each occurring but once, and during this time others were sung that he lacked time to record. The versatility of Bachman's Sparrow is well known; it is at least semicontinuous. (See Robbins et al.) Descriptions of the weak song of the Brewer's Sparrow (*Spizella breweri*) imply marked continuity *and* variety (R. Hoffman 1927: 331; Swarth 1930: 255f.). (See also Robbins.) The Song Sparrow of course has wonderful variety (6 to 24 songs in each individual repertoire), but chiefly of the eventual kind, each song being sung a number of times—on occasion as many as 70—before another is used (Nice 1943: 124). However, slight variations are introduced. In a "highly stimulated state," a singer may reach 10 times per minute, using the same song for two or three minutes. This is semicontinuous singing (45 percent); the cumulative approach to monotony, one may surmise, causes the bird to draw on his repertoire, whereas a species without this recourse, but otherwise comparable, must gain more complete refreshment from slightly longer pauses as he goes along.

The Black-throated Sparrow (*Amphispiza bilineata*) is "semi-continuous and semi-versatile," alternating two somewhat variable songs and reaching a maximum of 52 percent of the performance time (Heckenlively 1970).

The Black-throated Green Warbler (*Dendroica virens*) sings its two-second song from 5 to 8 times per minute (Nice and Nice 1932: 169–71); and many others in the family similarly space out their brief and relatively unvarying songs—as I have observed at various times of day and season in northern Michigan.

In sharp contrast is the Yellow-breasted Chat, the most consistently continuous, or nearly continuous, singer in the family, and the only consistently versatile one. Usually 7 different phrases, in no fixed order, are used (Bent 1953: 593) at a rate of 10 phrases in 25 seconds (Saunders 1951: 213). Phrases are short, giving a continuity of perhaps a little over 40 percent. Considering the extreme simplicity of most of the phrases, versatility seems also medium high.

Wrens are intermediate in continuity and in immediate variety, except for the Canyon and Cactus species, which are repetitive and discontinuous. Also intermediate in both dimensions are the cardinal grosbeaks and their allies, the least continuous-versatile being the Rose-breasted Grosbeak (*Pheucticus ludovicianus*), in some contrast to the Black-headed (*P. melanocephalus*). Of the kinglets (*Regulus calendula* and *R. satrapa*), the former, or Ruby-crowned, is the more versatile and continuous. Troupials, or the oriole-blackbird family (Icteridae) practice monotony avoidance. Their immediate variety is either low, and with it their continuity, or they are intermediate in both respects.

According to Dixon (1969) the Plain Titmouse (*Parus inornatus*) and according to Gomperz (1961) the Great Tit in England (*P. major*) illustrate anti-monotony.

C. Species with Two Modes of Monotony Avoidance

The American Redstart (*Setophaga ruticilla*) is noted for its versatility. In Cheboygan County, Michigan, usually at dawn, I have often heard it singing 12, and sometimes 13, 15, or even 17 times per minute, also 9 times in 30 seconds. These high rates were with conspicuously versatile singing, although as Saunders (1951) remarks, Redstarts sometimes sing the same song over and over. When they do so, the rate is generally 7, 8, or 9, occasionally 10 or 11; but when they (irregularly) "alternate" two or more songs, the rate, while sometimes low, is more commonly 9, 10, 11, sometimes 12, and up to 17 per minute. Moreover, a bird has several times shifted, as I listened to him, from repetitious to versatile, or from versatile to more versatile singing (by the addition of one or two more songs to the shuffle back and forth), and therewith the rate per minute has also risen sharply.

The two types of singing, repetitious-discontinuous and versatile-continuous, are illustrated even more clearly by the Canada Warbler (*Wilsonia canadensis*). Kendeigh (1945: 159) mentions a rate of six songs per minute. In mid-June 1954, two individuals near the University of Michigan Biological Station sang repetitiously at this very rate; and at the same spot in early July one sang eight times per minute, also without variations. However, late in June a Canada greeted me with almost fully continuous and amply versatile singing—9 times in 30 seconds, maintaining approximately this rate for several minutes, chipping or "tsacking" rhythmically between songs. I have heard no other species of warbler sing so continuously, nor—considering the complexity of songs—so versatilely. The versatility has been noted by Saunders (Bent 1953: 652) and the continuity by Allen (Bent, loc. cit.). What has not been noted is the sharply dual personality of the bird, combining two rather different modes of singing. Two other warblers (Tennessee, *Vermivora peregrina,* and Cape May, *Dendroica tigrina*) have been reported as singing in the two ways (Bent 1953, part 1). Also the two Nearctic species of marsh wrens (*Cistothorus* spp.) fit their degrees of continuity to their variety.

Recently recordings by Coffey, Frisch, and Hartshorne have made accessible a positively startling illustration of monotony avoidance, this time in contrasts between local dialects of (allegedly) one species, rather than between different species, or the same individual at different times. The Nightingale Wren has in some local groups a highly developed song, in others a much more primitive one. There are gradations of the difference and the entire set is as though made to order for our present purposes. The following are the songs (see spectrograms in Appendix D):

(1) Mexico, Costa Rica, recorded by B. B. Coffey and E. P. Edwards. "Leisurely rambling affair that alternately rises and falls in an arresting manner." (Slud 1958, 1960.) The song sometimes begins with several notes on the same pitch, not as loud as the remainder of the song. After that, not only does the pitch change each time but the direction of pitch change alters every second or third time. Only the tempo is constant, a fairly even rate of nearly 3 *notes per second,* so that a 17-second song has about 50 notes, with 45 pitch changes! Of how many songs can one say that?

(2) Brazil, recorded by Frisch. The song moves up and down in pitch as in (1), except that each pitch is usually repeated once or twice before a rise or drop to a different pitch. The rate is *one note per second.*

(3) Costa Rica, description by Slud. The opening notes rise in pitch, then there is a "long series of successively lower-pitched notes separated from one another by long pauses," the *pauses* increasing in length *up to at least 10 seconds!* (The notes, too, are longer, but the main change is in the pauses.) The drop in pitch is a small fraction of a tone. A similar song was described by Stolzmann long ago (Taczanowski 1884): "Simple, first some melodic notes then simple sounds repeated in 6–8 second intervals, dropping in pitch, but less than a half tone each time." In Amazonian Ecuador, without seeing the bird, I heard such a song, except that I was not aware of the drop in pitch (or did the bird omit it?). On Skutch's estate in Costa Rica, this species, as I heard and recorded it, omitted the pitch changes at the beginning, and in this case too I was not and am not aware of a fall in pitch. Certainly

there were none of the striking changes in direction of pitch change occurring in (1) and (2).

Here are three (or four?) different song-types, (1) and (3) seeming, as Slud says, "entirely different." (They do not correspond to even subspecific morphological differences, according to Slud.) Note how the pace drops with the fall in immediate variety: With a pitch change for nearly every sound we have 3 notes per second; with pitch changes about half as frequent, 1 note per second; with either very slight or perhaps no changes the pace falls again 400% to 4 or more (5 in my recording) seconds per note. This seems to be a made-to-order example of the anti-monotony principle, whether or not the birds are all one species.

It is also an extreme case of divergence of song, apparently without morphological difference. Also (1) is found both in Costa Rica and (in somewhat slower, less versatile form) in Brazil, while (3) in its extremest form is also in Costa Rica and (again in milder form) in Amazonian Ecuador! Still even the extremes of (1) and (3) are not really entirely different. The tone quality is much the same in all, although in the first two types some notes are richer than those in the more monotonous songs; the pace is deliberate, as bird songs go, since even 3 notes per second is a slow rate for this class of animal; there is an absence of marked rhythm, since notes and pauses tend to be roughly equal through a song, or the pauses tend to increase slowly. Slud believes the differences have inhibited interbreeding, and they certainly are very great, at least in musical complexity.

D. Species Less Sensitive to Monotony

Of all the Oscines I know about the most monotonous is Hutton's Vireo, which reiterates its kittenlike "me-ow" (said of the subspecies *stephensi*) or its "quid-id" about once a second for minutes at a time (Willard 1908: 232; Bent 1950: 246–47). Yet, Bent quotes an observer who noted a "change of key" every minute or two. Also, the actual singing of the phrase, evidently as unmusical as any vireo's, seems to occupy no more than ⅓ second. It has some small changes in its repetitive declamations. However, let us accept this species as V/CCC. Its high tolerance for monotony fits its musical insensitivity in other re-

spects. But how rare all this is among Oscines! The other vireos con-
form reasonably well to the anti-monotony principle.

Two further recalcitrant cases are the Chipping Sparrow and the
White-breasted Nuthatch (*Sitta carolinensis*). In these cases a rather
unmusical two-note phrase (not clearly discernible as such to the
human ear because of speed or slurring) is reiterated; and the reiterations are definitely grouped into series of rather variable length con-
stituting "songs." Pauses between songs may be of discontinuous mag-
nitude, but the Chippy in early morning may use pauses "as short as
or shorter than the song" (Saunders 1951); and I have heard the Nuthatch singing, as nearly as I could tell without a stop watch, 40 percent
of the performance time. The lack of a fixed number of phrases in each
song and the variations in the length of pauses constitute the only versatility. The fact that the basic simple phrase is merely repeated means
that the procedure can be carried out automatically, as in the act of
walking or flying, while attention is largely elsewhere. The Chippy, at
least, sings with little intensity compared, for example, with the Ovenbird. In both cases, the lack of what seems adequate contrast (or
pauses) between successive utterances of the phrase matches the pov-
erty of well-defined variety within the phrase.

More drastic exceptions to my anti-monotony principle occur outside
the Oscine suborder and are more extreme cases of the same characteristics. Thus in the early morning the Least Flycatcher repeats an
unmusical "ti-beck" or "che-bec" hundreds of times, almost without
substantial pauses, though not without slight modulations of rhythm.
It is a species which lives about clearings, pairs being close together
and in fairly good view of one another. Skutch (1960) tells about a
number of similarly monotonous dawn songs in this Suboscine family.
However, these songs are not continued through the day and usually
last less than a half hour, as though the singing were a chore to be
endured only while the light is too dim for anything else, such as
chasing insects. (For a startling exception see Skutch 1960: 563, and
compare with Chapter 8D below.) The Eastern Phoebe (*Sayornis
phoebe*) sings a dawn song consisting of two mildly contrasting
phrases, alternating irregularly, "phoebe" and "phoebleet." It is a musically dull performance, in the themes as well as in their excessive reiteration, yet in both respects superior to the Chebec.

In sharp contrast to these egregious repeaters is the most musical nonoscine species in North America, the Eastern Wood Peewee, which excels not only in the musical sweetness and effective contrasts within and between its three principal phrases, but also in the optimal variety, as already pointed out, in the order of their occurrence.

E. Monotony in the Primitive Orders

The grossest exceptions to anti-monotony are outside the Passeriformes. Thus the Whippoorwill (*Caprimulgus vociferus*) has a *slightly musical* phrase of five notes, and this phrase is repeated, sometimes hundreds of times, in fairly quick succession. The arrangement of the three chief pitches, 2–1–3, that is, a fall and a sharp rise, seems to call for the drop back to the opening note, and so the thing seems to keep itself going musically with almost hypnotic effect. In this case, as in that of the Chebec, there is some rhythmic modulation, the bird pausing ever so slightly here and there, making a break in the mechanical precision of repetition.

Some rails (Rallidae), nightjars, barbets ("tinkerbirds") (*Pogoniulus* spp.), radically exceed the true Songbirds in tolerance of monotony. My suggestion is that they are less specialized not only for controlling but also for discriminative hearing of sounds. The most musical bird related to the nightjars, the Potoo of South America, and the most musical tinkerbird in my experience (see Chapter 11), avoid monotony by pausing or number juggling. In both cases the voice is much superior, and I am not alone in admiring these songs.

Oring (1968) has shown that the Green Sandpiper (*Tringa ochropus*) sings nonversatilely, yet, at times, continuously. In this respect the bird is in a class with the Whippoorwill. Oring also remarks that the song does have some musical quality, and so seems to conflict with a remark of mine that birds which repeat a song monotonously also show a lack of musical sense in the internal structure of the song itself. However, it may be significant that, of the two versions of its song, the one which this species reiterates most continuously is also the one Oring (rightly, so far as the spectrograms show) terms less musical. It is also the one which is more crassly and immediately utilitarian (more strictly confined to the breeding season, used to appeal directly to the female, etc.). Finally, it is the one particularly sung in flight.

Flight singing should be less sensitive to monotony: for (a) the listening bird experiences changes in the direction of sounds if nothing else; (b) the singing bird experiences changes in his muscular activity other than singing, and also in his field of vision. I believe it is a fact that flight singers go a little farther in immediate repetition than others. A very fine flight-singer, the Red-winged Bush-lark (*Mirafra hypermetra*) (Chapter 10) shows this tendency strikingly (recorded by North). The Skylark, too, shows it, though much less, and one can see it in other African larks recorded by North. (Since nightjars sing mostly when sitting on a branch or the ground this explanation of monotony does not apply to them.)

The point of the anti-monotony principle is not that birds cannot sing mechanically, merely repetitively, somewhat as they can fly, and they and we can walk. The point is that they can, and rather generally do, sing nonmechanically, more or less aesthetically. The simpler the song, and the Green Sandpiper's song is simple enough, the more readily can it be sung without aesthetic feeling, with the bird's attention elsewhere. Barbets, which tend to be monotonous (with some exceptions, see Chapter 11), are not flight-singers. But their songs are mostly extremely primitive in every way except volume. Singing is more a matter of routine in such cases, not of attentive experience, though one cannot deny that considerable energy is going into it. (But then this is true of flying.)

Intermediate between the largely monotony-avoiding Oscines and the often monotonous nightjars, rails, barbets, and the like are the tyrant flycatchers, many of which sing a dawn song in decidedly monotonous fashion, but for a short time and in most cases a short season. Such singing seems a tour de force, rather sharply contrasting with the self-reinforcing performance of versatile singers like the Mockingbird, which tends to sing much and with high continuity in the middle of hot days. But the Eastern Wood Pewee sings through the day, and in its musicality and observance of anti-monotony acts like an Oscine. The relative, some would say absolute, lack of imitation in truly primitive groups (parrots are not primitive but intermediate in syringial development) confirms the supposition that in these groups aesthetic feeling for sounds is much weaker than in Oscines. This does not mean that it is no force at all. There is room for innumerable degrees in this force.

F. Conclusion

However one views the seeming exceptions to the rule against repetitive continuous singing, in the main the rule stands. The exceptions, chiefly among primitive types, physically unspecialized for song, indicate a limited musical sensitivity—as is also shown by the quality of the songs and the absence, so far as is known, of learning by imitation in these cases. Some nightjars sing as primitively as any insect, with no clear use of pitch contrast at all. Since they are not insects, but presumably much more intelligent, I assume that their main interest is elsewhere than in the sounds themselves.

My conclusion is that the evolution of song has been toward increasing sensitivity to the value of contrast and unexpectedness as balancing the value of sameness and repetition.

This essay in its original form (Hartshorne 1956a) was a contribution from the University of Michigan Biological Station. I am grateful for observational and research opportunities at that admirable institution, which I twice visited as Independent Investigator; and to Dr. Olin Sewall Pettingill, Jr., for helpful criticisms and advice. I also wish to thank Margaret Morse Nice and Aretas A. Saunders for information given in conversation and correspondence.

8

Song-Development and
Amount of Singing

❦

A. In British Oscines

In the *Handbook of British Birds* (Witherby et al. 1938, 1943) is to be found probably the most careful study ever made of the parts of the year during which the various birds of a region sing (a) regularly and frequently, (b) regularly but infrequently, (c) irregularly, and (d) virtually not at all. This accuracy (which of course has its limits) has a potential value beyond its mere convenience for bird watchers. Quantitative studies of variables are the means for discovering the order of nature, provided covariations can be found connecting the variables. One such relation seems obvious: A bird does something frequently and during much of the year only if it serves an important and continuing need of the species. Song must have unusual importance for the Robin, which sings freely during more of the year than any other British bird. And in fact Robins (like American Mockingbirds) practice territoriality almost the year through, and we know that song in this species is closely linked with territorial defense. So here, as in general, amount of singing corresponds with intensity and duration of the need for auditory announcement of territory.

There is another correlation which is almost as obvious. When an animal does something a great deal because it has a persistent need to do it, it also does that something with unusual skill and efficiency. Woodpeckers, treecreepers (Certhiidae), tropical woodhewers (Dendrocolaptidae), and nuthatches (Sittidae) spend most of their lives walking on trunks or large branches of trees. Many other kinds of birds may occasionally be seen clinging to the trunk of a tree to feed on an insect there, but they do it only incidentally, and as to their skill in this activity one can say little more than that they can do it. The professional bark-clingers not only do it but they also exhibit a high level of control and effortless versatility. Similarly, all sorts of birds now and then pursue and capture an insect in flight, but only the habitual "flycatchers" (including swifts [Apodidae] and swallows [Hirundinidae]) exhibit the maximum skill in this activity. The human eye detects the aerial skill of such birds almost at a glance.

Singing is the one avian activity that anyone has ever supposed exempt from the rule that doing a thing much and doing it well go together. One difficulty of course is to know what is meant by "singing well." Our forefathers had little doubt that the human listener can detect various degrees of singing skill. In Chapter 6 we saw some evidence that they were right. In this chapter, taking English Songbirds as our first statistical sample, we shall see additional evidence of this.

To avoid the charge of bias, I have taken ratings of songs already in the literature, made by writers who had no idea of giving support to any theory of mine. My own ratings give broadly similar results (I have heard about one-third of the British Oscines sing in the wild and have studied recorded songs of nearly all of them), but these ratings will not be appealed to in what follows.

Two English writers have treated the question of song-development in British birds comprehensively and with systematic care, and they agree rather well with one another, and with some other writers who were less comprehensive and had less adequate data. Alexander and Nicholson (see Nicholson and Koch 1936: 20, 70) both group British birds into four classes in order of decreasing power, complexity, and other indices of singing skill (they do not use this term). Nicholson's Class I is simply Alexander's I, his nine songs of "power and variety," plus a member of his second class, the Sedge Warbler. On Classes II and III there is agreement in nearly half the cases. Nicholson's Class IV has but three Oscine members (for reasons to be specified, I shall limit myself to Oscines). These species—tits (Paridae)—are all in Alexander's 3rd class. Thus we have the following six groups: I-I, I-II, II-II, II-III, III-III, and III-IV, where the first number represents one writer (no matter which) and the second the other. Note that all disagreements are between neighboring classes; I-III, II-IV, I-IV, do not occur. This again shows a considerable measure of agreement. Since I wish to be impartial between the two men, I compromise their disagreements as follows: I-I counts as 6 points, II-II as 4, and III-III as 2, while the intermediate or mixed cases (I-II, II-III, and III-IV) count as 5, 3, and 1. Thus odd numbers indicate (mild) disagreement.

In the seasonal chart given in Witherby's *Handbook*, solid lines indicate abundant singing; broken lines, abundant but still regular singing; dotted lines, irregular and infrequent singing. For statistical use I have translated these three indices into numerical values, allowing 1.0 for solid lines, 0.4 per month for broken lines, and 0.1 for dotted lines. With this understanding, and some additional items about to be explained, the 63 species with their quality or Q values from 1 to 6 and their months of song are as given in Appendix A. I list the species in order of decreasing seasons. Migrant species which are in England only for breeding are marked V (for visitors); the rest are permanent residents. (Nonbreeding migrants are omitted, since comparable data on their seasons are not given.)

Under "extras" some factors are listed which enhance or reduce the probable amounts of singing as implied by season-lengths. These factors are continuity C, night-singing N, and singing while the summer visitor is outside of England (perhaps while wintering in Africa) W. Fractions and multiples of these factors are also used, and under "total extras" the sum of these items is given, except that C (pausing more than 2 and less than 4 times the song length) is taken as normal, rather than extra, and that V counts as one unit extra. Seasonal figures derived from observations covering months in England of song by birds which spend over half the year out of England are plainly not immediately comparable to figures for species in England all year. Moreover, even taking W singing into account is not enough to balance the incompleteness of data for visitors, since summering species have their seasons close to the peak of the year's daylight (May, June), whereas resident seasons include proportionately many more weeks when days are short (October–February) or only average (March–April). In high latitudes a week in May or June may give nearly three times as much singing time as a week in January or February. In addition, the abundance of food in the first case may make much shorter foraging periods possible.

Some highly discontinuous species never actually sing more than 5 minutes in an hour of performance. Even if it performs nearly all day, such a bird still produces a smaller total output than that of a Skylark in the first two hours of many a day. Continuity figures are unfortunately not available for all the species. Night-singing and visitors' winter singing are more difficult to ascertain with precision, but rough indications can be given for most English species.

The incompleteness and possible inaccuracies in Appendix A are at worst random rather than unfairly selective, since I have made the table as complete and accurate as I could from the available data, using the *Handbook* for seasons and also (with minor supplementation from other sources) for out-of-England singing (W) of nonpermanent breeding residents (V), Nicholson and Alexander for quality ratings (Q), and Nicholson (for the most part) for continuity. Continuity is estimated by multiplying the average rate per minute by the song-length in seconds and dividing by 60. Ratios of at least ⅛ but not over ½ count as CC, and those below ⅛ as a fraction of C. I accept Nicholson's figures for frequency per minute, using the median between the extremes he gives, but I try in some cases to be more definite as to song-lengths. From "two or three seconds" one might guess an average of 2½. But perhaps in some such cases the real average is 2.10 and in others 2.9. With a frequency figure of 6 per minute, the first gives a continuity ratio of slightly over ⅕, the second a ratio of almost ⅓. With very short songs this source of error is still greater. Unluckily one can seldom use phonograph records for determining frequency, since pauses are usually shortened by the editing process. However, records do give some idea of song-lengths. By playing recordings at half or quarter speed and dividing the result by 2 or 4, one can somewhat reduce the percentage of inaccuracy inherent in the use of a stop watch. Spectrograms are the most accurate method and are now available for many North American and some European species. The diagrams of song by Saunders were the most accurate, prior to instrumental methods.

The only other writer I have found who has faced the question of comparative continuity in a quantitative way is Colquhoun (1940). Using Nicholson's data (Nicholson and Koch 1936) he calculates what he calls the "absolute song" of 10 species, meaning by this the number of seconds in a minute (or minutes in an hour, supposing the performance lasts that long) a bird actually sings. His results are:

Chiffchaff (*Phylloscopus collybita*) and Hedge Sparrow (*Prunella modularis*), 30 seconds/minute
Willow Warbler and Reed Bunting, 24
Blackcap, 23
Yellow Bunting, Goldcrest (*Regulus regulus*), and Blackbird, 21
Wren, 20
Chaffinch, 18

Trying to follow his method of deriving the figures from what Nicholson says, I get rather similar results, except that the Blackbird scores 27 (i.e., it sings not much less than half the performance time) and the Hedge Sparrow, 26. It is also to be noted that the Wren sometimes sings close to 30 seconds per minute (Armstrong 1955: 54, 56), and that nearly all the most continuous, and also 7 out of 9 of the most developed, songsters of Britain happen to be omitted from the list, which to this extent is unrepresentative.

Colquhoun ignores the distinction I have proposed (Chapter 6A) between pauses separating successive instances of the same pattern and those separating contrasting patterns and hence perhaps to be regarded as musical "rests." In what follows I have not made full use of this distinction since it seems a moot point. It results in a somewhat magnified version of the superiority in continuity of the more highly developed styles of singing, but it does not produce that superiority.

I have used the *Handbook*'s (Alexander's) tables for seasons rather than Nicholson's (which are not very different), because, Armstrong assures me, they are more accurate.

Since residents are a majority, and also, for statistical purposes, in a class by themselves, let us first analyze the figures for them (Table IV), provisionally ignoring the "extras." (Details are given in Appendix A.)

The visitors (Table V) yield a different picture. The poorest singers have the shortest seasons, but the middling and moderately good, not the best, singers have the longest. Yet note that this sample is much smaller than the previous, highly correlated one; and the slight negative correlation suggested by the figures for $Q = 3\text{-}6$ is almost negligible compared to the smooth, steep progression from $Q = 1$ to $Q = 6$ in Table IV. To see this consider the two groups of singers taken together in Table VI.

The seasons of the nine best singers are 2½ times as long as those of the nine poorest, and compare to the seasons of the 20 poorest ($Q =$

TABLE IV

Residents

Number of species	Quality (Q)	Average season (months)
4	1	2.5
11	2	4.8
11	3	6.3
8	4	7.1
0	5	—
5	6	7.5
Total 39		*Overall average* 5.8

For the residents the correlation between length of season and quality of singing is 0.50 (furnished by the statistician Dorothy C. Lowry, according to whom the "probability of this result by chance is less than 1%").

TABLE V

Visitors

Number of species	Quality (Q)	Average season (months)
5	1	1.5
0	2	—
6	3	3.3
8	4	2.8
1	5	3.2
4	6	2.3
Total 24		*Overall average* 2.6

TABLE VI

Residents and Visitors

Number of species	Quality (Q)	Average season (months)
9	1	2.0
11	2	4.8
17	3	5.1
16	4	5.0
1	5	3.2
9	6	5.2
Total 63		*Overall average* 4.6

1, 2) as 5.2 : 3.5. Moreover, if we take "extras" into account, we find that it is largely the good singers that have substantial totals of these. Thus the Song Thrush, Skylark, Woodlark, Willow Warbler, Blackcap, Garden Warbler (*Sylvia borin*), Nightingale, and Marsh Warbler average 3.6, which is far more than all the rest for which the facts are at all complete. And the two remaining singers rated Q = 6 have one unit each of extras. Note particularly (Appendix A, p. 230) that the five species rated Q = 5 or Q = 6 with short seasons (under 4 months) average 5.3 extras, and that the Nightingale and the Marsh Warbler, good singers with singularly short seasons, have 7 and 4.5 units, respectively. In my opinion this removes the chief anomaly in the short end of the table, and shows the indecisiveness of Armstrong's objections to my earlier discussion of this topic (Armstrong 1963: 243–44; Hartshorne 1958b: 441). Concerning the most striking anomalies in the long end: item 2 (the Hedge Sparrow) is inferior in continuity to the better singers with comparable seasons; in item 3 (the Starling) the singing seems to me largely subsong with loud bits now and then (subsong takes less energy, is less indicative of a bird's interest in what it is doing); item 9 (the House Sparrow, *Passer domesticus*) is said by Nicholson (and Saunders in New England) to sing little; none of the other singers with seasons longer than 5 months and ratings under Q = 6 are known to be outstanding in continuity, except perhaps the Wren (which I think most people would rate as Q = 5, not 4). On the contrary the five species rating Q = 6 with such seasons average 1.4 extra C units, and include the only pronouncedly nocturnal species with a long season and at least two others with some night song.

Thus the broad statistical support which season-lengths alone give to the correlation of quantity and quality of singing is strongly confirmed when known subsidiary factors are taken into account. If one includes under nocturnal singing performing extremely early at dawn or extremely late at dusk, the better singers excel in that also. Indeed, in the world generally, according to data I have been able to find, while some poor singers are observed to sing extra early or late, or in the night, proportionately more good singers are listed under these heads. By this indication also, good singing extends over more of the bird's life than poor singing.

That the Nightingale, in spite of its short season, produces a large output of song, even in England, is supported by the following observations of Morris (1925: 81–83). He heard "hundreds" of these birds singing at night during migration "in a lonely spot on our downs. . . . Every thornbush, every patch of gorse around, was replete with birds which had not long crossed the water, and which were gathered here in countless numbers to recruit their strength before dispersing to their breeding haunts." Also: "The song is uttered by day or night with equal persistency, especially on first arrival, and perhaps there is no songster which crowds more melody into the few weeks which elapse before the advent of the young brood." He says, too, that there is some song in August. And it has been heard in Africa (Bannerman 1953) "as early as January 3."

The Chiffchaff has the longest V season. In terms of my theory this is an anomaly. However, the rating of 3 on a scale 1–6 is in my opinion the lowest reasonable one. The song does not in fact consist of only two elements, corresponding to chiff and chaff, as the name has ludicrously enough misled even Eliot Howard and Nicholson (of all people) to suppose. But even if it did, one would malign the song in taking it to be a mere reiteration of chiff-chaff, chiff-chaff. Rather, monotony is avoided by changing the order: chiff-chaff-chaff-chiff-chaff-chiff-chiff. Also the tone quality is poorly represented by the English syllables, as compared to the more appropriate German Zilp-zalp. But actually the song consists of three or four elements: "Chip, chap, chep, chop" (Garstang), "chif-chef, chif-chef, chif-chaf" (Morris). See also North and Sims (1958).

Observers of many individuals in Germany and Spain, using recorders and sonagraphs, declare that "no Zilp-zalp deserves its name," since there are always more than two and sometimes, counting five variations, as many as nine elements (Thielcke and Linsenmair 1963). Even three variations or elements give nine binary relations: AB, BA, AC, CA, BC, and CB, as well as AA, BB, and CC, compared to only four with but two elements. With four elements there are 16 binary relations. I rate the song 768.562:34, well above the Cirl Bunting (*Emberiza cirlus*), the Corn Bunting, or the Lesser Whitethroat (*Sylvia curruca*), for instance, which rate not much above 18 or 20 on my scale, which runs from 6 to 54.

A partly uncontrolled variable in our account is the amount of daily performance represented by Alexander's unbroken lines. They are not likely to report the same amounts for all species. From many detailed observations in widely separated parts of the U.S. and elsewhere I am convinced that good singers perform more liberally each day as well as with higher continuity and for more of the year than poor ones.

A third British author (Turnbull 1943) distinguishes "major" and "minor" songsters. Apart from nonoscines and one species omitted from Alexander's chart, the majors are Alexander's Class I plus three sensible additions, the twelve species averaging 5.5 months of song. The 33 minors average just under 5 months, besides rating lower in continuity or other extras. The remaining "occasional voices and otherwise" are obviously regarded as third class, both in quality and in quantity. So here again the thesis of mere subjectivity shows itself to be statistically invalid. The correlation holds independently of the particular observer.

Birds with primitive syrinxes, nonoscines, of course tend to be musically inferior. To include them does not, I think, upset the correlation we are dealing with. But it complicates the issues, and I am less clear about the facts where such birds are concerned. Some qualification of the generalization may be needed for nonoscines. However, large numbers of primitive birds confine their singing to a short breeding season and, in the Neotropics especially, many confine it to brief dawn songs. So far as my data go there is a pronounced tendency for the better-singing primitives (e.g., tinamous [Tinamidae]) to have longer seasons or to persist more through the day or to have higher continuity, or all of these.

B. In North American Oscines

For North America, not including Mexico, we have much information concerning song-lengths and rates of singing per minute. From these data continuity is deducible. Conveniently, a good deal of this is contained in one handy volume (Robbins et al. 1966). Bent is also often helpful.

Much as in England, there is fair agreement as to which species sing the best. About 16 species are praised by most authors. One of these, the Solitaire, has been too little studied, especially as to continuity, to be used in the present analysis. (It does have a long season.) For the other 15 we know at least the continuity with fair precision. It varies from 0.2 in the Western Meadowlark to 0.8+ in the Brown Thrasher (*Toxostoma rufum*), Sage Thrasher (*Oreoscoptes montanus*), and

Mockingbird. The average continuity is 0.42, and the average season 5.3 months. The product of the two chief indices of amount of singing is 2.3. All other species for which adequate data are available (67 species) average 0.26 and 3.2, giving as product 0.8. Thus the indications are that the output of the best singers is nearly three times that of the others—among whom there are, of course, some rather good singers.

There are many poor singers in North America, especially wood warblers and "sparrows" (buntings) which have rather short seasons, 2–3 months, and low continuity, say 1/4 or 1/5, giving a product of 0.4–0.6. No very good singer in all the world is like this, so far as I can learn. Henslow's Sparrow has a continuity of 1/15 and a season of at most 3.8 months, product 0.26. By comparison, the European Marsh Warbler, with a season of 1.5 months and a continuity of 0.8+ has a product of 1.2, not counting night-singing. LeConte's Sparrow (*Passerherbulus caudacutus*), with one of the poorest of all songs, has a continuity of 1/8 (Bent 1968).

Saunders (1947, 1948, 1951), though he does not distinguish as definitely as the English do between periods of abundant and less-frequent singing and does not rank songs in a systematic way, still does nearly always give total seasons and plain enough indications of what songs he finds highly, moderately, or little developed; and the seasonal indications correlate with the others, even without taking continuity into consideration, but especially with such consideration. Supplementing his information with that of others, I think it is safe to say that the Mockingbird (whose song is "a wonderful performance") sings at least as much as any other bird in North America (perhaps in the world) and the Cardinal (a "great artist"), Carolina Wren, the two meadowlarks, and Bachman's Sparrow ("high among birdsongs") are among the closest competitors in output as in quality. (Quotations from Saunders 1951: 128, 241, 302. Note also Saunders 1929: 94–97.)

The only species with short seasons that Saunders rates high are the Brown Thrasher and the Bobolink. Adding the Sage Thrasher (out of his region), we have three superior singers with rather short seasons. Two are exceedingly continuous, and the third, the Bobolink, is not especially discontinuous, and besides sings in fairly high latitudes at a time of very long days. By contrast, numerous wood warblers, though some sing in high latitudes, combine short seasons with low continuity and mediocre or poor songs. This is also true of many finches, whose season may be somewhat longer but whose continuity may be even less. Tits have long seasons, but most have neither high continuity nor liberal performance periods.

In the high Sierras I found no species singing as much through the summer as the Hermit Thrush (which Saunders puts highest of all) or the Fox Sparrow, and in the coastal regions of central California none as much as the Mockingbird, Meadowlark, and Swainson's Thrush (*Catharus ustulatus*). These are all rated good singers. I have lived for years with Wood Thrushes (a species which is next to the Hermit according to Saunders) and have found them to sing abundantly, with much higher continuity and for several weeks more than most warblers. (All around the world, thrushes, especially the more musical forest species, mostly sing more than 2½ months and always with fairly high continuity. Some genera sing 6 months or more, e.g., solitaires, *Myadestes* spp. Wrens mostly sing well and all year round, with middling continuity.)

Of all the North American species that seem to sing much, the Tufted Titmouse perhaps is the poorest singer. It is heard in most months of the year, if not in all. Its continuity is middling rather than low. It seems to me to perform more liberally than the Cactus Wren, which also sings through the year. How poor a singer is the Titmouse? I rate it middling, not poor. Its voice is loud and clear, and an individual seems to have about three songs, each of which gains several variations through number juggling. So 856.552:31 is perhaps fair enough.

C. Worldwide Statistical Sample

Having heard songs in several parts of each of the six zoogeographical regions, and in most of the states of the U.S., I have selected 81 species from 14 countries for special consideration (Appendix B, p. 234). I have tried to get a statistically fair sample, i.e., neither including items because they support a correlation nor excluding any because they fail to support one, but only on the basis of their meeting or failing to meet two requirements: (a) their seeming to me clear cases of very high, very low, or middling song-development (43 or more, 17 or less, 29–31 points, respectively); and (b) the availability of information about song season and other probable indications of

song-output. Having judged songs for many more years than I have
been concerned with the correlation now under consideration, I believe my rating habits are independent of information about seasons.

In listing poor singers, I largely ignore whisper songs, subsongs, and
songs extremely difficult to distinguish from mere calls, as with the
House Sparrow. There seems to be considerable disagreement as to
how much this species sings. In my experience, little. Perhaps this is
not true if the "social singing" (Summers-Smith 1963: 26–29) or choral
performing, e.g., in the process of roosting, is taken into account. The
Starling (a far better singer) is another species whose performances
are hard to classify. Much of its output seems subsong to me. And I
also omit nonoscine singers. They seem to fit the main thesis, but they
introduce complications calling for lengthy discussion. It is one thing
biologically to ask if a sparrow, or bunting, with good syringial muscles for singing, sings well, and another thing to ask this about a woodpecker, with primitive muscles. But to deal adequately with such
points requires space. Also I have observed nonoscine singing with
less care. I have put lyrebirds under superior singers because they are
closely related to Oscines, their habits are well known, and there is
no serious disagreement as to the superiority of their singing.

For similar reasons of simplicity I have omitted species whose song
ratings (18–28, 32–42 points) fall between the middling and the extreme values. Ample experiment has shown that these two groups add
nothing essential.

Estimates of song seasons for British birds are taken from Alexander's data as given in Witherby's *Handbook of British Birds*; for
North American species, chiefly from Saunders (1947, 1948, 1951),
with some consideration of observations by G. R. Mayfield (1940–41),
Baerg (1930), and of course myself. For Japanese birds, Austin and
Kuroda (1953) were helpful, for Australia, Halafoff (correspondence),
for Central America, Skutch, for Europe, Géroudet (1961). I have also
profited by the remarkably extensive and accurate field knowledge of
Edgar Kincaid of Austin. I have had direct experience of 70 of the
species and have heard recordings of most of the rest. Hundreds of
species have been studied in recordings. Innumerable descriptions
have been read in regional guides.

My "good" singers are famous on this account and my "poor" ones
have not, I think, been rated highly by anyone. There could always
be debate as to details, but some of the debate turns on objective facts.

Thus, the Yellow Bunting (see Table VII) has up to 7 songs in individual cases. I ask the reader to remember that "good" does not mean merely that some like the song, and "poor" that some dislike it, but that the song has a high or low degree of the six parameters of song-development: Loudness (L), Variety, complexity, scope (V), Continuity (C), Tonal purity (T), Organization (O), and Imitativeness (I). In Table VII and in Appendix B, p. 234, (Song) Development (D) represents the sum of the values of these six variables; (Song) Season (S) is the number of days of singing in the region where the bird nests; and Continuity Fraction (Cf) is the length of a song divided by the length of the song-pause cycle. Effective Season (ES) is expressed by the formula

$$ES = Cf \times [F + \frac{(S - F) \pm L + N + W}{3}]$$

in which F means the season of full or abundant song; L, the excess or deficiency of daylight (extra-long or extra-short days in high latitudes); N, nocturnal song; and W, song by migrants in winter quarters or during the part of the year not covered by S. ES is thus the number of days in S, suitably modified because of Cf, and also by: the part of S in which singing is not abundant, night-singing, singing outside the breeding region, and location of the season in the part of the year with extra-long (or short) days—the last four factors discounted to ⅓. Numerically Cf is by far the the greatest of these modifying factors.

For ease of comprehension I consider in Table VII only six examples out of the 81 in Appendix B, omitting some of the less important variables as well. Note the sharp decrease, in the middling and poor singers, of the average song season, continuity, and effective season, and hence, according to probability, in total output of song.

It might be objected that continuity is counted twice, in rating quality and also in estimating effective season and annual output. However, (1) continuity makes only a minor difference in quality rating and a major one in the estimation of quantity. Besides, (2) since the higher continuities go with high immediate variety and are to a considerable extent, as we shall see, correlated with all the dimensions of excellence, the correlations we obtain would still hold even if we did not include continuity in quality ratings. We obtain correlations between quality and season even as unmodified by continuity, S rather than ES. Thus the argument is not basically weakened by the apparent circularity.

TABLE VII

	LVC.TOI:D	S	Cf	ES
Very Good Singers				
Blackbird	978.895:46	169	3/4	127
Brown Thrasher	989.775:45	75	1	65
General averages for 35 species		199	0.69	103
Middling Singers				
Yellow Bunting, Yellowhammer	854.562:30	198	1/4	53
House Wren	756.553:31	104	1/3+	45
General averages for 14 species		150	0.44	58
Very Poor Singers				
Reed Bunting	723.121:16	183	1/4	36
Worm-eating Warbler	233.121:12	67	1/5	15
General averages for 32 species		114	0.18	17

I grant that other observers using my rating system would give somewhat different numerical values. Even the same observer, or I myself (as can be seen by comparing ratings I have given of certain birds in different chapters in this book), would not always come to the same values on repeated ratings of a species. However, the differences in my case are usually slight. And the self-consistency of a given observer has some value for statistical purposes. Also another observer might agree that my very good, very poor, and middling songsters deserve these classifications, yet reach higher scores for the first class and lower scores for the third. The essential thing is that ratings should be carefully based on the singing, not on factors (e.g., season-length) whose correlation with singing skill is in question.

Some Spearman rank correlation coefficients calculated by computer (courtesy of R. Selander, to whom I owe valuable suggestions) from data concerning the 81 species are given in Table VIII.

TABLE VIII

(1) D:S = 0.48; D:ES = 0.85
(2) L:S = 0.42; L:ES = 0.71
(3) V:S = 0.40; V:ES = 0.85
(4) C:S = 0.44; C:ES = 0.91
(5) T:S = 0.40; T:ES = 0.68
(6) O:S = 0.41; O:ES = 0.67
(7) I:S = 0.39; I:ES = 0.83
(8) V:C = 0.87; C:I = 0.87; V:I = 0.92
(9) T:O = 0.92; V:O = 0.75; O:I = 0.72; T:I = 0.77; T:V = 0.76

These coefficients are of course very high. (1) shows that while song-development correlates definitely with total season, it correlates still more positively with the effective song season, in which continuity, etc., are taken into account.

(2) to (7) support this contention and show that, except for variety and continuity, the separate variables are less closely correlated than their sum with annual amounts of singing. Since continuity, which covaries with variety—see (8)—is the chief factor distinguishing ES from S, it is inevitable that it correlates well with ES.

(5) and (6) show musical exquisiteness and order to be less strongly correlated with annual amounts of singing (the presumed correlate of ES) than the other variables, especially continuity and variety. Continuity and complexity are more obviously important biologically than tonal purity and organization (as judged by the human ear). Yet the latter, by sharpening the distinctiveness and *Gestalt* closure of the song, also have their utility.

(8) confirms my anti-monotony principle, since it shows that V, which includes "immediate" as well as "eventual" variety—the former removing the need for pauses to retain the effectiveness of the stimulus—covaries with continuity, and that imitative singers, which of course have immediate variety, are continuous ones.

(9) shows that birds favoring pure single notes also favor musical relations between them, and that it is the noisier singers which have the looser organization. Also, that, while musical "perfection" acts almost as a single variable, it correlates only moderately strongly with variety and imitativeness. Birds with enormous repertoires, subject to additions through imitation, will achieve less musical integration than many of those which limit their variety somewhat. Still, all the variables tend to increase together, although each species specializes in its emphasis.

Between the very good and the very poor singers, total seasons decrease from 199 days to 114, continuity fractions from 0.69 to 0.18, and effective seasons from 103 days to 17. Night- and (with visitors) winter-singing also decrease slightly. However, since more of the poor singers considered have their seasons in the period of long days, the decrease in ES is essentially due to the short seasons and low continuity.

Assuming Rollin's figure of 186 for the Skylark, one may guess that on the average each unit of ES corresponds to at least two hours of annual singing.

For song-pause cycles I have sometimes relied on personal observations, or on Nicholson or Reynard, or on information assembled in Bent
(1946–68); also on unedited tapes and recordings in which pauses are
kept intact. For song-length Saunders (1951) is very helpful. Spectrograms, the ideal means, have been used in a few cases. Of course, an
individual varies its continuity somewhat. I try to arrive at the most
usual ratio. With some species (Chapter 7C) an individual has two
modes of singing: a rather discontinuous one, a single song being repeated over and over at intervals (illustrating the "anti-monotony
principle"); and a relatively continuous one (perhaps used only at
dawn), with several songs following each other in varying order (thus
also illustrating the principle). Craig's favorite, the Wood Pewee, is
one example.

My ranking system is inessential. Others may devise a system better
for them, and I should not expect them to get the same values in particular cases, even using my system, but I should expect them to confirm similar correlations.

D. Singing at Narrowly Limited Times

There are species—but no first-class songsters known to me—which
sing at random times of the year, yet "never very much at any time,"
e.g., Gnatcatcher (*Polioptila caerulea*), Loggerhead Shrike (*Lanius
ludovicianus*), and Blue Jay (*Cyanocitta cristata*) (Baerg 1930). Of
tropical tanagers Skutch (1954: 218, 124, 190) says, "Many species sing
so little and have such poorly-developed voices." The few tanagers
which sing rather well are not said to sing little. There are species, all
rather poor singers, which sing only at dawn. Thus, the Blue (or Red-
legged) Honeycreeper (*Cyanerpes cyaneus*), "like many another bird
with a poorly-developed voice . . . has a dawn song which he rarely
if ever utters after sunrise" (ibid.: 390). I agree with Armstrong that
there are some life histories in Skutch's works which seem counter-
instances to the quantity-quality correlation. But the confirming instances to be found there are more numerous.

There are species—but no highly rated ones—which sing, if at all,
only until they secure a mate (Quaintance 1938), which some individuals may do by visual means alone (Rand and Rand 1943). In contrast, Song Sparrows, e.g., reduce singing sharply when a mate is

gained, but still sing a good deal thereafter (Nice 1943, 1964). There are species—again not highly rated—which sing rather freely at night but (some say) not very freely by day, e.g., the English Grasshopper Warbler.

At the opposite extreme are species, mostly with highly developed songs, which sing freely at normal times, but in addition much at night, or much in winter quarters (Bannerman 1954; Archer and God-man 1961; Chapin 1953; Wayne 1910: 124, 128, 129, 184, 197, 202), or extremely early at dawn (Clark 1938; Ball 1945), or at night in winter (Wayne: 127), or at night while migrating in spring (Morris 1925: 81–83) and even in autumn (Hazen 1928).

That singers with high ratings sing more is supported also by the results of a method of spot sampling not presented here in detail. During a short walk, or while remaining in a very limited area, I try to ascertain what species that are singers at all are present, which ones sing abundantly, which in moderate amounts, and which little or not at all, taking continuity into account in estimating abundance or lack of it. Almost universally I have found that the proportion of high-rating species singing abundantly has been higher, and the proportion of low-rating species singing abundantly has been lower, than their ratio to the total number of species present. This has been true even if continuity was left out of account, much more so when it was considered. These results were obtained in Georgia, Texas, and the San Francisco Bay area, Stanford, and the central high Sierras of California. Nowhere has it been sharply contradicted by any statistically significant number of species. Of course it may sometimes happen that one hears but one or a very few songs by a poor singer or two and nothing else. But it is more common to hear only a very good singer, say a Mockingbird. At the height of the spring, outside the tropics, nearly every bird sings abundantly by its standards, and at such times only continuity may distinguish the high-rated species. But at times of substantial but not climactic singing the better singers do more than their statistical share, even neglecting continuity. With continuity there is scarcely any room for doubt.

On the whole it is as if birds which seem to man to sing better have a more persistent impulse to sing. True enough, the singers with long seasons are also those for which the utility of singing extends over more of the year (as in the territorial behavior of English Robins). But as we have seen (Chapter 1D) there is no conflict between "birds sing for pleasure" and "they sing to maintain territory or attract mates." The more essential an activity in the whole life of the bird, the greater the portion of the bird's pleasure which is realized in that activity. Presumably swifts enjoy flying more than some terrestrial and weakly flying species do. So the star singers of nature particularly enjoy singing, and fill as many seconds, hours, days, months, as other preoccupations and pressures leave room for. All this may be somewhat anthropomorphic. But it does have a broad relation to a great mass of facts.

There has been some experimentation (Konishi and Nottebohm, in Hinde 1969) on the effects of deafening upon a bird's singing, or the presence or absence of "auditory feedback." It gives some support to the notion that hearing themselves sing encourages birds to keep on singing. Kinaesthetic feedback is also involved, but a deaf bird lacks the stimulation of hearing itself and others.

E. Amounts of Singing by Nonoscines

It must be admitted that our argument so far is incomplete, in that nonoscines have been ignored. I have made some attempts to deal with them, and on the whole the results seem positive. However, the data are less adequate, and the distinctions between good, middling, and poor songs are more difficult to clarify. The Oscines are the fullest expression of the possibilities of song, and we cannot expect that the principles involved would be as clear in the more primitive forms.

A recent study (Snow 1968) will serve to illustrate the difficulties. The Little Hermit Hummingbird (*Phaethornis longuemareus*) has a song which is sung a very great deal indeed—apparently up to 12,000 times a day for many months. Since the song is one second long, this means many hundreds of hours of actual singing in a year. Is it a good song? What is a good performance by a bird of this type? Not many hummingbird songs are in any definite sense better; so perhaps it is quite good. But is it an aesthetic affair for the bird? Perhaps so. However, the singing situation is not at all typical, taking birds in general. We have a company of polygamous males not far from each other singing to such females as may be interested. They are receiving constant stimulation from each other. The seemingly tedious simplicity and lack of versatility of one individual's performance, the same song every other second, with omission of the last element about the only variation, is perhaps not apparent to the bird, since it is hearing its fellows all the time. That it is listening to them is proved by the way the birds fall into groups in each of which there is the same song type. The shortness of the pauses, only equal to the songs, yet without versatility, is another example of the partial failure of the anti-monotony and other aesthetic principles to apply to primitive singers. Evolution toward the Oscine climax is in part, I hold, a progress toward increased aesthetic sensitivity, hence diminished tolerance of unrelieved repetition.

One of the most glaring apparent exceptions to my generalization that I know of among Suboscines is the Ochre-bellied Flycatcher (*Pipromorpha oleaginea*), which, says Skutch (1960), sings at all times of day for six months. In comparison with Oscines we can hardly rate it above 21 points. However, allowing for its primitive syrinx we might reasonably raise this to 30, and call it a middling singer. If it performs 2 hours daily for 180 days and has a continuity fraction of ⅓—which may well be much too high—then its total quantity is 120 hours, which is still far short of the output of some of the best singers. However, Skutch's account suggests that it performs more than 2 hours. So the bird may be an extreme exception. Some of the tropical barbets also may be exceptions.

In East Africa, in early September one of the persistent singers was the Golden-rumped Tinkerbird, a barbet (*Pogoniulus bilineatus*). North asked, did this not violate my rule? I found, however (see Chapter 11), that there was no reasonable way to rate this bird other than middling, rather than poor. I have listened to this bird a lot, partly because of Myles North's kindness in giving me a fine taping of it. I do not know its season length.

F. Summary

In this chapter statistical evidence has been presented to show that amounts of singing per year and quality of singing, as judged by various authors, or by myself using a six-dimensional rating system, and whether in England (A.), North America (B.), or the world over (C., D., E.), are positively correlated. This supplements evidence given in the previous four chapters to show that quality of singing as humanly assessed correlates with objective, functionally important factors—such as the proportion of a bird's life spent in singing, or the intensity of the need for acoustical advertisement. From this I take it to follow that these assessments disclose with some reliability, though not with sharp accuracy, a significant variable of avian biology.

9

The Well-Equipped Singers (Oscines)

❦

A. *The Families and Their Regions*

Relationships among the 4000 species of true Songbirds, birds with good muscles for voice control, are in many cases extremely puzzling. I follow Austin's family groupings (1967) as at least convenient. They are roughly those of Wetmore (see Thomson 1964: 13–20) and most recent American authorities, except that Austin, unlike Mayr, Delacour, and some others, keeps thrushes, babblers, Old World warblers, and some other groups as separate families, instead of reducing them to subfamilies of an extended Muscicapidae.

The following abbreviations designate, with some additions and qualifications, the usual zoogeographical divisions of the world, largely due to Sclater and Wallace (see Thomson 1964, "Distribution, Geographical"):

Au   Australia
Eth   Ethiopian: tropical Africa (below the Sahara)
Haw   Hawaii
Ha   Holarctic: the nontropical Northern Hemisphere
Na   Nearctic: the nontropical New World—North America
           (including the Mexican Plateau)
Na^e Eastern North America
Na^w Western North America
NG   New Guinea
Nt   Neotropical: the tropical New World

Nt^n   Northern Neotropical: Middle and Central America, the
        West Indies, and the Northern Andean region in
        South America

Nt^s   South America, except the Northern Andes (which, espe-
        cially in songs, have much in common with Central
        America)

NW   New World, the Americas

NZ   New Zealand

Or   Oriental: the Asian tropics (South of the higher Hima-
        layas) including the Philippines and Indonesia

OW   Old World: the Eastern Hemisphere

Pa   Palearctic: nontropical Eurasia

Pa^w   Europe and Africa north of the Sahara

Pa^e   Nontropical Asia, including Japan

Pac   Pacific Isles

Pt   Paleotropical: the Old World Tropics

W   World

In Table IX *spp. means species with highly developed or superior
songs, as shown by their rating 42 or more in my six-dimensional rating
system. (In some cases my ratings have to be based on descriptions by
others.) An asterisk after a family name means that at least 7% of the
family have highly developed songs. Two asterisks mean that at least
20% of a family large enough to be statistically significant, with say 20
or more members, have superior songs.

The places listed under Region are only those to which the birds
have, so far as is known, found their way without help from man—
apart from the now nearly ubiquitous starlings (no. 33). Regions in
parentheses are those in which the family is but slightly represented.

The first two families are Suboscine, but they are above other Suboscine families in vocal equipment; so I include them.

The starred, or musical, families are nos. 1, 3, 9, 11, 19, 21, 22, 23, 24.
It seems to follow that, if (a controversial point) the linear order has
much evolutionary significance, the general trend has been somewhat
away from acoustical and toward visual modes of communication.
This may possibly be because some seed- and fruit-yielding plants or
trees—or the birds nourished by them—are late arrivals, and because
(see section B) feeding on vegetable products rather than on insects
is favorable to feeding in the open or above ground, where light is

TABLE IX

Families and Their Regions

Family	No. spp.	*spp.	%	Region
1. lyrebirds, Menuridae*	2	2	100	Au
2. scrub-birds, Atrichornithidae	2	0	0	Au
3. larks, Alaudidae*	75	10	13	OW (Na)
4. swallows, Hirundinidae	79	0	0	W exc. NZ
5. cuckoo-shrikes, Campephagidae	70	1?	?	Pt
6. drongos, Dicruridae	20	0? 1?	0–5	Pt
7. OW orioles, Oriolidae	28	0	0	Pt
8. crows and jays, Corvidae	102	0	0	W
9. wattlebirds, Callaeidae*	3	0? 1?	0–33	NZ
10. mudnest builders, Grallinidae	4	0	0	NG-Au
11. butcherbirds and bell-magpies, Cracticidae*	10	3?	30?	NG-Au
12. bowerbirds, Ptilonorhynchidae	17	0? 2?	0–13	NG-Au
13. birds of paradise, Paradisaeidae	40	0	0	NG (Au)
14. titmice, Paridae	62	0	0	Ha-Nt^n-Eth
15. creepers, Certhiidae	5	0	0	Ha (Nt^n)
16. nuthatches, etc., Sittidae	32	0	0	Ha-Or-Au
17. babblers, etc., Timaliidae	287	12	4	Pt (Na^w)
18. bulbuls, Pycnonotidae	119	5	4	Eth-Or-Japan
19. leafbirds, etc., Irenidae*	14	2	14	Or
20. dippers, Cinclidae	4	0? 1?	0–25	Pa, Na^w, Nt
21. wrens, Troglodytidae**	59	14	24	NW (Pa)
22. mockingbirds and thrashers, Mimidae**	31	11	36	NW
23. thrushes, Turdidae**	307	65	21	W
24. OW warblers, Sylviidae*	398	28	7	OW (NW)
25. OW flycatchers, Muscicapidae	378	9	2.4	OW
26. accentors, Prunellidae	12	0	0	Pa
27. pipits and wagtails, Motacillidae	54	0–2	0–4	W
28. waxwings, etc., Bombycillidae	8	0	0	Ha
29. Palmchat, Dulidae	1	0	0	Nt^n (Hispaniola)
30. wood-swallows, Artamidae	10	0	0	Or-Au
31. vanga-shrikes, Vangidae	13	0	0	Eth (Madagascar)
32. shrikes, Laniidae	73	1–2	2	Eth (W exc. NG, Au)
33. starlings, Sturnidae	111	0–1	0?	Pt (W)

TABLE IX (*Continued*)

Family	No. spp.	*spp.	%	Region
34. honeyeaters, Meliphagidae	162	5?	3?	Au-NG-NZ-Pac
35. sunbirds, Nectariniidae	104	1–2	0–2	Pt-Pac
36. flowerpeckers, Dicaeidae	54	0	0	Or-Au
37. white-eyes, Zosteropidae	85	1–3	2?	Pt (Pac, NZ)
38. vireos, Vireonidae	42	0	0	NW
39. Hawaiian honeycreepers, Drepanididae	22	0–1?	0?	Haw
40. wood warblers, Parulidae	119	0–1?	0?	NW
41. icterids (NW orioles), Icteridae	94	4–6?	5?	NW
42. tanagers, Thraupidae	223	0–2?	0?	Nt (Na)
43. NW seedeaters, Fringillidae	315	8?	3	W (exc. NG, Au)
44. OW seedeaters, Ploceidae	375	3?	1?	W
total	4025†			

† Figures in this column are open to debate. "Lumpers" give lower ones; "splitters" give higher ones. (See Rand 1967.)

more abundant or where visual exposure is less dangerous, or both. Vegetable feeding is much more important in families coming after no. 27 than in those preceding it. It is notable that the three double-starred, large families, nos. 21, 22, 23, are closely related insectivorous, ground- or low-foraging birds, and that at least the two larger families are mostly sylvan. Comprising less than ⅒ of the species, they furnish about ½ of the superior singers. Nearest to these three in their contributions to the company of star singers are nos. 3 and 24. Both are largely insectivorous, and, while the larks are ground-feeding, the warblers are sylvan, or live in reeds and dense high grasses. Comprising 12% of the Oscines, they furnish 20% of the superior singers. This is a much inferior (though still supernormal) showing compared to that of the first three families. Why? Larks are open-country and in many cases arid-country birds, and warblers are mostly either high-foragers or live in brilliant light in tropical grasses. Balanced against these factors are the predominance of concealing coloration and/or the denseness of the growth in which they forage. All five families are highly territorial. Together they furnish a majority of the world's superior songsters, and thus form the main peak of the development of subhuman music.

B. An Ecological-Behavioral Classification of Songbirds

Although Oscines are, as a group, anatomically specialized for song, the extent to which song is actually developed varies as widely among them as among birds in general. The explanation cannot lie in anatomical differences, unless it is in brain structures too subtle to be discerned. Since taxonomical groupings are anatomically based, they do not throw any direct light upon differences in Oscine musical skill or virtuosity. Thus thrushes are very different from OW flycatchers in degree of song-development, though closely related to them taxonomically. Since song has its functions in relation to the bird's mode of life and environment, and since these vary enormously among Songbirds, it seems clear that a classification at least partly in behavioral and ecological terms must be more helpful for our purposes of explaining song phenomena than a purely taxonomic one. Table X is such a partly ecological classification. Its chief criteria are not the gross anatomical differences and geographical locations but rather the different habits and types of habitat of the birds.

The crucial factors in a bird's life seem to be its type of food, the habitats in which this food is usually found, and the social patterns involved in its finding and in reproduction and the care of young. As we saw in Chapter 2A, the type of food may influence song by determining the amount of surplus time and energy the bird disposes of. Moreover, the conditions under which the food is obtained may have even more influence. Fruit-eating, seed-eating—especially the latter (Lack 1968: 70–71, 306–14)—and nectar-sipping species are likely to be at least somewhat gregarious, and are also likely to spend much of their time in well-lighted places, for that is where the fruit, seeds, or nectar are mostly to be found; but species which live on insects occurring chiefly on or near the forest floor must live much of the time under conditions of poor visibility. They will probably also be protectively colored because of predators. Hence it is not surprising that most of the better songsters of the world are of this kind.

Species feeding on the ground in the open are a more complex problem. On the one hand, they live in well-lighted places; on the other hand, their danger from hawks must be great, so that conspicuous colorations seem out of the question. (This is especially true of nongregarious species. It has been shown that hawks hesitate to dive into a compact flock.) And though such birds are not in deep shade, still, unless the vegetation is very sparse indeed, they are likely to be quite invisible to one another much of the time as they run or walk among grasses and small plants. Thus we can perhaps explain the rather musical character of the lark family. It is another question why the larks are so much superior to the pipits.

There is some ambiguity in the term "gregarious." Some groups, such as the babblers (no. 17), nest territorially; but outside the breeding season they tend to go in flocks or "parties." I consider these "somewhat" gregarious, and I find that in general such birds are not the most musical. Although some thrushes behave similarly (among them the American Robin), these are not the most musical thrushes. And I believe that the majority of the family are individualistic all year round. Bulbuls, in contrast, are "not strongly territorial" (Austin) and the pairs are very chummy. These traits also are unfavorable to song. The isolated and, at least when feeding, invisible individual is the typical singer, in touch with even one other of his kind only by voice.

That a bird may sing in a conspicuous position, or have rather rich coloring, does not make it essentially a conspicuous type of bird if while foraging for food it is seldom visible to others of its kind. Much of the time the others in question will themselves be inside the foliage or in undergrowth or grass, where they will be unable to see very far. Thus in the main they will have to keep track of rivals or mate by hearing. The American Cardinal is a somewhat brilliantly colored bird, but one can be in a region where at least one bird is audible wherever one goes yet only rarely see a glimpse of red, or occasionally a singing bird. But if Baltimore Orioles are around, flashes of fiery color will be frequent, for they are considerably brighter than Cardinals and they forage higher and in better light. Their songs are musical but simple, with almost no repertoire, and they have little of the Cardinal's gift for treating a song as a theme for a goodly number of variations.

From Table X it seems apparent that singing skill is favored by territoriality, dull or protective plumage, insectivorous diet, ground-feeding, sylvan habitat, and the absence of visually identifying habits (note tits in IIb, flycatchers in VIa, also IV, V).

Of these factors the case for territoriality and ground-feeding is rather clear. That for sylvan habitat is obscured by the vagueness of "sylvan." Does it mean primary (or "climax") continuous forest, or are

TABLE X

Families and Their Sources of Food

Habitat, habits (plumage)		Family	Quality of song
	Animal Matter		
I. On and near ground in forest			
(a) territorial	1.†	lyrebirds*	complex, imitative, refined
	2.	scrub-birds	noisy, imitative
	21.	wrens**	very good except in continuity and imitativeness
(b) many species somewhat gregarious	17.	babblers	gossipy, some musical
II. Mostly in trees			
(a) territorial, many in grass	24.	OW warblers*	many good, some very good
dense foliage	32.	(some African) shrikes	a few very good
	38.	vireos	fair or rather good
(rather bright plumage)	40.	wood warblers	slight, fair, some good
(b) somewhat gregarious (visually revealing actions)	14.	titmice	slight, fair
(brilliant plumage)	5.	cuckoo-shrikes, minivets	slight
(c) highly gregarious, conspicuous plumage	31, 32.	vanga- and some other shrikes (see VI.)	nearly songless
III. On or near ground in rather open country			
(a) territorial	22.	mockers, thrashers**	complex, some imitative
(b) mildly territorial†† (cf. VIII, no. 3)	27.	pipits, wagtails	simple, some good
(c) somewhat gregarious	26.	accentors	fair
	24.	Au "Fairy wrens"	slight
(d) very gregarious	17.	Parrotbills, Bearded Tit‡	nearly songless
IV. In streams	20.	dippers	at least fair, perhaps one very good

† The numbers are those assigned in Table IX, p. 159.
†† Baker 1942: 142.
‡ *Panurus biarmicus.*

TABLE X *(Continued)*

Habitat, habits (plumage)		Family	Quality of song
V. Bark (trunk and branch)	15, 16.	creepers, nuthatches	slight
VI. Observation-post flight-feeders, mostly in woods			
(a) territorial (dull plumage)	6.	drongos	middling, one or two very good
	25.	OW flycatchers	slight, fair, a few very good
	32.	Ha shrikes	middling
(showy plumage)	25.	monarch fly-catchers	rather poor
(b) rather gregarious, conspicuous	28.	silky flycatchers	slight
VII. Wholly aerial feeders, mostly very gregari-ous	4.	swallows	somewhat musical twitter
	30.	wood-swallows	somewhat musical twitter
Animal Matter and Seeds			
VIII. Open country			
(a) mostly territorial	3.	larks*	fair, good, or very good
(b) somewhat gregarious	10.	mudnest builders	rather crude, one species duets
Chiefly Seeds			
IX. Mostly in woods			
(a) territorial	43i.	cardinal finches	fair or good
(b) mildly gregarious	44i.	cardueline finches	slight, fair
X. Mostly open country			
(a) mostly territorial (some bright)	43ii.	buntings, NW sparrows	a few very good
(b) most species very gregarious (many very bright)	44.	waxbills, weavers, etc.	fair, crude, or none
Animal Matter, Some Fruit			
XI. In forest chiefly, near ground			
(a) territorial (mostly dull plumage)	23.	most thrushes**	nearly all at least fair, many very good
(b) group territories	9.	wattlebirds*	one species superior
	11.	Au bellmagpies*	several superior

TABLE X (*Continued*)

Habitat, habits (plumage)		Family	Quality of song

Half Fruit, Some Nectar, Insects

XII. Forest and open country arboreal, somewhat gregarious	18.	bulbuls	mostly simple, a few good

Chiefly Fruit

XIII. In forest or open country			
(a) territorial (bright)	7.	orioles	musical but simple
(protective color)	19.	leafbirds*	some highly imitative
(b) mildly gregarious (bright)	36.	flowerpeckers	almost songless
(c) bowerbuilders, somewhat gregarious (some bright)	12.	bowerbirds	loud, unmusical, imitative
(d) gregarious when not nesting (visual display)	42.	Swallow Tanager†	"little developed," "poor," "no song"
(e) polygamous (very showy plumage)	13.	birds of paradise	largely songless
XIV. Mostly in open country			
(a) most species gregarious (conspicuous), some species largely insectivorous	33.	starlings	slight, some imitation
(b) very gregarious	28, 29.	waxwings, Palmchat	nearly songless
XV. Forest or gardens, somewhat gregarious (sober colors)	37.	white-eyes	mostly fair, one or two very good
(bright colors)	35.	sunbirds	slight or fair, a few good
	34.	honeyeaters	slight, fair, a few very good
	42.	honeycreepers	slight

Miscellaneous Foods

XVI. Mostly in forest and territorial	39.	Hawaiian honeycreepers	poor, fair, one good
XVII. Arid isles	43 iii.	Darwin's finches††	rather poor

† *Tersina viridis.*
†† Geospizinae.

TABLE X (Continued)

Habitat, habits (plumage)	Family	Quality of song
XVIII. Ubiquitous		
(a) many species territorial (most species conspicuous)	41. icterids	usually fair, a few very good
(b) gregarious (conspicuous)	8. crows and jays	some slight songs or subsong, none good

patches of thicket or half-grown replacement woods enough? Must the forest be tall, requiring good rainfall, or will stunted xerophytes do? The essential factor seems to be low visibility, for which tall climax forest is not necessary, though it does produce it. Probably only a minority of highly developed songs are sung in mature forest. (This is fortunate since man's expansion in numbers and in appetites threatens most, if not nearly all, such forest with extinction. The threat to Song-birds does not stop there, alas.)

If tall moist forest favors song by making birds invisible and by hampering the transmission of sounds so that utterances must be loud and distinctive to be effective at a distance, very arid open country can favor it for a different reason, by causing birds to space unusually far apart from one another in order to find sufficient food (Linsdale 1938a). Possibly this is why Western Meadowlarks in the drier parts of North America have more powerful, lower-pitched, and longer, some say more beautiful, songs than Eastern Meadowlarks in the moister portions. Perhaps also relevant here is the fact that the most powerful, and one of the two most musical, of all true lark songs is that of the Bifasciated Lark of the desert belt stretching from North Africa to the western edge of the Oriental region. The other most musical lark, the Woodlark, is better hidden by bushes and trees than most larks (Welty 1962: 191, citing Pernau). The Black-throated Sparrows of our Southwest, living in very barren creosote-bush flats, space themselves wide apart and have a more distinctive, far-carrying song than most bunting-type birds (Heckenlively 1970). This applies even more to the Lark Bunting (*Calamospiza melanocorys*), though this bird is in less arid country. The Crested Bellbird of arid Australia is another suggestive case. With small territories, the thin, somewhat transparent, stunted vegetation might not require maximally effective song, but the territories presumably cannot be small. The thrashers of our Southwest are also to be considered here, though most of them are not comparable in song to the Brown Thrasher of the moist East.

The correlation of song with territoriality and inconspicuousness and, I believe, with foraging on or near the ground, is easier to establish than the relation to this or that type of precipitation and vegetation. The amount and variety of song-development on the planet depends chiefly on the existence and variety of adequate niches in which territorial birds can live, under conditions and with habits which render visual means radically insufficient to attract and hold mates and secure territorial privacy.

C. Evolutionary Relationships

The evolution of the Oscines (Table XI), taking into account only some of the more probable relationships implied by the diagram in Fisher and Peterson (1966: 48), is illuminating.

TABLE XI

Hypothetical Evolutionary Tree

Arrows, but not commas, indicate presumed evolutionary derivatives from groups (or their proximate ancestors) immediately preceding on the left.

(1) (a) OW warblers → OW flycatchers → starlings, accentors, swallows
   (b)   OW flycatchers → thrushes → dippers, mimids
(2) OW warblers
   (a) *Cisticola*, grass warblers → creepers, titmice, nuthatches, wrens
   (b) *Cisticola*   → Bearded Tit, babblers, larks, pipits
   (c) *Cisticola*   → whistlers, drongos, shrikes, bellmagpies, magpie-larks, wood-swallows, monarch flycatchers
   (d) *Cisticola*   → widowbirds, weavers, waxbills and true sparrows, vireos, buntings and American sparrows, wood warblers, troupials, finches, tanagers → (cardinals, honeycreepers, Hawaiian honeycreepers, Swallow Tanager, Plushcapped Finch†)
   (e) *Cisticola*   → honeyeaters
(3) OW warblers → bulbuls → cuckoo-shrikes, waxwings, Palmchat, leafbirds, wattlebirds, birds of paradise, bowerbirds
(4) OW warblers → OW orioles, crows
(5) OW warblers → white-eyes, flowerpeckers, sunbirds

† *Catamblyrhynchus diadema.*

OW warblers occur in numerous species in a given area and are territorial, but, being arboreal or grass-inhabiting, are less than maximally well hidden. Their singing averages above normal, but not in comparison with thrushes or wrens. From them, or something like them, derive the OW (Oscine) flycatchers, which are insectivorous, aerially —hence conspicuously—foraging, but territorial and mildly musical. From flycatcher stock came the mostly rather gregarious, conspicuous, and musically mediocre starlings, accentors, and swallows; but also (1b) the mostly ground-feeding, concealed, and territorial thrushes. From related stock came the mimids, strongly territorial, low-foraging, and fairly inconspicuous, and the dippers, living in long, somewhat open, noisy stream-beds, visually distinctive by their habits, and the least highly developed in song of these three groups. Thrushes, the best hidden (in most genera), have more exquisite, but mimids more consistently imitative songs. Why?

Cisticolas, or grass warblers, may be hidden while feeding but can easily rise to a conspicuous position in brilliant light. Their territories, I assume, are not large. They sing interestingly enough, but with limited volume, refinement, and complexity.

From *Cisticola* stock (2) came several groups, of which only the wrens sing well, and only they feed on or near the ground, mostly in forest. Wrens are also the dullest-colored and are more territorial, at least than the tits. Their feeding habits have less obvious peculiarities.

In (2b) occur the rather gregarious, and in some cases conspicuous babblers (including parrotbills, Paradoxornithinae); also the wagtails (*Motacilla* spp.) and pipits (*Anthus* spp.) (not rich in good song), and the larks, which, more definitely territorial, more uniformly dull-colored and inconspicuous in foraging habits than the wagtails, and more consistently ground-feeding than the babblers, are between warblers and thrushes in proportion of superior singers.

In (2c) the scarcely musical monarch flycatchers (Monarchinae), wood-swallows, magpie-larks (Grallinidae), and vanga-shrikes (the last three gregarious, all four conspicuous) should be contrasted to the family of bellmagpies (Cracticidae), which are largely ground-feeding and, though gregarious in some species, include some with individual and one or two with group territories, which are defended by excellent song in both cases. It is somewhat surprising that such large birds, relatively strongly marked in black and white patterns, should sing so well. The size of their territories is probably the explanation. Whistlers (Pachycephalinae) are territorial, and some, including several superior singers, are largely ground-feeding or dull-colored, or both. Also some drongos live in dense forest, and these are the good singers in their group. Some African shrikes, e.g., Boubou Shrike, Nicator (*Nicator chloris*), Rufous-breasted Bush-shrike (*Chlorophoneus rubiginosus*), with striking songs are rather plain-colored, and live in very dense vegetation (on insects, not fruits).

In (2d) there are many colorful, high-foraging or open-country, often very gregarious, groups: weavers and widowbirds (Ploceinae), wood warblers, etc., all second- or third-rate acoustically. But somehow this branch produced the buntings and American sparrows, and a few of these are highly territorial, well-hidden, low-foraging, and dull-colored birds. That among these are some excellent songs, the best of all by one of the dullest, most-hidden birds, the Bachman's or Pinewoods Sparrow, should not surprise us. African canaries (*Serinus* spp.) and some American seedeaters mostly sing in almost superior fashion, which is perhaps congruous with their not excessively showy coloration and to some extent open-country habitats. In any case the percentage of altogether superior songs in the buntings is not high.

The tanagers are mostly arboreal, brilliant in color, and not very territorial; they eat much fruit or (in the honeycreepers) nectar. But four species (Skutch 1954) are rather exceptional in these respects: the two ant-tanagers (*Habia* spp.), the Thrush Tanager (*Rhodinocichla rosea*), and the Gray-headed Tanager (*Eucometis penicillata*). These are found well down in dense growth, are nongregarious and, in their habitat, inconspicuous birds. All have, for tanagers, unusually complex and impressive songs. The Thrush Tanager duets. I tried vainly for some time to see a duetting pair close by in a small, slender, though dense tree but saw nothing until I played back the song, whereupon one flew out to see the intruder. The nontropical Scarlet Tanager (*Piranga olivacea*), with a fair song, is largely insectivorous, not gregarious, and rather well hidden in foliage much of the time. The tropical Scarlet-rumped Tanager (*Rhamphocelus passerinii*) has a song of 3–4 notes, which it sings much though monotonously (Skutch 1954). It is gregarious, frugivorous, and not very well hidden. Its singing posts are near the roost rather than the nest. Its season is long, over six months. It seems to be a mild exception to a number of rules.

Saltators (*Saltator* spp.) live in open woods or forest edges. They are "essentially" frugivorous, though somewhat dull-colored, and slightly beyond tanager standards in song. The remaining cardinal finches (Richmondeninae) are farther from the tanager origins, much less frugivorous, much more territorial, darker-colored, and better hidden. They include a number of species at least close to superior status in song-development: two *Pyrrhuloxia* species, the Blue-black Grosbeak (*Cyanocompsa cyanoides*), several *Pheucticus* species (perhaps best *aureoventris,* the Black-backed Grosbeak, or *melanocephalus,* the Black-headed), and *Rhodothraupis celaeno,* the Crimson-collared Grosbeak, which has a lovely song. The first three, at least, are low-foraging and fairly well hidden; the next two are rather dull-colored, and the last is in mature rain forest.

The least elaborate singers of the cardinals are in the colorful *Passerina* genus. The Painted Bunting (*Passerina ciris*) has a rather weak little song. The Indigo Bunting (*P. cyanea*), much darker and probably less conspicuous, sings more impressively.

Honeyeaters (2e) are in general near average, rather than superior in song (contrary to the usually reliable Austin). They are mostly "rather gregarious" and conspicuous, but many species need to distinguish themselves from one another. Why the New Zealand Tui and Bellbird (*Anthornis melanura*) sing so much better than most of the family is hard to say, unless it is because of the cloudy, foggy climate and the dense growth of the habitat, both in contrast to most of Australia, the main home of the family.

Some branches in (3, 4, 5) specialized in fruit or nectar and hence tended to live in well-lighted places—while the rather gregarious crows went in for versatility in eating methods. These groups produced little superior song. Some groups developed visual display enormously (cuckoo-shrikes, birds of paradise); some are highly gregarious (waxwings and the Palmchat). The best song in the fruit-eaters is in the bulbuls and leafbirds (mostly green, in dense foliage, and territorial) and the wattlebirds (ground- and branch-feeders in lush forest).

D. Wood Warblers: A Case Study

Of all the sizable families of Songbirds, perhaps none has been more carefully studied than the wood warblers (no. 40). (See the monograph by Griscom and Sprunt 1957; also Ficken and Ficken 1962.) Though the family includes few if any superior songsters, it does present a wide range of singing abilities, from very poor to almost superior, and it also contains a fairly wide range of habits and habitats. It should be instructive, therefore, to consider the distribution of degrees of singing skill in this group from the ecological standpoint.

The family almost strikes a balance between visual and acoustical display but inclines toward the visual side. Whereas European warblers look much alike but sound very different, wood warblers tend to sound alike but to look very different. Two-thirds, or 71 species, are sexually isomorphic, but some of these and nearly all of the dimorphic species are rather brightly colored. Still they are fairly well hidden in vegetation. Territorial song is pervasive and unmistakable, but rarely very complex or extremely musical. (If there are any to be rated superior, they are tropical species other than those I have heard.) Nevertheless, some sing much better than others. Since none of the birds are gregarious (though their territories are not large), inequalities in their singing ability are to be explained by varying degrees of conspicuousness, high- or low-foraging in trees or bushes, visual or auditory orientation, presence or absence of dimorphism, brightness of coloration, etc. The first two factors tend to vary together, the low-foraging birds being more protectively colored and compelled to rely more upon sound to detect danger. Perhaps high-foragers have weaker songs in part because there are fewer obstructions to sound waves higher up.

In Tables XII and XIII the numbers after the birds' names represent degrees of inconspicuousness in terms of low- (or high-) foraging, L.f.; sexual indistinguishability, S.i.; and other factors making for invisibility, Inv. In the first column 3 stands for low-, 2 for medium-, and 1 for high-foraging, as indicated in Griscom and Sprunt (1957: 41). I use pluses and minuses to take ambiguities in foraging ranges into account. In adding, these in part cancel out. In the second column 3 registers the lack and 1 the presence of sexual dimorphism, while in the third, 3, 2, 1 stand for least, medium, and maximal visibility, as estimated from factors other than those measured in the first two columns, e.g., protective or display coloration other than sexual, denseness of vegetation, and average lighting (lower in cloud forests). This column is the only one in which my own judgment is expressed. The others are derived, through the conventions just explained, from data in Griscom and Sprunt.

If it is correct that low visibility increases pressure for song-development, then the higher the sum for the three numbers, especially the first two (which are more objective), the better the bird should sing.

In the fourth column (Exp. for my experience of the song), f means that I have sufficient field experience of the bird to know how it sings, and r that I have studied recordings of its song. Under Reg. (for region) tr means that the bird is tropical. In the last column, Authority, JB is for James Bond, taking account both of his own book (1947) and of remarks in Griscom and Sprunt (1957); Gr is for Griscom, as in Griscom and Sprunt; Sk is for Skutch, as in Griscom and Sprunt and in Skutch (1954, 1967); MM is for Margaret Mitchell (1957); CH for myself as the only person who seems to have studied the song; and T(S) for Taczanowski (quoting Stolzmann) (1884).

Table XII contains the "musical," "superb," "varied," "complex," "loud" songs, so far as the literature and my experience indicate. All but one song have been rather highly praised, and that one (no. 13) has not been discussed by anyone but me. None has been called poor, so far as I know.

Table XIII contains the "unmusical," "weak," "thin," "wiry," "buzzy," "insect-like," "colorless," "fricative," "poor" songs, according to the literature and my experience. None has been strongly praised, that I know of.

An examination of the spectrograms will show that these classifications of warbler songs into more and less highly developed are not merely arbitrary. For example, in the spectrograms of four species shown in the booklet included with the Borror and Gunn recordings (also in the *Bulletin of the Federation of Ontario Naturalists,* December 1958: 20–21), the thick or vertical lines and lack of clear-cut patterns in the graphs of Parula and Blue-winged Warblers, in comparison to those of the Kentucky, are obvious. Or one might (Robbins et al. 1966) compare spectrograms of nos. 1, 2, 3, 5, 6, 7, 8, 10, 11, 12, 13 of List B with nos. 2, 3, 4, 5, 6, 7, 8, 10 of List A. There are the following differences: The B species average 1.3 seconds in length, while the A species, even if the Ovenbird (which has indefinite length) is not considered, average 1.6, and only one of them is less than 1.5 seconds. The chief pitches (in kc) of the B songs average 5.9, of the A songs 4.1. (cf. Ficken and Ficken 1962: 113.) Noisy sounds are more prominent in the B graphs, and pitch contrasts are less striking (almost nonexistent in nos. 1 and 13).

TABLE XII

Wood Warblers: List A

	L.f.	S.i.	Inv.	Exp.	Reg.	Authority
1. Swainson's (*Limnothlypis swainsonii*)	3	3	3	f		Gr
2. Ovenbird (*Seiurus aurocapillus*)	3—	3	2	f		
3. Louisiana Waterthrush (*S. motacilla*)	3—	3	2	f		Gr
4. Kentucky (*Oporornis formosus*)	3	3	2—	f		Gr
5. Connecticut (*O. agilis*)	3	1	3			Gr
6. Mourning (*O. philadelphia*)	3	1	3	f		Gr
7. McGillivray's (*O. tolmiei*)	3	1	2			Gr
8. Yellow-breasted Chat (*Icteria virens*)	3	3	2	f		Gr
9. Fan-tailed (*Euthlypis lachrymosa*)	3	1	2		tr	Sk
10. Hooded (*Wilsonia citrina*)	3	1	1	f		Gr
11. Ground-chat (*Chamaethlypis poliocephala*)	3	1	3	f	tr	
12. Whistling (*Catharopeza bishopi*)	2	3	3		tr	JB
13. Rufous-capped (*Basileuterus rufifrons*)	3—	3	1	f	tr	CH
14. Buff-rumped (*B. rivularis* or *fulvicauda*)	3	3	2	f	tr	Sk
15. White-browed (*B. leucoblepharus*)	3	3	3	f	tr	MM
16. Two-banded (*B. bivittatus*)†	3	3	2		tr	?
17. Russet-crowned (*B. coronatus*)	3	3	2		tr	T(S)
18. Collared Redstart (*Myioborus torquatus*)	2—	3	2	r	tr	Sk
19. Chiriqui Yellowthroat (*Geothlypis chiriquensis*)	3	1	3		tr	Sk
20. Olive-crowned Yellowthroat (*G. semiflava*)	3	1	3		tr	Sk
21. Painted Redstart (*Setophaga picta*)	2+	3	1		tr	Sk
Averages	2.8	2.2	2.2			

† "Rich, tumbling, House-wren like."

Table XIII

Wood Warblers: List B

	L.f.	*S.i.*	*Inv.*	*Exp.*	*Reg.*	*Authority*
1. Worm-eating (*Helmitheros vermivorus*)	3	3	3—	r		Gr
2. Golden-winged (*Vermivora chrysoptera*)	2	1	1	f		Gr
3. Blue-winged (*V. pinus*)	2	1	1	f		Gr
4. Bachman's (*V. bachmanii*)	3—	1	3—			Gr
5. Orange-crowned (*V. celata*)	2—	3	2	f		Gr
6. Parula (*Parula americana*)	2—	1	2	f		Gr
7. Cape May (*Dendroica tigrina*)	1	1	1	r		Gr
8. Black-thr. Blue (*D. caerulescens*)	2	1	2	f		Gr
9. Myrtle (*D. coronata*)	2	1	2	f		Gr
10. Cerulean (*D. cerulea*)	1	1	1	r		Gr
11. Blackburnian (*D. fusca*)	1	1	1	f		Gr
12. Bay-breasted (*D. castanea*)	1	1	1	r		Gr
13. Blackpoll (*D. striata*)	1	1	2	f		Gr
14. Palm (*D. palmarum*)	3—	3	2	r		Gr
15. Olive-capped (*D. pityophila*)	2—	1	2		tr	JB
16. Arrow-headed (*D. pharetra*)	2	3	2		tr	JB
17. Green-tailed Ground (*Microligea palustris*)	2	3	2		tr	JB
18. White-winged Ground (*M. montana*)	3—	3	2		tr	JB
19. Oriente (*Teretistris fornsi*)	2	3	2		tr	JB
20. Yellow-headed (*T. fernandinae*)	2	3	2		tr	JB
21. Crescent-chested, Hartlaub's (*Vermivora superciliosa*)	2	1	1		tr	Sk
22. Flame-throated (*V. gutturalis*)	1	3	1		tr	Sk
23. Black-cheeked (*Basileuterus melanogenys*)	3	3	2		tr	Sk
Averages	2.0	1.9	1.7			

Swainson's Warbler has not been graphed, but it is the most highly praised of all nontropical songsters of the family. (See Bent 1953.) I recall the song as over 2 seconds in length, and the lowest-pitched song I have heard from the family. It has both rhythmic and pitch contrasts and clear musical tones. The bird is extremely terrestrial, in dense moist growth.

The Yellow-breasted Chat, which haunts dense thickets, has some noisy sounds but also some clear tones. Loudness, complexity, continuity, and contrast are its chief merits. The Hooded Warbler's lovely song appears with extremely delicate thin lines, just sufficiently off the vertical to be rapidly slurred tones rather than noises. There is a neat contrast between the two parts of the song. In addition this species has a repertoire of two songs sung more or less alternately and with rather high continuity.

The two lists show that the stronger and more musical singers are also, on the whole, the ones with more need to sing; their habits, coloration, and habitats having forced them to rely more on sound and less on sight. The strongest correlation is with low-foraging. Low-foraging wood warblers simply do sing better, as judged by human listeners, than high-foraging ones. This cannot be because the treetop birds are too far off for us to hear them well, for modern tape-recording can overcome that. The treetop songs still sound poor. There is no human reason, but an obvious ornithological one, why invisible creatures must have better acoustical signals than visible creatures do. And just as human eyes can judge the high development of visual display in birds of paradise, so human ears can judge the high development of acoustical display in well-hidden and territorial species.

Why some good singers have low figures and some poor ones high I do not know. Biology is full of complexities, uncertainties, and (I believe) elements of sheer historical evolutionary accident. Still, on a broad statistical basis I am confident that the correlation of territoriality and visual obscurity with humanly perceptible good singing will hold.

As a check I have computed averages in the first two columns for the remaining species in this family not in either list, because their songs are neither very good nor very poor, but of which the foraging ranges are given. These averages are 2.2 and 1.9, thus (in combination), intermediate between the A and B figures, but still rather close to the mean between the possible extremes. This is what one might expect. For this family is a mean between songless birds and highly developed songsters. None of the 13 high-ranging species listed in Griscom and Sprunt have ever been at all highly praised by anyone, but of the 37 low-ranging ones at least half have been so praised.

Another point nicely illustrated by this family is that duetting is a tropical phenomenon. The Buff-rumped Warbler duets, according to Skutch, though when I heard it the unison was so perfect that I did not know it was a duet, if in those few instances it actually was. The male's part of the song is about like that of a waterthrush, but the female adds a "beautiful warble." Still another point is that definite, ritualized song means territory. Wood warblers are essentially non-gregarious, even in winter. And song, though often slight, is unmistakably present in all cases, save perhaps a few little-studied West Indian species. Nor is visibility extreme, in spite of the somewhat brilliant coloration. There are much more visible birds.

An obvious implication of the two lists is that the tropical members of the family sing at least as well as the nontropical. This is true of a good many families, in spite of an old prejudice.

None of the poorer singers is reported to sing more than 4 months, while three of list A sing at least 5 months: nos. 1 and 10 (Wayne 1910) and 14 (Skutch). This agrees with the view, defined and defended in Chapters 6 and 8, that the better singers sing more. Moreover, while the highest continuity I have been able to find for list B is ¼, several members of list A are semicontinuous, and hence they probably sing more even if their seasons are not longer.

Among well-known North American warblers not listed above are the following: The Golden-cheeked Warbler (*Dendroica chrysoparia*) of the Edwards Plateau in Texas is a bird of restricted habitat (which some people are trying to save from destruction); it lives in better-lighted forest than its near relative the Black-throated Green (*Dendroica virens*), is more brilliant—really beautiful—in plumage, and has a weaker, less musical song and a short season. Kirtland's Warbler (*Dendroica kirtlandii*) lives in open but, because of climate, less sunny scrub, has quiet protective colors, and feeds much on the ground. Its song is strong for a wood warbler.

E. Thrushes and Chats (Turdidae): 68 *Singers

This group illustrates the basic principles of song-development with great clarity. Ten of the 46 genera (here following Ripley's divisions

—1952) are ecologically atypical, in being birds of more or less open country: *Phoenicurus, Sialia, Enicurus, Cercotrichas, Cercomela, Saxicola, Myrmecocichla, Oenanthe, Prunella, Monticola.* (A stream, the haunt of some redstarts (*Phoenicurus* spp.) and the forktails (*Enicurus* spp.), unless very small, is somewhat open. Also these are birds of striking appearances.) Only 1 in 17 of these 86 nontypical thrushes is a *singer, compared to nearly 1 in 3 of the remaining species. The probability of singing very well is thus multiplied 5 times by the forest habitat.

Grandala coelicolor is a highly atypical thrush with apparently no song. It is essentially frugivorous and gregarious. *Irania gutturalis* is atypical in being a treetop forager, largely frugivorous. Its song is only fairly good.

The family is nearly ⅔ tropical, and the tropical portion has about ⅔ of the *singers. Nearly half of these tropical fine singers are definitely mountain birds, and only a minority live at really low elevations. Good song tends to move upward near the equator. Still, shamas (*Copsychus* spp.) are low-altitude birds and there are no finer singers. Much the same could be said of many wrens.

Only two genera outside the thrushes compare in number and quality of good singers with *Erithacus* (*Luscinia*), *Cossypha, Copsychus, Myadestes, Catharus* (including *Hylocichla*), and *Turdus.* Of the two others, *Thryothorus* and *Mimus*, both are low-foraging, and one is forest-loving. All tend to be plain, protectively colored.

F. Wrens (Troglodytidae): 14 *Singers

This very musical family tends to duplicate the thrushes on a smaller scale (smaller in size, fewer species, fewer countries in which they are found). Like the thrushes, wrens are of two kinds, those dwelling in more open, better-lighted places, and those in humid dark forest. The former are: the House Wren (*Troglodytes aedon*), most of the 11 species of cactus wrens (to a lesser extent), marsh wrens, the Rock Wren (*Salpinctes obsoletus*), the Plain Wren (*Thryothorus modestus*), and the Timberline Wren (*Troglodytes browni*). Nearly one-third of the family, they have *at most* one or two of the 14 superior singers. In this open-country group itself, the best singers seem to be the well-hidden Long-billed Marsh Wren and the cactus wrens *Campylorhynchus rufinucha* and *C. gularis.* The Marsh Wren has been shown by

spectrograms to be one of the most versatile of singers, the second
wren has been highly praised by several writers, and it and the third
are the only two which Selander (1964), in his detailed study of the
genus, terms "melodious." *Gularis* he calls "highly melodious," and
says that it haunts the densest growth of the group. *Rufinucha* seems
to go in about as dense growth as any of the other nine species. The
species in this genus in the most exposed position is *C. brunneicapillus*,
and it has nearly as poor a song as any, a harsh monotone (Robbins et
al.). The Rock Wren is exposed, but it blends with the rocks in color,
and must often be invisible among its stones. Its arid territory may also
be large for a wren's. It is a highly versatile, moderately powerful,
somewhat musical singer (D. Kroodsma, unpublished work).

The forest-loving wrens, in some respects the most typical songsters
of all, have the highest proportion of species that sing well of any
sizable group of birds, though nearly the same proportion as the forest
thrushes. They are territorial, hard in every way to see and distinguish
visually, and essentially isomorphic. Unlike flycatchers or wagtails they
have no obvious visually classifying habits or gestures, even though
the usually tiny tail may be held erect a good deal. They are in many
cases more exquisitely musical than any of the mimids, but lack their
imitative gifts. (Oddly enough there is no well-documented case of
imitation of alien species among wrens, though many among thrushes.)
The proportion of good singers is about the same in the tropical and
nontropical species. But since the family is largely tropical, the very
best, and also the poorest, songs might be expected to be and are
mostly tropical.

Unlike thrushes, the better-singing wrens live at low or moderate
altitudes. The high-altitude singers are weaker, less highly developed.
They live in less dense vegetation. Since wrens are mostly tropical, it
is not surprising that male-female duetting is found in many species.
This may be a reason why continuity is usually not very high. Duetting
pairs want to keep track of each other all day and sometimes all year,
and they can do this most easily by snatches of song at intervals.
Connected with the moderate continuity is the tendency toward eventual variety, though one finds a fair amount of immediate variation,
too. That (miscellaneous) imitation is apparently absent goes well with
the other factors just mentioned. Imitation is most useful to produce
abundant immediate variety and consequently an unbroken flow of
song for minutes at a time, as in both lyrebirds and mockingbirds, and

indeed many others. Such singing is probably for rivals more than for mates.

G. Some Other Families

Within other families similar correlations obtain. The forest green-buls and brownbuls (Pycnonotidae) of Africa sing better than the more open-country bulbuls (Austin 1961). The forest-dwelling warblers are far superior to the grass warblers. It is hard to get any agreement on a single cisticola song as superior, but easy to get it for many forest warblers. Cisticolas can use visual display in intense light at the top of the grass. The monarch flycatchers, more gaudy and dimorphic than other flycatchers, have none of the *species. Of the few whistlers (flycatcher family) that have taken to ground-feeding, nearly all sing better than the average flycatcher or arboreal whistler. They are of course more protectively colored and isomorphic. The few bowerbirds which come close to being good singers (by their imitations) are among the dullest colored. This is also true of the honeyeaters. The few ploceids whose songs are praised in Bannerman's two-volume edition (1953) of his great work are exceptions to the gregariousness of the family. Three of the four or five best singers among the icterids are the two meadowlarks and the Bobolink, ground-feeding, and on the whole rather less gaudy and better hidden when feeding than most of the family, as well as less gregarious than many. The helmet-shrikes, Prionopinae, are the least musical group of their family and the most gregarious as well as rather gaudy. The few superior singers among the babblers are in the nongregarious portion of the family, and very well hidden. Some gregarious species are nearly superior but very well hidden indeed, while some conspicuous open-country gregarious ones (as anyone can see in India or northern Australia) are entirely nonmusical. The open-country, but territorial, drongos are poor in song. Only the forest species are at all distinguished.

The duller-colored genera among the cuckoo-shrikes (*Coracina, Lalage*) have the only claimants to fame as musicians; the flaming minivets (*Pericrocotus* spp.) have none. The starling whose song has in my reading been most highly praised is a "tree starling" of the New Guinea forest. The two best honeyeater singers, by far the most famous, are relatively dark-colored birds of dense forests given to cloudy weather, in New Zealand. The most highly praised bulbul, *zeylanicus*, the Yellow-crowned, is not only quite dull colored, but, unlike some bulbuls, keeps well hidden, as I found on several occasions when I got but a single glimpse out of more than two hours of looking. The song, a famous one, is immediately impressive. Are the mates in this species less chummy than in the family generally?

Larks and warblers have a much higher percentage of superior singers in cloudy Europe than in Africa, where they live for the most part in brighter sunshine and often more arid conditions, with sparser vegetation. More than half of European or Asian larks are at least nearly superior, but nothing like this percentage of African larks are. Similar conditions distinguish the warblers of much of Europe from the African warblers, which, on the average, certainly sing less well.

Warblers in various densely forested Pacific Islands and the moister parts of Australia tend to sing well, those in African savannahs less well, delightful though a few of these songs are.

"Australian warblers" or "fairy wrens" (*Malurus* spp.) are gorgeously colored, live mostly in well-lighted places, and sing insignificantly.

Since many babbling thrushes (Timaliidae) nest territorially and are also mostly well hidden, it is puzzling that so few are superior singers. The group is not very well known in many of its haunts, and my estimate of 5% superior singers may be too low. Nor do I know what proportion of the family is free from the out-of-season gregariousness which undoubtedly sets limits to the song-development of most of its members. Of the two nongregarious species I know best, the Red-billed Leiothrix (*Leiothrix lutea calipyga*) and the Hwamei (*Garrulax canorus*), the former sings charmingly but rather simply, and is somewhat brilliantly colored for a singer; the other sings in energetic, complex, but not exquisitely musical fashion, apparently with imitations, and is dull colored, living in dense growth.

Pipits (but not the wagtail members of the family) might be expected to do better than they do at singing, considering the larks. Yet since there are twice as many larks as pipits, one need not have expected more than perhaps four superior pipits. Also, territoriality seems less intense, and this may account for there being but one pipit, in Argentina, whose claims to superior status are at all impressive. Sprague's Pipit (*Anthus spragueii*) has been overpraised by some; it is only a middling singer. As for the ten wagtails, "tailwagging," being a means of visual signaling, is in itself unfavorable to song. (Where a given means suffices, evolution does not produce another.) And territoriality is mild in wagtails, being confined to the breeding season.

Why the vireos fail to rise above the upper limits of "middling" song development I cannot imagine, unless it is because they are well up in trees and are visually a little better distinguished as species than some of the best singers, for instance, among the European warblers. Also the latter live in less sunny climates than most vireos.

The three largest very unmusical groups—waxbills et al., tanagers, and starlings—are seed- or fruit-eaters, with showy, often dimorphic plumage; they are mostly gregarious, some intensely so. Thus communication can be short-range, with much aid from vision, and with few other species near enough to make confusion likely.

Aerial feeders, treetop and outer-foliage feeders, feeding partly on fruit or nectar, are not only more visible than those hidden in the understory, or in the grass, or well inside a tree canopy; they perhaps also spend more energy foraging than species which hop or walk on the ground. Bark-feeders identify their species to some extent by their peculiar foraging habits, and much of the time are rather exposed to view. They do not excel in song.

A puzzling group from the standpoint of song-development is the American so-called sparrows. That the two clearly best singers among these are the Bachman's and Song Sparrows fits the requirements we have accepted. But it is much harder to see why the Lark Sparrow and the Lark Bunting should sing as well as they do, in comparison with LeConte's and Henslow's Sparrows, for instance. That sparrows living in swamps sing poorly or mediocrely, e.g., the Sharp-tailed (*Ammospiza caudacuta*), is perhaps to be explained by a combination of much light, small territories, and the small number of species present and needing to be distinguished in such a specialized habitat. But the "wet, weedy fields" of LeConte's should conceal it well and are less specialized. Similarly with Henslow's. The latter is said to be not very territorial. (Yet this helps less than one might wish, for there are aspects of gregariousness in Lark Sparrows and Lark Buntings.) Taking things broadly and statistically, I believe it could be shown that the good singers (Song, Bachman's, White-throated, Fox) among the woods or thicket sparrows with strong territoriality represent a far higher percentage than those found in the open-country, on the whole

more nearly colonial, species in this fringilline group. But there are
many puzzles. Some races of Song Sparrows, for instance, are swamp
birds.

The argument is more easily made in terms of very poor singers. The
"neither loud nor impressive" song of Baird's Sparrow (*Ammodramus
bairdii*) (Bent 1968) has been called the best singer among "grass
sparrows," far better than the Grasshopper, LeConte's, Henslow's,
Savannah (*Passerculus sandwichensis*), or Sharp-tailed. Here are six
rather primitive types of song which could not be matched by sparrows
living in forests or more or less wooded country. I add that Lark Sparrows generally live where there are some trees or bushes, and Lark
Buntings, in tall prairie grass. (On territory size in sparrows see Potter
1972: 54.)

H. Summary

The families of Songbirds (A.) differ ecologically (B.), and to some
extent (C.) in their presumed evolutionary ancestors, in ways that
correlate well in general with their degree of song-development.
Within families similar correlations can reasonably be made, particularly in the wood warblers (D.), thrushes (E.), and wrens (F.).

CHAPTER

10

Highly Developed or

"Superior" Songs

❦

A. The Concept of Superior Singer

In Chapter 6 I tried to show that singing skill has degrees and that these degrees can be roughly measured somewhat objectively in terms of six parameters: Loudness or carrying power, Scope (variety and complexity), Continuity (shortness of pauses in a standard performance), Tone quality (shown by narrow bands in a spectrogram), Organization or Order (*Gestalt* closure, musical coherence), and Imitative ability. The qualifications "roughly" and "somewhat" are necessary concessions to the element of truth in the rather pervasive conviction that evaluation of song must be hopelessly relative and subjective. The "relative" and "subjective" are to be admitted, but not the "hopelessly." Many concepts used in biology are more or less relative or subjective, for example, "territorial" or "subspecies." It is a question of degree whether the limitations of a concept render it useless, or merely one to be handled with care. White-crowned Sparrows (Mulligan, personal communication) space out fairly well in nesting but are rather "permissive" to trespassers. Just how territorial are they? Imprecise concepts cannot be avoided in dealing with some aspects of nature. And it is arguable that apart from pure mathematics there are no wholly precise and objective conceptions.

Since song-development or singing skill cannot be precisely measured, one should not claim seriously to know which is *the* most skilled or "best" singer. (Could anyone name "the most territorial" avian species? Yet there are, in nature, degrees of avian territoriality.) Many birds have been called "the best" in the world. The Nightingale is but one of these. Others are the Mockingbird, the Hermit Thrush, the Shama, the Tui, the White-banded Mockingbird, the Eastern or Thrush Nightingale, the Pied Butcherbird (*Cracticus nigrogularis*), and the Slate-colored Solitaire. No one has talked about "the most territorial" species partly because territoriality is a much less obvious trait of birds (indeed it has only been generally recognized since 1920) and so it has escaped the uncritical application of prescientific habits of thought, as of course song could not have done. Also, territoriality is not felt so clearly to be an excellence as is singing ability. (After all, sociability, group cooperation, are positive capacities.) And we have a tendency to ask not merely what is good or great, but what is best or greatest. Yet only concepts capable of very precise objective application, e.g., the height of a mountain top above sea level, make it reasonable to ask which individual or specific instance surpasses all the others. Only scientific instruments could give pertinence to the question, Which peak is highest of all? Yet there could well have been a prescientific basis for the judgment that the Himalayas are higher than the Andes, and certainly that both are higher than the Rockies. Similarly we can say that thrushes in general have much more skill in singing than bulbuls, or *a fortiori* than weaver finches. But it seems unlikely that any amount of science will give the notion of singing skill sufficient precision to make it sensible to ask which species in the world sings most skillfully. The Mockingbird of North America has never been described in more glowing terms than Hudson (1920) uses of *Mimus triurus* of southern South America; and Hartert, who knew both Nightingales, preferred the eastern (or northern) species to the other. (So does Jean C. Roché.) Also, at least four writers have preferred the Woodlark to other European songsters.

Our numerical rating system is, in fact, less pretentious in its implied claim to accuracy than it may at first thought appear to be. It recognizes 40 gradations (8–48), but these are not insisted upon except for judicious statistical uses, for instance, to show that in certain families song-development goes much farther than in certain others, or that song-development is almost independent of size or, within wide limits, of climate, or that species with the most highly developed songs spend the most time actually singing, or that such species are relatively inconspicuous and territorial.

It is to be remembered that one species can be much more exquisite musically than another and still not score so high in its total rating, because of low levels of complexity, continuity, or imitativeness. Contrariwise, a musically exquisite species with a simple, rather discontinuous, non-imitative song rating 9 in the fourth and fifth places can compare favorably overall with one which sings a complex, continuous, and imitative song consisting mostly of harsh noisy sounds and with low degree of organization. Thus the six-variable system gives a profile of the strengths and weaknesses of a specific manner of singing. Crude and coarse as it is, it is less so, and is more analytic and objective, than any available alternative. (The only other published attempts at measuring song-development objectively are found in Nicholson 1936.)

If we cannot say which is precisely the very best or most-developed song, neither can we say which songs are the ten or one hundred or two hundred best. Yet a representative list of highly developed songs, say 175 or 200, can have biological relevance. It would not be, but would be something like, the most highly developed 5% of the Oscines, or the most highly developed 4% of singing birds generally. There could never be full agreement as to which species belong on such a list. However, many species would, I think, be on almost any list made by a person with wide knowledge of the world's birds and thoughtful criteria of highly developed or good song. That A thinks a species is somewhat above and B thinks it is somewhat below the lower boundary of superiority, as defined by "among the best 5%," is no evidence that either A's or B's list is foolish or useless. One is seeking not an absolutely definite, but only a highly representative, group of "very good singers," species with high degrees of singing skill. If the list is to be representative, species must not be included or excluded for irrelevant or purely question-begging reasons, such as that the species fits a theory that the list is to be used to test, or that it is well or little known to most readers, or is the subject of an appealing poem, or that it is associated with one's own youth or a charming environment, or belongs to one's own country. For we wish to make "superior singer" a biologically useful, reasonably impersonal or objective concept, analogous to "territorial," say.

Quite apart from the vagueness or subjectivity of "good singer," we face the difficulty that many songs are not available in recordings, or even in careful descriptions, and that no one person can have heard more than a minority of the world's songsters. I might have limited my list to songs I have heard myself. But then some rather large parts of the world would be scarcely represented, and some large families extremely inadequately so. Besides, to take my personal experience as decisive is to imply that we are dealing with a concept that is devoid of objective applicability. So I have taken the opinions of others on trust in a good many cases. I have tried to strike a sensible compromise between such trust and skepticism.

Some authors tend toward enthusiasm about songs and some toward condescension ("cheerful little song," e.g.). I have done the best I could with this problem. There are also species belonging to genera otherwise rather musical whose habits and songs are not described at all. A few of these may be *singers. Thus my list, in the words of Colonel Meinertzhagen concerning his *Birds of Arabia,* is "full of gaps and surmises." But it may be better than no list at all. And though the conclusions I draw from it cannot be regarded as proved, they may be suggestive and stimulate further thought and observation.

In terms of my rating system, as I am able to apply it, the number of points to be assigned to the superior songsters is 42–48. I arrived at these figures in the following way. The nine species of English songsters most widely recognized as complex and otherwise excellent have this range of values, in my estimation. Using the same criteria I find eighteen species in the contiguous United States (the same for North America, neglecting an Asiatic species or two spilling over into Alaska) with the same range of values. My educated guess is that if one knew the world's birds as well as some now know those of England or North America one would find something like 175 or 200 species whose singing is equally complex, musical, and otherwise skilled as the English or American species just referred to. It might be 150 or 250; but hardly 100 or 300, and certainly not 50 or 500. The number 50 would mean that England and North America, which together have less than 1/10 of the world's birds, had half of the best singers; the number 500 would mean that among 1/10 of the world's birds there were only 1/20 of the best singers. There is no reason to suppose the two regions either so favored or so disfavored. Rather, there is a reason to take English birds as having a somewhat, but not extremely, disproportionately high percentage of good singers, and North American as only about average, so that the two together are somewhat above average. In South America, because of the very numerous Suboscines, the very good singers are quite certainly a much smaller fraction of the avifauna than in most parts of the world.

The reader should bear in mind that many species fall just under the 42-point rating, as I take these matters. Hence the omission of an item does not imply that I think it even a mediocre, much less a poor singer. For example, I rate the Black-headed Grosbeak of Na^w 877.765:40, and the English Sedge Warbler 889.457:41. Hence I omit them. Also, since no conclusive reason can ever be given for assigning a certain value to a song under a given dimension, it is necessary to make persistent efforts to avoid systematic leaning one way or another in doubtful cases. Thus if one always gave the highest plausible value to birds of one's own country or some favored foreign country; or to temperate-zone birds vs. tropical birds, or vice versa; or to wrens or thrushes; or to small birds and hence higher-pitched songs, or to large birds and hence lower-pitched songs; or to forest birds vs. open-country ones; or bright-colored vs. somber-colored species, it would then be invalid to apply statistical reasoning to the results in order to support a generalization about the groups mentioned. I have tried hard to avoid such systematic distortion of ratings. One way of doing this is to suspect any list of superior songsters unless an almost comparably numerous list of nearly superior or much better than middling songsters can be credibly drawn up from the same large group, whether regional, taxonomic, or whatever. Thus besides the nine superior songsters of Britain one can propose the following nearly superior ones: Sedge Warbler, Wren, Willow Warbler, Tree Pipit (*Anthus trivialis*), Pied Flycatcher (*Ficedula [Muscicapa] hypoleuca*), Mistle Thrush, perhaps Dipper (*Cinclus cinclus*) and Linnet (*Carduelis cannabina*). These all have recognized merits as singers, yet are generally thought not quite equal to the nine others. They are "runners up" for first class.

Besides the 18 *singers of the 48 contiguous states of the U.S. we have, as much better than mediocre, 9 finches: Rose-breasted and Black-headed Grosbeaks, Fox Sparrow, White-throated Sparrow (*Zonotrichia albicollis*), Pyrrhuloxia (*Pyrrhuloxia sinuata*), Lark Bunting, the eastern form of the Purple Finch (*Carpodacus p. purpureus*), House Finch (*Carpodacus mexicanus*), Pine Grosbeak (*Pinicola enucleator*); 2 thrushes: Swainson's and the Veery (*Catharus fuscescens*); the Catbird; 4 thrashers: Bendire's (*Toxostoma bendirei*), California, Long-billed (*T. longirostre*), and Curve-billed (*T. curvirostre*); Solitary Vireo; finally Canyon Wren and perhaps Long-billed

Marsh Wren (the former loud, musical, and well patterned; the latter
very versatile and continuous). In Australia for the 22 superior singers
we can adduce as near rivals several additional honeyeaters, whistlers,
warblers, one or two additional butcherbirds, the "delightful" Wedgebill or "Chimes-bird" (*Sphenostoma cristatum*), the Singing Bushlark
(*Mirafra javanica*), two or three additional shrike-flycatchers, the
White-winged Triller (*Lalage sueurii*), and the Striated Field-wren
(*Calamanthus fuliginosus*). The 40 or more superior singers of tropical
Africa are the presumed best of 70 to 90 fine songsters. One of the best
known of these is the African Pied Wagtail (*Motacilla aguimp*). To
include the secondary lists in these countries would, by the same criteria, imply a proportionally expanded list for the world, something
like 1/10 of the Oscines, instead of 1/20. Similarly, to double or sharply
increase the number of thrushes would imply additional warblers,
wrens, larks, bulbuls, etc., and would mean that some families not
rated as having any highly developed songs, e.g., the cuckoo-shrikes,
would have one or more. For in all these other groups there are species
that one is tempted to include just as one is tempted to include additional thrushes. What seems genuinely objective is not the precise list
of thrushes, warblers, or larks, but the proportions, when similar criteria are used on all groups.

B. World List of Superior Singers

In Table XIV, families are numbered as in Chapter 9A; fractions
and decimals given after the family names show the proportion between the *singers and the total number of species in a family;
zoogeographical regions are abbreviated as in Chapter 9A. Other symbols used are:

L	Large, longer than 9″ (22.8 cm.).
S	Small, less than 7″ (17.7 cm.).
M	Medium, 7″–9″ inclusive.
* *	Rating 44 or more points.
* * *	Rating 46–48 points. (It is understood that all items in the list "deserve" at least one star.)
Ev	Eventual rather than immediate variety. (Variety is im- mediate in most *singers.)

D   Male-female duets.

Tr   One or more trills in song. (Trill = a rapidly repeated note or rapid oscillations between two notes.)

Tr^2 Song largely composed of trills.

W   Warble—"quavering modulation of the voice" (more complex than a trill).

F   Field experience. (I have heard the bird sing.)

F^r I have recorded the bird's song.

F^c Experience of a singing caged bird.

R   I have heard recordings (T if in tape form only).

Where no symbols follow the six-dimensional ratings, the bird is included solely on the basis of evaluations or descriptions by others. Practically all the species listed have been evaluated or described by someone in the literature, usually by a number of writers. This scarcely applies to item 89, but Delacour, who presumably knew this bird, says that members of this genus are among the world's best songsters. I have my own notes on its remarkable singing.

I do not attempt six-dimensional numerical ratings of species whose songs are known to me only through descriptions insufficiently definite for this purpose. Their inclusion only means that I believe, on the basis of others' appreciation of them, that they would probably rate at least 42 in overall quality.

C. Discussion

More complete familiarity with the better singers over the world would of course incline one to omit some items from the above list, but also to add some to it. My guess is that the list would be slightly but not greatly enlarged. However, very good singers attract attention, and I may have taken a writer's praise (or my own favorable but inadequate experience) of a singer too seriously more often than I have missed very good singers that have not been convincingly praised.

To arrive at or evaluate any such list one needs (a) criteria for superior or highly developed song; (b) personal observations in diverse parts of the world; (c) study of regional bird books (see Austin 1961: Bibliography, also Thomson 1964: Article Bibliography, and References, I, p. 256 of this book); (d) study of numerous recordings (see

TABLE XIV

World List of Superior Singers

1. Lyrebirds (2/2 = 1.00)

1.	Au^e	L	*Menura superba*, Superb Lyrebird.*** Tr. 999.669:48. F, R.
2.	Au^e	L	*M. alberti*, Prince Albert Lyrebird.*** 999.559:46. F, R.

3. Larks (10/75 = 0.13)

3.	Eth	M	*Mirafra nigricans*, Dusky Bush-lark, Red-tailed Lark.**
4.	Eth	M	*M. hypermetra*. Red-winged Bush-lark.** Ev. 988.875:45. R.
5.	Pa	M	*Alaemon alaudipes*, Bifasciated Lark.** Tr. 977.985:45. R.
6.	Pa^w	M	*Melanocorypha calandra*, Calandra Lark.** 989.567:44. R.
7.	Pa^e	M	*M. mongolica*, Mongolian Lark.
8.	Pa^e	M	*M. yeltoniensis*, Black Lark.
9.	Pa^w	S	*Galerida theklae*, Thekla Crested Lark. 787.866:42. R.
10.	Pa^w	S	*Lullula arborea*, Woodlark.*** 989.895:48. F, R.
11.	Pa	S	*Alauda arvensis*, Skylark.** 989.666:44. F, R.
12.	Or	S	*A. gulgula*, Indian Skylark.

6. Drongos (1/19 = 0.05)

13.	Or	L	*Dicrurus paradiseus*, Great Racket-tailed Drongo. 988.548:42.

9. Wattlebirds (1/2 = 0.50)

14.	NZ	L	*Callaeas cinerea*, Wattled Crow. 966.984:42.

11. Bellmagpies (3/10 = 0.30)

15.	Au	L	*Cracticus nigrogularis*, Pied Butcherbird.** D. Tr. 977.975:44. F, R.
16.	Au	L	*C. quoyi*, Black Butcherbird.
17.	Au	L	*Gymnorhina tibicen*, Bellmagpie. 977.775:42. F, R.

12. Bowerbirds (2/17 = 0.12)

18.	Au	L	*Chlamydera maculata*, Spotted Bowerbird. 999.438:42.

TABLE XIV (*Continued*)

19.	Au	L	*Scenopœetes dentirostris*, Tooth-billed Bowerbird. 999.537:42.

17. Babblers (12/258 = 0.05)

20.	Or	S	*Pellorneum ruficeps*, Spotted Babbler. 887.775:42.
21.	Or	L	*Napothera crispifrons*, Limestone Wren-babbler.
22.	Or	L	*Garrulax merulinus*, Spotted-breasted Laughing Thrush.
23.	Pa[e]	L	*G. canorus*, Brown Laughing Thrush, Hwamei.** 779.677:43. F[r], R.
24.	Or	L	*G. austeni*, Brown-capped Laughing Thrush.
25.	Or	L	*G. milnei*, Red-tailed Laughing Thrush.
26.	Or	S	*Alcippe nipalensis*, Nun Babbler. F[r].
27.	Eth	S	*A. abyssinica*, Abyssinian Hill-babbler.
28.	Eth	S	*Parophasma galinieri*, Abyssinian Catbird.
29.	Or[e]	S	*Yuhina nigrimenta*, Pale Yuhina.
30.	Eth	S	*Horizorhinus dohrni*, Thrush Babbler (Principe Isle).
31.	Au	L	*Psophodes olivaceus*, Whipbird (Lamington Plateau, Queensland). 976.785:42. F, R. (Peters puts this in the Orthonychinae, logrunners.)

18. Bulbuls (5/119 = 0.04)

32.	Or	L	*Pycnonotus zeylanicus*, Yellow-crowned Bulbul. 977.775:42. F[r].
33.	Eth	M	*P. tephrolaema*, Mountain Greenbul.
34.	Eth	M	*P. gracilirostris*, Slender-billed Greenbul.
35.	Eth	S	*P. virens*, Little Greenbul.
36.	Eth	S	*Chlorocichla laetissima*, Joyful Greenbul.

19. Leafbirds (2/14 = 0.14)

37.	Or	M	*Chloropsis hardwickii*, Orange-bellied Chloropsis.
38.	Or	M	*C. aurifrons*, Gold-fronted Chloropsis. 898.658:44. F[c].

21. Wrens (14/59 = 0.24)

39.	Na[s,w]	S	*Thryomanes bewickii*, Bewick's Wren.** Tr[2] 777.995:44. F, R.
40.	Nt[e]	S	*Ferminia cerverai*, Zapata Wren.
41.	Nt[n]	S	*Thryothorus atrogularis*, Black-throated Wren. D, Tr. 677.995:43. F[r], R.
42.	Nt[n]	S	*Th. fasciatoventris*, Black-bellied Wren.** Ev. 977.885:44. F[r].

Table XIV (*Continued*)

43.	Nt	S	*Thryothorus genibarbis*, Moustached Wren.** 977.885:44. R.
44.	Nt[n]	S	*Th. coraya*, Coraya Wren. Tr. 978.775:43.
45.	Nt[n]	S	*Th. nigricapillus*, Black-headed, Bay, Wren.** D, Tr. 988.785:45. F[r].
46.	Nt[n]	S	*Th. pleurostictus*, Banded Wren.*** Tr². 878.995:46. F, R.
47.	Na[se]	S	*Th. ludovicianus*, Carolina Wren.*** Ev. 987.895:46. F[r], R.
48.	Nt[n]	S	*Th. rufalbus*, Rufous and White Wren.** Tr². 778.895:44. F[r], R.
49.	Nt[n]	S	*Th. sinaloa*, Bar-vented Wren. 777.895:43. R.
50.	Na	S	*Troglodytes t. hiemalis*, Winter Wren. Tr². 877.884:42. F, R.
51.	Nt	S	*Cyphorhinus aradus*, Musician Wren, Organbird.** 777.995:44. F[r], R.
52.	Nt	S	*Microcerculus marginatus*, Nightingale Wren (some races). 777.885:42. F, R.

22. Thrashers and Mockers (11/31 = 0.35)

53.	Na	M	*Mimus polyglottos*, Mockingbird.*** 899.677:46. F, R.
54.	Nt[n]	L	*M. gilvus*, Tropical Mockingbird.** 788.786:44. F[r], R.
55.	Nt[s]	L	*M. thenca*, Chilean Mockingbird.
56.	Nt[s]	L	*M. saturninus*, Chalk-browed, Calandra, Mockingbird.*** 899.677:46. R.
57.	Nt[s]	L	*M. triurus*, White-banded Mockingbird.*** 999.678:48.
58.	Nt[s]	L	*M. longicaudatus*, Long-tailed Mockingbird. 789.567:42. R.
59.	Nt[s]	L	*M. patagonicus*, Patagonian Mockingbird.
60.	Na[w]	M	*Oreoscoptes montanus*, Sage Thrasher. 779.875:43. R.
61.	Na[e]	L	*Toxostoma rufum*, Brown Thrasher. 889.666:43. F, R.
62.	Na[sw]	L	*T. dorsale*, Crissal Thrasher. 888.675:42. R.

23. Thrushes and Chats (65/303 = 0.21)

63.	Or	S	*Brachypteryx major*, Rufous-bellied Shortwing.
64.	Or	S	*B. montana*, White-browed Shortwing.

TABLE XIV (*Continued*)

65.	Eth	S	*Erythropygia leucophrys*, White-browed Scrub-robin. 877.785:42. R.
66.	Eth	S	*E. barbata*, Bearded (including Eastern Bearded?) Scrub-robin.** 989.775:45. R.
67.	Eth	S	*E. hartlaubi*, Brown-backed Scrub-robin.
68.	Eth	S	*E. leucosticta*, Gold-coast Scrub-robin. 866.895:42.
69.	Pa[w]	S	*Erithacus rubecula*, Robin.** 788.785:43. F, R.
70.	Pa[w]	S	*E. [Luscinia] megarhynchos*, Nightingale.*** Tr. 988.795:46. F, R.
71.	Pa	S	*E. [Luscinia] luscinia*, Thrush Nightingale.*** Tr. 989.795:47. R.
72.	Pa	S	*E. svecicus*, Bluethroat.** 888.776:44. R.
73.	Pa[e]	S	*E. [Luscinia] cyane*, Blue Robin. Tr². 778.785:42. F[r], R.
74.	Pa[e]	S	*E. [Luscinia] akahige*, Japanese Robin, Komadori.** Tr². 977.984:44. F, R.
75.	Pa[e]	S	*E. komadori*, Ryukyu Robin, Akahige.** Tr². 778.895:44. R.
76.	Eth	M	*Cossypha heuglini*, Heuglin's, White-browed, Robin-chat.*** 899.796:48. F, R.
77.	Eth[s]	M	*C. dichroa*, Chorister Robin-chat.*** 999.667:46. R.
78.	Eth	M	*C. natalensis*, Red-capped Robin-chat.** 788.777:44. T.
79.	Eth	M	*C. semirufa*, Rüppell's Robin-chat.*** 998.677:46. F, R.
80.	Eth	M	*C. niveicapilla*, Snowy-headed Robin-chat.*** 899.777:47. F, R.
81.	Eth[w]	M	*C. cyanocampter*, Blue-shouldered Robin-chat.**
82.	Eth	M	*C. humeralis*, White-throated Robin-chat.** 888.885:45. R.
83.	Eth	S	*Modulatrix strictigula*, Spot-throat.
84.	Eth	S	*Cichladusa guttata*, Spotted Morning Warbler.** 998.667:45. F, R.
85.	Eth	S	*C. ruficauda*, Rufous-tailed Morning Warbler.
86.	Eth	M	*Cercotrichas podobe*, Black Bush-robin.
87.	Or	M	*Copsychus saularis*, Magpie Robin, Dyal.** 877.995:45. F[r].
88.	Or	L	*C. malabaricus*, Shama, White-rumped Shama.*** Tr. 899.787:48. F[r], R.

Table XIV (*Continued*)

89.	Or	M	*Copsychus luzoniensis*, White-eyebrowed Shama.** Tr. 778.995:45. F.
90.	Or	M	*C. pyrropygus*, Orange-tailed Shama.
91.	Eth	M	*C. albospecularis*, Madagascar Magpie Robin.
92.	Or	M	*Cinclidium* [*Myiomela, Muscisylvia*] *leucurum*, White-tailed Blue Robin.** 967.995:45. F^r.
93.	Na^w	M	*Myadestes townsendi*, Townsend's Solitaire.** Tr. 977.885:44. F, R.
94.	Na^s	M	*M. obscurus*, Brown-backed Solitaire.** 977.885:44. F, R, T.
95.	Nt^n	M	*M. unicolor*, Slate-colored Solitaire.*** Tr. 987.895:46. F^c, R.
96.	Nt^{ne}	M	*M. elisabeth*, Cuban Solitaire.
97.	Nt^{ne}	M	*M. genibarbis*, Rufous-throated Solitaire. Tr. 777.885:42. F, R.
98.	Nt^n	M	*M. ralloides*, Andean Solitaire. 768.994:43. F^r, T.
99.	Eth		*Myrmecocichla nigra.* Sooty Ant-chat. 779.775:42. R.
100.	Eth	M	*Thamnolaea cinnamomeiventris*, Cliff-chat.**
101.	Eth	M	*Oenanthe monticola*, Mountain Wheatear.
102.	Eth^s	M	*O. pileata*, Capped Wheatear.
103.	Pa^w	M	*Monticola saxatilis*, Rock Thrush.** 888.895:46.
104.	Or	L	*Myiophoneus horsfieldii*, Malabar Whistling Thrush.**
105.	Or	L	*M. caeruleus*, Blue Whistling Thrush. 966.975:42. F^r.
106.	Or	M	*Zoothera* [*Geocichla*] *citrina*, Orange-throated Ground Thrush.** 899.666:44. F^r.
107.	Or	M	*Z. spiloptera*, Spotted-winged Ground Thrush.
108.	Eth	M	*Z. crossleyi*, Crossley's Ground Thrush.
109.	Eth	M	*Z. guttata*, Spotted Ground Thrush.
110.	Pac	M	*Phaeornis obscurus myadestinus*, Large Kauai Thrush, Kamau. 667.995:42
111.	Nt^n	S	*Catharus frantzii* (Phillips 1969), Ruddy-capped Nightingale-thrush. 688.885:43. F^r, R.
112.	Nt^n	S	*C. fuscater*, Black-billed Nightingale-thrush.
113.	Nt^n	S	*C. dryas*, Spotted Nightingale-thrush.
114.	Na^n	S	*C.* [*Hylocichla*] *guttatus*, Hermit Thrush.*** 988.995:48. F, R.
115.	Na^e	M	*Hylocichla* [*Turdus*] *mustelina*, Wood Thrush.*** 978.995:47. F, R.

TABLE XIV (*Continued*)

116.	Or	M	*Turdus dissimilis* (incl. *hortulorum*), Black-breasted Thrush.
117.	Or	L	*T. albocinctus*, White-collared Blackbird. 888.676:43.
118.	Or	L	*T. boulboul*, Grey-winged Blackbird.**
119.	Pa^e	M	*T. cardis*, Grey Thrush.** 988.785:45. F^r, R.
120.	Pa^e	M	*T. rubrocanus*, Grey-headed Thrush.**(?)
121.	Pa^e	L	*T. ruficollis* (incl. *atrogularis*), Red-throated Thrush.**(?)
122.	Pa^e	?	*T. mupinensis*, Verreaux's Thrush.
123.	Pa^w	M	*T. philomelos* [*ericetorum*], Song Thrush, Throstle.** 999.666:45. F, R.
124.	Pa,Or	L	*T. merula*, Blackbird.*** 988.885:46. F, R.
125.	Nt^n	M	*T. serranus*, Black Thrush.** 899.667:45. F.
126.	Nt^n	L	*T. grayi*, Clay-colored Robin. 878.784:42. F, R.
127.	Nt^e	L	*T. jamaicensis*, White-eyed Thrush. 979.675:43. F.

24. Old World Warblers (28/398 = 0.07)

128.	Pa^e	S	*Cettia diphone*, Short-winged Bush Warbler.** 978.885:45. F^r, R.
129.	Pa^w	S	*Acrocephalus palustris*, Marsh Warbler.** 789.677:44. R.
130.	Pa^{nw}	S	*A. dumetorum*, Blythe's Reed Warbler.** 989.676:45. R.
131.	Pa^{e}Au	S	*A. stentoreus*, Southern Great Reed Warbler. 789.775:43. F.
132.	Pa^e	S	*A. aedon*, Thick-billed Reed Warbler.
133.	Pa^e	S	*A. agricola*, Paddy-field Warbler.
134.	Pa^w	S	*Hippolais icterina*, Icterine Warbler. 999.557:44. R.
135.	Pa	S	*H. caligata*, Booted Warbler.** 878.886:45.
136.	Pa^w	S	*Sylvia nisoria*, Barred Warbler. 789.667:43. R.
137.	Pa^w	S	*S. hortensis*, Orphean Warbler.*** 988.885:46.
138.	Pa^w	S	*S. borin*, Garden Warbler. W. 867.885:42. F, R.
139.	Pa^w	S	*S. atricapilla*, Blackcap.** W. 976.896:45. F, R.

TABLE XIV (*Continued*)

140.	Pa^{ne}	S	*Phylloscopus proregulus*, Pallas's Warbler.** 987.785:44.
141.	Pa^e	S	*Rhopophilus pekinensis*, White-browed Chinese Warbler.
142.	Or	S	*Orthotomus cucullatus*, Mountain Tailorbird.** 778.994:44. F^r.
143.	Pac	S	*Psamathia annae*, Palau Bush Warbler.
144.	Au	S	*Acanthiza pusilla*, Brown Thornbill.
145.	Au	S	*A. uropygialis*, Chestnut-tailed Thornbill.
146.	Au	S	*Pyrrholaemus brunneus*, Redthroat.** 787.887:45.
147.	Eth	S	*Seicercus umbrovirens*, Brown Woodland Warbler. 777.885:42. R.
148.	Eth	S	*Eminia lepida*, Grey-capped Warbler. Tr². 977.775:42. F, R.
149.	Eth	S	*Cisticola lateralis*, Whistling Cisticola.
150.	Eth^s	S	*Bradypterus sylvaticus*, Knysna Scrub Warbler. 877.885:43. R.
151.	Pac	S	*Conopodera caffra*, Tahitian Warbler
152.	Au	S	*Gerygone cantator*, Mangrove Warbler.** 877.995:45. F.
153.	Au	S	*G. olivacea*, White-throated Warbler.
154.	NZ	S	*G. igata*, Grey Warbler. Tr. 677.994:42. F, R.
155.	Au	S	*Hylacola pyrrhopygia*, Heath-wren.** Tr. 787.787:44. F.

25a. Old World Flycatchers (9/378 = 0.024)

156.	Eth	M	*Fraseria ocreata*, Forest Flycatcher.
157.	Eth	S	*Platysteira cyanea*, Wattle-eye. 967.794:42. R.
158.	Eth	S	*Chloropeta similis*, Mountain Yellow Flycatcher.
159.	Eth	S	*Parisoma subcaeruleum*, Tit-babbler. 877.776:42. R.
160.	Or	S	*Muscicapa pallipes*, White-bellied Blue Flycatcher.
161.	Pa^e	S	*Ficedula [Muscicapa] narcissina*, Narcissus Flycatcher. 978.675:42. F^r, R.
162.	Pa^e	S	*Cyanoptila [Muscicapa] cyanomelana*, Blue and White Flycatcher.** 877.985:44. F, R.
163.	NZ	M	*Petroica australis*, New Zealand Robin.** 988.775:44. F, R.

25b. Whistlers (6/49 = 0.12)

164.	Au	M	*Colluricincla harmonica*, Grey Shrike-flycatcher.** Ev. 976.995:45. F, R.

TABLE XIV (*Continued*)

165.	Au	M	*Colluricincla boweri*, Stripe-breasted Shrike-flycatcher.**
166.	Au	S	*C. woodwardi*, Sandstone Shrike-flycatcher.
167.	Pac	S	*C. tenebrosa*, Palau Morning Bird.
168.	Au	M	*Pachycephala olivacea macphersoniana*, Queensland Olive Whistler.** Ev. 867.995:44. F.
169.	Au	M	*Oreoica gutturalis*, Crested Bellbird.** Ev. 877.995:45. F, R.

27. Pipits and Wagtails (1/53 = 0.02)

170.	Nt^s	S	*Anthus correndera*, Cachila Pipit. 777.885:42.

32. Shrikes (1/74 = 0.01)

171.	Eth	M	*Laniarius ferrugineus ambiguus*, Tropical Boubou.** D. 977.886:45. F, R.

34. Honeyeaters (5/158 = 0.03)

172.	Au	S	*Gliciphila indistincta*, Brown Honeyeater. Tr. 978.675:42. F, R.
173.	Au	S	*Melithreptus gularis*, Black-chinned Honeyeater.
174.	Pac	M	*Foulehaio carunculata*, Wattled Honeyeater.
175.	NZ	M	*Anthornis melanura*, Bellbird.*** Ev. 977.995:46. F, R.
176.	NZ	L	*Prosthemadera novaeseelandiae*, Tui.*** Ev. 987.996:48. F, R.

35. Sunbirds (1/105 = 0.01)

177.	Eth	S	*Cyanomitra olivacea*, Olive Sunbird. 778.785:42.

37. White-eyes (2/78 = 0.03)

178.	Au	S	*Zosterops lateralis*, Grey-breasted White-eye.** 969.884:44. F.
179.	Eth	S	*Speirops lugubris*, Black-capped Speirops.

41. Icterids (4/88 = 0.05)

180.	Nt^n	M	*Icterus mesomelas*, Yellow-tailed Oriole.** D. 967.994:44. F, R.
181.	Na^{e}Nt^n	M	*Sturnella magna*, Eastern Meadowlark.** Ev. 986.885:44. F, R.
182.	Na^w	M	*S. neglecta*, Western Meadowlark.** Ev. 985.995:45. F, R.

TABLE XIV (*Continued*)

| 183. | Naⁿ | M | *Dolichonyx oryzivorus*, Bobolink. 966.984:42. F, R. |

43a. Cardinals and Their Allies (4/110 = 0.04)

184.	Naᵉ	M	*Pyrrhuloxia* [*Richmondena*] *cardinalis*, Cardinal. Ev. 977.785:43. F, R.
185.	Naˢʷ	M	*P. sinuata*, Pyrrhuloxia. Ev. 977.775:42. F, R.
186.	Nt	M	*Pheucticus aureoventris*, Black-backed Grosbeak. 878.775:42. R.
187.	Nt	S	*Cyanocompsa cyanoides*, Blue-black Grosbeak. 867.994:43. Tr.

43b. Buntings and American Sparrows (5/183 = 0.03)

188.	Naʷ	S	*Chondestes grammacus*, Lark Sparrow. Tr². 688.785:42. F, R.
189.	Naˢᵉ	S	*Aimophila aestivalis*, Bachman's Sparrow.** 887.895:45. F, R.
190.	Na	S	*Melospiza melodia*, Song Sparrow.** Ev, Tr. 887.895:45. F, R.
191.	Paᵉ	S	*Emberiza elegans*, Yellow-throated Bunting.

44i. Cardueline Finches (3/123 = 0.02)

192.	Ethⁿ	S	*Serinus leucopygius*, White-rumped, Grey, Seed-eater.
193.	Paʷ	S	*S. canarius*, Canary. Tr. 877.875:42. F.
194.	Eth	S	*S. atrogularis*, Black-throated Canary.

Thomson: "Sound Recordings," and Boswall 1961, 1964, also References, II, p. 270); (e) scanning of ornithological journals for accounts of songs, often now with sonagrams.

The 22 triple-starred species might be termed "superlative songsters." They are about ½ of 1% of the Oscines. The 61 double-starred species may be termed "superb" or "clearly superior." With the superlative singers they form close to 2% of all Oscines. The remaining 111 species include a good many borderline cases such that I could have rated them a point or two higher or lower and also a good many whose ratings are based on scanty information and little or no direct acquaintance. With more complete knowledge some might be double-

or triple-starred, and others dropped from the list of the 5% most highly developed songsters.

About 75 items (not marked "F" or "R") are included on the authority of others, since I have heard neither the bird itself directly nor a recording of its voice, and also have not seen sonagrams of such a recording. To have excluded these items would have made the list too much a mere matter of my autobiography. To include them was to run a risk of overestimating the powers of observation and discrimination of others. I thought the latter the less objectionable evil.

I have heard about 67 species in their habitats ("F") or (in several cases) in a cage. About 90 species have been recorded by others. Of my recordings ("Fʳ")—most of them technically poor, alas—about ten are of otherwise unrecorded species. Thus about 100 seem to have been recorded. Some of the remaining 94 items are rare, or even perhaps endangered, species. I hope they will be recorded.

The table throws light upon the relation of song to size. About half the species are small (S, under 7″, or 17.7 cm.). Since the world over the small species constitute 60% of the Oscines, it seems that extreme smallness is not a factor favorable to song. Nor is being over 9″, or 22.8 cm., an unfavorable factor. The 34 large (L) species are close to their statistical ratio, taking Oscines in general. It may be that small songsters are more readily overlooked, or, because of their high-pitched voices, more easily underestimated. Still we can, I think, be confident that smallness is not particularly conducive to skill in singing. Nor (see Chapter 2C) is there any clear reason why it should be. True, small size lowers visibility, but it also makes territories smaller, pitch range less extensive, and—I believe—reduces brain capacity and hence ability to grasp complex patterns. The size most favorable to song is apparently that indicated by "M." Such birds require fair-sized territories and can have much greater pitch ranges and perhaps better brains than very small birds. These advantages outweigh the negative factors that the medium size somewhat increases visibility and somewhat reduces the number of related species or individuals to be distinguished. The more powerful voice tending to go with large size correlates with the larger territories. But when size passes a certain point the negative factors mentioned (and perhaps others) predominate.

It is hardly necessary to remark that the *species are scattered somewhat evenly over the world, definitely including tropical areas, and all zoogeographical regions. The radical selectivity is effected, not by climate or region, but, as we saw in the previous chapter, by ecological and social differences between families that occur together in the same climate or area. That singing skill is so widely distributed shows the basic importance of song in bird life. Some niches in nature can be taken advantage of without song, but many, found in extremely diverse climates, the occupants of which are sometimes only remotely connected genetically, cannot. There are songless birds and there are flightless birds; but still the typical bird flies and sings, and the ability to do both appears everywhere. Also everywhere this double ability has various degrees—the maximal degree being everywhere the exception. Nevertheless, everywhere, if land birds in variety are present, it does occur.

D. Summary

(A.) The idea of highly developed or superior songster is capable of being made sufficiently definite and objective to be useful.

(B.) Nearly two hundred such songsters, scattered over the world, are listed, their singing skill on six dimensions (see Chapter 6) rated from 42 to 48 points out of a possible 54, their size and zoogeographical regions indicated, and a few conclusions suggested.

CHAPTER

11

The Less Well-Equipped Singers

❦

A. Singing in the "Primitive" Orders

Of the 27 orders into which birds are classified, all except the order of perching birds, Passeriformes, are sometimes termed "primitive." From the standpoint of song this has a definite meaning; for only in the perching birds has the organ for singing, the syrinx, with its controlling muscles, reached its peak of development. But even in this order there is a marked division into primitive and highly evolved birds. The less advanced groups, which used to be appropriately called Clamatores (the term now has a somewhat narrower meaning), and may also be referred to as Suboscines, include 1100 to 1200 species, all but a handful of which are in the Americas, and form by far the most distinctive element of American, especially South American, birds. They mostly have one pair of muscles to control sound production, compared to four for the Oscines. The lyrebirds are in between with three pairs. There is considerable singing by the less-advanced types, both in and outside of the perching birds order. Also many Oscines, or "true Songbirds" (e.g., waxwings) are songless or virtually so.

If there are something like 5000 species which could be called "singing birds," the number depending upon the criteria for "singing," they are divided among the groups mentioned somewhat as follows:

	Primitive Orders	Perching Birds (Passeriformes) Suboscines	Oscines or Songbirds		
Nonsingers	2500	400	800		
Singers	1000?	800?	3200?		
Totals	3500 +	1200 +	4000 =	8700

Just as most "nonperching" or primitive birds do perch, but without benefit of the special arrangement of toes which facilitates this operation in the Passeriformes, so many species which are not Songbirds in the fullest anatomical or oscinine sense do nevertheless sing. They do so with a comparative handicap, that is all. Some manage quite well. And many Oscines, whose ancestors must have sung (for the organs are there), have found a mode of life which makes song functionless, and so they have largely or entirely dropped the activity (for example, some members of the crow family). Their extra muscles for voice control may still be useful in making a great variety of call notes possible. But even this capacity may not be used. This is an example of the general truth that the musical skill of a particular species depends largely not upon gross anatomy but upon ecology (and no doubt presently unknown brain structures).

In this chapter we shall consider singing, especially relatively good singing, in birds below the Songbird (or rather lyrebird) level. In these groups (to which in my bird-observing I have given little heed) the difference between songs and mere calls is often hard, perhaps sometimes impossible, to make. However, there are utterances that have one or both of the two great functions of song: attracting or arousing a mate, and warning off territorial rivals. The crow of the cock Chicken (*Gallus gallus*) (originally, and in some regions, still a bird of dense tropical forest) is definitely a song (except that it seems to develop normally in spite of early deafening—Konishi 1963), and a powerful one, though not very complex, and somewhat noisy rather than pure in its tones.

Several groups of primitives are physically incapable of more than very crude utterances, because they have no internal syringial muscles. These voiceless birds are storks (Ciconiidae), vultures (Cathartidae), the Ostrich (*Struthio camelus*) and several related species (not rheas, Rheidae), and "most Pelecaniformes" or pelican-like birds. In this way some 60 species can be set aside as making virtually no contribution to animal music, even though their hisses, grunts, and the like can be good to hear as indications of vitality. They rank low in the social-behavioral-ecological traits that favor song, such as territoriality or inconspicuousness.

In other primitive groups there is a single pair of syringial muscles, except that "some hummingbirds" (Trochilidae, Thomson 1964) and the hawk genus *Falco* have two pairs, and the parrots have three. If song, properly so-called, is not much in evidence in these three groups, it is chiefly for behavioral-ecological reasons to be mentioned presently. That parrots are rather well equipped for voice control is not surprising, partly for reasons suggested in Chapter 4. And hummingbirds have much more need to sing than their relatives the swifts (Apodidae). But the case of the falcons is indeed surprising.

Seabirds (about 230 species, not counting the voiceless among the pelicans), e.g., penguins (Spheniscidae), albatrosses (Diomedeidae), gulls (Laridae), skuas (Stercorariidae), could hardly be expected to sing, since they are as conspicuous, and also nearly as gregarious, as birds well could be. Nor has any appreciable approach to music been claimed for them. Then there are some tall, mostly open-country gregarious birds (about 15 species), including herons (Ardeidae) and flamingos (Phoenicopteri), which also have little need to sing. Their size not only makes them conspicuous, but it makes them distinctive by the depth and power of their utterances, so that a mere shriek may almost suffice to distinguish them from the necessarily few, if any other, comparably large species in an area. Perhaps the best "music" in these groups is in the bitterns (Botaurinae), nongregarious and also, especially *Ixobrychus exilis* [Na],† smallish for their kind, protectively colored, and inhabitants of dense growth. The Reddish Egret (*Dichromanassa rufescens*) [Naᵉ] is said to have a "bugle call." It seems not to be especially well hidden, but is certainly less conspicuous than some of its relatives.

Cranes, rails, and the like (Gruiformes, 199 species) are partly similar to the above. However, rails are well hidden (but their restricted habitat is almost diagnostic), as are Kagus (*Rhynochetos jubatus*). Trumpeters (Psophiidae) are extremely gregarious. All the birds just mentioned are partly nocturnal. Since few birds make sounds at night, the need for acoustical distinctiveness is to that extent diminished. Crude, simple, monotonous utterances characterize these species. The most respectable song seems to be by the Gray-necked Wood Rail (*Aramides cajanea*) (Nt) (recording by Davis). It inhabits wooded swamps and mangroves, hence lives in diminished light and visibility. The small Sora Rail (*Porzana carolina*) [Na] is especially hard to see and has a rather pleasing song. In West Africa (Bannerman 1953) the largely invisible White-spotted Pygmy Rail (*Sarothrura pulchra*) ut-

† Bracketed abbreviations in the rest of this chapter refer to the zoogeographical regions as explained at the beginning of Chapter 9.

ters a ringing "goong-goong-goong-goong." How far it varies its numbers from four goongs is a question, but six are also mentioned. The Yellow Rail (*Coturnicops noveboracensis*) "clicks" as follows: || ||| || ||| etc., an occasional |||| breaking the monotony. The narrow vertical lines indicate very brief and unmusical sounds. In this song rhythm is the only musical quality.

In India my wife and I spent a month with a White-breasted Waterhen (*Amaurornis phoenicurus*) pair just by our house on the campus of Banaras Hindu University. (There was no marsh, only some water running off at times from sinks or baths.) These birds sang what sounded like a duet, extremely raucous and rather formless, from a dense bush, but they walked out in plain sight to feed in the bare garden. This was an extreme of conspicuousness for this type of bird.

Rails are so alike ecologically that one could hardly expect them to vary greatly in singing ability. Nearly all are well hidden and protectively colored. Why then do they not sing better? In one respect the marsh habitat is unfavorable to song-development: Only a few species are to be expected in the middle of a marsh; hence the pressure for distinctiveness is to that extent not great.

The most consistently musical primitive group is the tinamous (Tinamidae). Here are about 40 species of ground-feeding, nongregarious, protectively and isomorphically colored, largely forest birds, with some species in savannahs. They have every reason to sing, and they do so. Their voices are mellow, and some songs are remarkably complex. The Little (or Pileated) Tinamou (*Crypturellus soui*) lives in dense second growth in wet tropics. I use my crude version of Saunders's notation to represent its song according to Friedman and Smith (1955) (Figure 8).

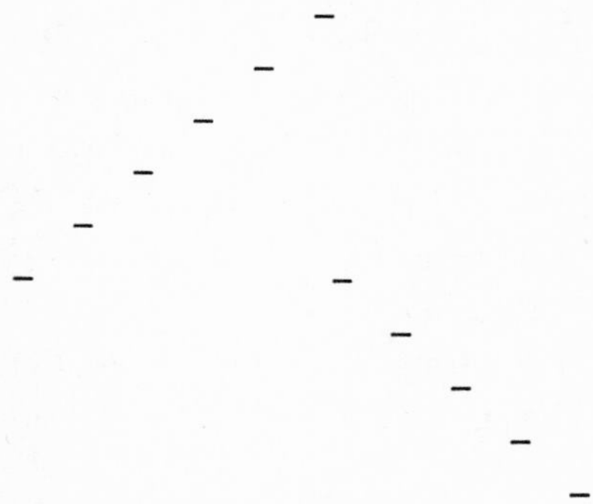

FIG. 8. *Song of the Little Tinamou (after Friedman and Smith)*

The quality is "zylophonic," also "bell-like." This bird is even more se-
cretive and hidden than tinamous in general (Leopold 1959). But
according to a sonagram made by Thorpe (1961: 3) from a Cornell
tape, the song has a different form (Figure 9). The sonagraph lines

FIG. 9. *Song of the Little Tinamou (after Thorpe)*

are thin, showing relatively pure or flute-like quality. The formula for
this pattern is that the notes get both higher and shorter; and the
second, descending part of the song described by Friedman and Smith
is lacking.

The Red-winged, Rufous, Tinamou (*Rhynchotus rufescens*) has
"perhaps the sweetest" song on the pampas (Hudson 1920). It is well
hidden in grass and sings all year. The Spotted Tinamou (*Nothura
maculosa*) sings all year as follows (Hudson): 20–30 powerful short
whistles and then 6 rapid notes, first loud, then falling away. It has also
a soft trill. It inhabits savannahs and is protectively colored.

The Tataupa Tinamou (*Crypturellus tataupa*) has a "powerful and
brilliant" song, again sung all year. The song is a unique type of accelerando (Azara, via Hudson): after the opening note a pause of 8
[*sic*] seconds, then the note is reiterated with ever shorter intervals
until it is a "trill," changing finally into three or four "chororos." If this
is really a fixed pattern, it must be one of the longest of all. The bird
lives in undergrowth in dense forest. Apparently all tinamous are, for
primitive birds, musical; all are protectively colored, and most are very
well hidden.

Waterfowl (Anseriformes) are, by contrast, a group of rather large
birds, mostly in good light, with rather showy colors, and more or less
gregarious, which scarcely produce music. Oldsquaws (*Clangula
hyemalis*) are said to yodel pleasantly. Screamers (Anhimidae) are very
vocal and indeed somewhat musical. They are less aquatic than ducks
(Anatidae) and feed much in grasses. Sylvan birds, they are rather

dull-colored. They are, however, gregarious. Geese and swans (Anserinae) may perhaps be termed slightly musical in quality of voice, but not otherwise.

Grebes (Podicipitidae) are like the waterfowl. Loons (*Gavia* spp.) [Ha] are spectacularly vocal; perhaps one should say crudely musical. Why they should be more so than ducks or grebes is not obvious, unless it is because they are partly nocturnal.

Diurnal birds of prey (Falconiformes) are largely aerial, hence visible. Also they are large, and a limited number of individuals and species occur in an area. Mere shrieks, without appreciable refinement or complexity, tend to suffice for their communication needs. Some have slightly musical whistles, e.g., the Laughing Falcon (*Herpetotheres cachinnans*) [Nt], which of course does not laugh, but does give an extremely crude falling cadence. It is a forest bird hunting largely below the treetops, often in wet tall forest. However, the Pale Chanting Goshawk of Africa (*Melierax musicus*) lives in open country. Very large hawks or eagles need so extensive a territory that, as Craig remarks, they could hardly make vocal proclamations of territory carry over the required distances. They can be seen soaring much farther off than they can be heard.

Shorebirds (Charadriiformes) are mostly rather small, protectively colored, and somewhat territorial. There are two monographs on the American species—Hall and Clement (1960) and Matthiessen and Palmer (1967). These birds seem to have a good deal of simple music. Some particularly exposed, gregarious, or visually distinctive, visually displaying species are deficient in this respect, e.g., the Avocet (*Recurvirostra americana*), Stilt (*Himantopus mexicanus*), Ruff (*Philomachus pugnax*), Buff-breasted Sandpiper (*Tryngites subruficollis*), Crab Plover (*Dromas ardeola*) [Pt], Ruddy Turnstone (*Arenaria interpres*) [Ha], Sanderling (*Crocethia alba*) [Ha], breeding on open beaches, and godwits (*Limosa* spp.) [Ha]. Killdeer (*Charadrius vociferus*), a bit closer to music, are perhaps a little less visible. The Upland Plover (Sandpiper) (*Bartramia longicauda*), thought by Thayer to be a notable example of protective coloration, has a melodious breeding song, a fluctuating, ascending and descending, clear whistle. The American Golden Plover (*Pluvialis dominica*) [Ha] sings well in dry tundra which must make it somewhat inconspicuous. Oystercatchers (*Haematopus* spp.) defend territory with powerful, vibrant voices audible above the surf. The dark-colored American Oystercatcher (*H. pallia-*

tus) is even said to sing beautifully in territorial defense. Perhaps against the wet rocks it is not conspicuous.

At least five species of the genus *Tringa* have noticeable songs. Perhaps the best of all is that of the Green Sandpiper (Oring 1968), which breeds in wooded swamps and has large territories and unusually concealing colors. The somewhat gregarious Wood Sandpiper (*Tringa glareola*) [Pa] and Solitary Sandpiper (*Tringa solitaria*) [Na] breed in more or less concealing habitats (muskeg, woods). The Greenshank (*Tringa nebularia*) [Pa] is solitary, in foggy, wet moors (Britain). The Redshank (*Tringa totanus*) [Pa] has an accelerando of pure sweet notes and breeds in grassland or heath.

The Lesser Yellowlegs (*Totanus flavipes*) [Ha] lives in woods and sings a series of *pill-e-wee* calls. The Stilt Sandpiper (*Micropalama himantopus* [Na] sings similarly in tundra. The Dunlin (*Calidris alpina*) [Pa] lives on wet, hummocky tundra and has accelerating, descending notes. The Short-billed Dowitcher (*Limnodromus griseus*) [Na], living in muskeg, has a rather complex tinkling song. The Rock Sandpiper (*Erolia ptilocnemis*) lives in tundra and has a pure, sweet song ascending an octave in a minor chord. The Least Sandpiper (*Erolia minutilla*) [Na], breeding in bogs or bushy uplands, has an impressive and sweet trill. The Collared Pratincole (*Glareola nuchalis*) in West Africa has a beautiful trill (Bannerman 1953). It lives in rocky riverbeds and islands. Curlews (*Numenius* spp.) [Ha], with concealing colors in grassy or hummocky areas, are rather melodious. On the Long-billed Curlew (*N. americanus*) see Forsythe (1970: 217). The Knot (*Calidris canutus*) has "beautiful, flute-like utterances on its territories in more or less well-vegetated tundra" (Manniche 1912).

A special case is the Woodcock, particularly the American species, *Philohela minor*. It is very well hidden, though visually distinctive, and sings a notable, in part musical, flight song with a mixture of wing whistling and twittering. Phalaropes (*Lobipes* et al. spp.) are rather colonial, feed much in sight of each other in water, and are unmusical. Jaçanas (Jacanidae) are conspicuous, visually eccentric, and vocally crude.

Fowl-like or gallinaceous birds (Galliformes) are ground-feeding, and vary greatly in plumage and habitat. Their singing skill also varies widely. Some inhabit dense forest, and of these some are protectively colored, while others are rather gaudy. The test as to the latter point is, as Beebe sagaciously says, whether the bird tends to fly or to crouch quietly to escape enemies. If it flies at the first sign of danger, it is not protectively colored. Peacocks (*Pavo* spp.), guinea fowl (Numididae), and some pheasants and partridges (Phasianidae) are conspicuous. They are notoriously not good singers. The Annam Ocellated Pheasant (*Rheinardia ocellata*) [Or] sings harmoniously and powerfully. It is beautiful but tends to blend with the forest floor, and lives in dense dim undergrowth (Beebe 1926: vol. 2).

The Singing Quail (*Dactylortyx thoracicus*) [Nt] lives only in forest (Leopold 1959), usually in thick undergrowth, and is extremely hard to see. It has one of the most melodious and complex songs of any gallinaceous bird (Warner and Harrell 1957: 139): 7–10 notes, with several pitch changes and an accelerando effect in the early part, finishing with a low twittering. It hides rather than flies. Fuertes (1914) speaks of the complicated, powerful songs of the protectively colored wood-quails (*Odontophorus* spp.) [Nt^n]. The Ferruginous Wood Partridge (*Caloperdix oculea*), at least in Borneo (Smythies 1960), has a complex ascending accelerating song. The Common Hill Partridge (*Arborophila torqueola*) [Or] lives in dense growth and (Deignan 1945; Ali 1949, 1962) sings well. The Rufous-throated Hill Partridge (*Arborophila rufogularis*) [Or] has a sweet, clear, ascending whistle; and the Red-breasted (*Arborophila hyperythra*) (Smythies 1960) is another good, well-hidden singer.

Pigeons vary widely in ecology and in singing ability. In general, they are much less gregarious than parrots. Since they feed either on the ground or in dense foliage, and are mostly dull-colored, in many cases matching the foliage, they are often hard to see. Their hearing seems to be inferior (Schwarzkopf 1955: 344). Most have very simple songs, but some have (for nonperching birds) rather good ones. The widespread Mourning Dove (*Zenaidura macroura*) is an example. It is somewhat territorial. The extremely gregarious Passenger Pigeon (*Ectopistes migratoria*), now extinct, had only "degenerated" music, its voice being loud but harsh. The North American White-winged Dove (*Zenaida asiatica*) feeds on the ground in bushy areas where it is often hard to see. It is weakly territorial, although territories are small and not foraging areas. Its song is termed "impressive." The song of the Tambourine Dove (*Tympanistria tympanistria*) of Africa is probably as developed as any pigeon song. The bird is hard to see and feeds mostly on the ground in forest. It is not gregarious. Its song is a ritardando in flute-like notes lasting 12 seconds or more (recording by

North). The Argentine Wood Pigeon (*Columba picazuro*) sings five notes, the last prolonged and mournful (Hudson). In the Philippines I heard and saw a green wood pigeon with a rather beautiful voice. It was certainly far from conspicuous in its trees.

Parrots in captivity seem among the gaudiest of birds. They also live well up in the vegetation where the light tends to be strong. Even so, most species probably blend fairly well with the mixed greens, flashes of sunlight, and fruit or flower colors around them. This would apply, I should think, least of all to the cockatoos (*Kakatoë* spp., e.g.) and macaws (*Ara* spp., e.g.), whose voices seem particularly crude. In their syrinx parrots are hardly "primitive"; rather, like lyrebirds, they are intermediate, with three muscle pairs. The main factor inhibiting song, in the primary territorial and musical sense, in this family is the gregariousness of the birds. As was argued in Chapter 4, they are chatterers. But they are chatterers *par excellence*. (The Hill Myna's greater precision in its duplications is to be credited to its superior muscular equipment.) Their lives are matters of flock talk and pair talk. And their forest habitats, after all, do set limits to visibility. Thus the rather plain-colored Grey Parrot lives in tall forest. Females in captivity imitate, so far as is known, as well as males (Finn 1919, Nottebohm 1970).

Parrots show signs of supernormal "intelligence." Impressive evidence is given by a number of writers, including Finn, that some captive parrots have had a rough sense of the meanings of words or short phrases, e.g., saying "Good night" when ready to sleep but not otherwise. The intense sociability of the family is shown by the volubility, even of females, and by the fact that, like some babblers and waxbills, and the Hill Mynas, parrots indulge in bill fondling (Finn). This is the opposite of the isolationism typical of the great songsters. But in another way it brings this family closest of all to ourselves. The most intelligent animals (e.g., dogs, apes, horses, elephants, dolphins) are also the most sociable, if one excludes the almost mechanical sociality of the insects and some fishes.

The King Parrot as I heard it in Queensland mountain forest had a simple (two-toned) musical song. The species is described as "not especially gregarious." It has a red head and front, but forest-green back and wings and dark tail. Perhaps this is as close to a singer as the family comes. Of course the imitative capacity includes ability to learn simple tunes. And Finn had a Budgerigar that learned to imitate a

Song Thrush, its companion in captivity, copying the song "perfectly" except for the quality of voice.

Owls (Strigiformes) seem most nearly comparable to hawks except for being in general smaller and usually hunting only by night. Living in dim light they are less visible to one another. And they certainly do come closer to music than their diurnal counterparts. But not much closer. Nocturnal foraging seems only mildly favorable to song, as one can see also from the nightjars. The number of bird noises is so greatly diminished that this alone reduces the need for distinctiveness. Owls have mostly very simple utterances, in voices ranging from crude to mildly musical. The most-developed songs are perhaps by the bush or woodland Pearl-spotted Owlet (*Glaucidium perlatum*) [Eth], with "beautiful" tones rising and falling in pitch, and two members of the genus *Aegolius,* the Boreal Owl (*funereus*) and Saw-whet Owl (*acadicus*). Living in forests, these have flute-like or bell-like voices.

The absurdly named goatsuckers (Caprimulgiformes), all nocturnal, have functional songs, but only a few have much musical refinement or complexity. The dim light explains the first fact; a possible reason for the second has been touched on above. However, the purely aerial feeding of the group is an additional factor. Taking all aerial feeders together, one finds little musical development. They are in the maximum of light for the given time, and they have the fewest chances of being behind opaque barriers. The most musical nocturnal species seem to be the following:

The Whippoorwill [Na^e] has a rather sweet whistled song of three notes, the second, lowest, the third, highest and slurred downward (spectrogram in Robbins et al.). The Little Nightjar (*Caprimulgus parvulus*) [Nt] (recording by Schwarz) has a delightful little zylophonic song dancing up and down in a lively way. The Common Potoo [Nt] has a rather thrilling slow song (recording by Schwarz) in falling cadence. Its voice is almost flute-like, and it has four, sometimes five or six, pitches, each below the last. This is a forest bird. Apparently it does not weaken the aesthetic effect by the endless quick reiterations, running into the hundreds, characteristic of the true nightjars. Significantly, like its relative the Great Potoo (*Nyctibius grandis*), it is a perch feeder, not a purely aerial forager.

The songs of the three species just mentioned are in great contrast to the harsh utterances of European nightjars. Perhaps the reason is the far greater variety of night sounds in the American tropics, putting pressure on distinctiveness. The Usambara Nightjar (*Caprimulgus poliocephalus*) [Eth] is said to have a melodious four-syllabled call, and the Great Eared Nightjar (*Eurostopodus macrotis*, Burma), a "lovely, clear whistle" (Smythies 1953). This is one of several families whose most musical members are tropical.

In the swift-like birds (Apodiformes) the extremely aerial swifts (Apodidae) are also gregarious. Their twittering seems to have little of the character or function of song and is scarcely even minimally musical. The closely related but somewhat less aerial and far less gregarious hummingbirds, foraging mostly in forest, are a rather different story. They mostly sing, though in primitive fashion, and usually with the thinnest possible voices. The music is almost entirely in the rhythm, which sometimes is a bit sophisticated, for example in the Jamaican Vervain Hummingbird (*Mellisuga minima*). There is a good deal of polygamy, but otherwise the family is not gregarious. However, territories are small. Though these birds are more gaudy than swifts, they are also much more likely to be hidden in vegetation and their dominant color is green. They also perch more. It seems on balance that they should be more songful, which they are. Yet it would be surprising if their songs were even as good as their tiny size makes possible. (Of course, a few are not at all tiny. But the larger ones still do not sing well.) Their combination of small size and unique hummingbird habits is visually diagnostic. According to Skutch (personal communication), the Band-tailed Barbthroat (*Threnetes ruckeri*) and the Wine-throated Hummingbird (*Atthis ellioti*) have fine songs, apart from the lack of volume [both Nt^n]. Beebe describes the song of the Rufous-breasted Hermit (*Glaucis hirsuta* [*Phaethornis episcopus*]) as a sweet trill, 12–15 notes, changing from slow to fast and rising in pitch. The genus feeds low down in forest. Greenewalt (1960) prefers the singing of the Wedge-billed Hummingbird (*Schistes geoffroyi*) [Nt^s]. It is one of the less showy in plumage (picture in Austin 1961) and is a forest bird. The White-eared's "silver bell" (Mexico), the tonal range of the Rufous-tailed, and the monotonous but attractive song of the Sparkling or Gould's Violet Ear (*Hylocharis leucotis*, *Amazilia tzacatl*, *Colibri coruscans*) have also been admired.

The forest-haunting trogons (Trogonidae) [Nt, Eth] might sing better if their colors were quieter. However, they blend rather well with the foliage. Their aerial foraging, even when they eat fruit, is a negative factor. Their voices are somewhat refined, but the songs have only the simplest patterns. Colies (or mousebirds) (Coliidae) [Eth] are dull-colored but highly gregarious, and they forage in an odd visually identifying fashion responsible for their second English name. Thus they do not need to sing. They either call harshly, or twitter insignificantly, or in some cases have a "trilling whistle in flight."

The kingfisher group (Coraciformes) [W] consists almost entirely of visually distinctive, poorly concealed birds, many of them fairly large. They are mostly without music. Laughing Kookaburras (*Dacelo* [*gigas*] *novaeguineae* [Au] certainly sing in amazing choral fashion, though in noisy, unmusical voices, and with rather crude patterns. They live in "open forests." Slightly musical are the White-breasted and Brown-headed Storkbilled Kingfishers of India (*Halcyon smyrnensis* and *Pelargopsis capensis*); also the Eurasian Kingfisher (*Alcedo atthis*).

The woodhoopoes (Upupidae) and some bee-eaters (Meropidae) are gregarious. They and the rollers (Coracidae) and todies (Todidae) are easily seen, partly because of their plumage and partly because of their habits. They are almost without music. Motmots (Momotidae) are rather sober-colored, unobtrusive, and sylvan, but still not very well hidden since they are observation-post feeders. They have mellow voices but ultrasimple patterns. The Blue-throated Motmot (*Aspatha gularis*) [Nt^n] has "delightfully clear and mellow notes" heard chiefly at dawn, the pair sometimes singing together (Skutch 1969). This species is smaller and plainer than the others, and is nearly all green. Dickey and van Rossem (1938) found one in very dense growth. It seemed to be nocturnal or at least crepuscular, spending much of the day in its nesting tunnel. It is a mountain bird, up to 10,000 ft. (1200–3200 meters).

Hornbills (Bucerotidae) [Eth, Or] are visually eccentric and large, but also mostly sylvan birds. They have loud crude songs, some sounding like a motorcycle; and one species, the Grey Hornbill (*Tockus nasutus*) [Eth], has a crude kind of melody of some complexity (recording by North). It is a forest bird of slightly soberer color than most. The Hoopoe (*Upupa epops*) [Or] is startlingly eccentric in appearance, but dull-colored and ground-feeding. It has one of the best songs in the group, but this is not saying very much.

Touracos [Eth] (Musophagidae) are gaudy, frugivorous, visually displaying birds, appropriately harsh in voice and with virtually no songs. In contrast, the related cuckoos (Cuculidae) [W] are rather plain colored, nongregarious though only mildly territorial (Baker 1942: 139–53), mostly arboreal, but insectivorous and sylvan birds, and nearly all have definite, though simple and rather monotonous songs.

Anis (Crotophaginae) [Nt] are more protectively colored but still rather visible and visually very distinctive birds, with simple wooden-sounding songs. Several cuckoos have fluty voices, including the one that says "cuckoo," *Cuculus canorus* [Pa]. The Indian Cuckoo (*C. micropterus*) has a musical though monotonously reiterated four-toned song (Figure 10).

$$-$$
$$-$$
$$-$$
$$-$$

FIG. 10. *Song of the Indian Cuckoo*

The Himalayan Cuckoo (*Cuculus saturatus*) has a flute-like voice but no pitch contrasts or rhythmic complexity. It merely repeats one note.

Cuckoos are little given to varying their songs. With barbets and nightjars they seem rather oblivious of my anti-monotony principle. I infer that their musical feeling is primitive. None of them sing outside the breeding season, as many tinamous do, nor are they known to imitate. One of the most interesting cuckoo songs is by the Black-billed Cuckoo [Na^e], nonparasitic and extremely well hidden. Its song has little melody but begins with a descending series of guttural notes and then repeats the same tone, in varying lengths, now singly, now in groups of 3 or 4. This is an unusually subtle form of rhythmic versatility, highly monotonous only to a careless listener.

A remarkable cuckoo song (recording by Davis) is the Rufous-rumped Ground-cuckoo's (*Morococcyx erythropygus*) of Middle America. It has a 14-second song with a nice ritardando. According to Blake (1953), it is rather hard to see, living "on or near the ground" in dense growth.

The woodpecker order (Piciformes) [W exc. Au] is inferior to the cuckoos in song-development. Woodpeckers themselves are visually distinctive through their habits and rather gaudy and constantly moving head plumage. Though mostly sylvan, they are not very well hidden or, most of the time, in anything like the dimmest light. Their drumming is partly a substitute for song or could be called a type of song. But it is a primitive type, since the rhythms are wholly uncomplicated. The "laughter" of the Green Woodpecker (*Picus viridis*) may be taken as a vague hint of melody. The Yellow-shafted Flicker (*Colaptes auratus*) has a simple reiterative spring song "cut-cut-cut," etc. The repetitiveness is within reason, not nightjar-like. Perhaps the most musical woodpecker song is that of the Olivaceous Piculet (*Picumnus olivaceus*) [Nt], a tiny, dull-colored bird usually in dense growth. Its trill is "at best melodious" (Skutch 1969). The Antillean Piculet (*Nesoctites micromegas*) has a similar reputation (ibid.: 551). Skutch reports two woodpecker species as drumming in duetting fashion. He also notes that ceremonial drumming is specifically different from species to species.

Toucans (Ramphastidae) [Nt] are among the most gorgeous of all forest birds, and among the most distinctive in shape. A glimpse of a bill identifies not only the family but the species as well. They are gregarious. They are rather large, and their voices stand out by sheer power from the mass of bird utterances. Altogether, their tunelessness seems in order, in spite of their forest habitat. Jacamars (Galbulidae) [Nt] are visually distinctive in a subtler way. They are observation-post feeders, and are not in deep forest as a rule. Yet they are not gregarious and, though their voices are weak, some have melodious little trilling songs (Austin 1961). Puffbirds (Bucconidae) [Nt], too, are visually peculiar, though not bright-colored, forest birds, feeding similarly. They are nearly tuneless, which is perhaps not altogether what one might expect. The last remark applies also to honeyguides (Indicatoridae) [Eth, Or], except that they have crude songs. They are dull-colored.

Barbets [Eth, Or] are as vocal as any of this order. Their reputation for monotony is in part richly deserved. Some of the species have few rivals in this respect. The quality of voice and pattern is usually unrefined. However, there is at least one very definite exception, the Golden-rumped Tinker-bird [Eth], an exception not overlooked; for one ornithologist (Jackson) said of the song, "personally I love it." So do I. There is a reason, an objective reason having nothing to do with any oddity of mine or Jackson's, unless it is odd to observe closely and precisely. This bird has a very clear subtle sense of rhythmic variation, and his voice is well tuned, as I think a sonagram would show. His song consists in the exactly timed repetitions of a clear "pop, pop, pop,

pop," often with excellent avoidance of monotony. He divides the reiterations sharply into groups, now four, now three, now two, now five, pops to a group. One never knows where he will stop for the little punctuating pause. Thus: pop-pop-pop, pop-pop-pop, pop-pop-pop-pop, pop-pop-pop, pop-pop-pop, pop-pop, pop-pop-pop-pop, pop-pop-pop-pop, pop-pop-pop-pop-pop, etc. The commas represent pauses, mostly of the length of one pop. This is one of the finest examples of variety through number juggling. But still, let us rate it only 3 in complexity. The species also lacks imitativeness; however, since there is good reason to suspect all singing birds of learning to sing, at least in some slight degree, by listening to others, even if only others of their own species, I habitually assign one point under this variable if no proof of imitation is available. However, let us lean over backward, and allow no value under this head. In loudness one cannot rate the song at less than 7; in continuity, also 7; in tone quality, not less than 5; and in coherence or unity not less than 7 (the rhythmic precision is fascinating). We thus have a score of 29, that is to say, a middling, not a low, rating.

The common barbet of Indian cities, the "Coppersmith" (*Megalaema haemacephala*), is another matter. All he knows musically is just to go on and on. For minutes at a time his brain has nothing to do, so far as his singing is concerned, until he finally decides to stop. Surely he must be putting his brain to some use other than singing! The Golden-rumped Tinker-bird is a precursor of the Songbirds in his appreciation of acoustical pattern. But the Indian bird has less pattern than some insects. This difference must have biological meaning. Most barbets are somewhat conspicuous in color and habit of feeding in outer branches. But the African bird is small, dull-colored, and tends to be hidden. There are also more closely-similar species in Africa than in India, which may add to the pressure for distinctiveness. Austin (1961) says that some barbets have pleasing low whistles.

Looking back over the primitive orders, we see that the most consistently musical group is the tinamous. It is also the only one which is consistently ground-feeding, nongregarious, and protectively colored (by Beebe's acid test of crouching not flying in case of danger), as well as mostly sylvan (in the largest nearly continuous region of heavy forest in the world). Those that are not sylvan have at least some grass or bushes to hide them and do not live, like some shorebirds, on bare sand or in open water. It ought to be and it is the most musical

primitive group. It is also, out of all birds whatever, the most numerous group (40 or more) of rather *large* species which practically all
sing moderately well. Their size is not huge, which would increase
visibility, but it is large enough to make territories large, which enhances the number of songs that must be distinguished. It shares with
wrens the tendency to sing all year round.

After the tinamous come fowls, or gallinaceous birds, and shorebirds, then pigeons or cuckoos—it is hard to say which. All are rather
middle-sized, most are protectively colored; the fowls, shorebirds, some
pigeons, and a few cuckoos are ground-feeding; many cuckoos, fowls,
and pigeons are sylvan, as are some shorebirds. Perhaps the best
singers are the *Tringa* sandpipers, the hill partridges (*Arborophila*
spp.) [Or], and some of the tropical wood pigeons [Eth].

The most consistently nonmusical groups are either very visible
(seabirds, soaring birds, large birds of open country, diurnal purely
aerial feeders, especially swifts, high-foragers) or brilliant in plumage,
eccentrically shaped, obviously exceptional in behavior (e.g., woodpeckers), or very gregarious, or several of these at once (parrots,
toucans).

B. Singing by Suboscine Perching Birds

I begin with some anatomical facts. The syringial differences among
Suboscine perching birds have recently been subjected to careful study
and lucid statement (Ames 1971). The results may for our purposes
be summarized as follows (departing little from relevant passages in
Ames's monograph):

(1) While the Oscines are relatively uniform in their syrinxes, the
Suboscines differ widely.

(2) In both Suboscines and Oscines, differences in song are mainly
conditioned by factors other than the structure of the syrinx: ecological and (presumably) neurological factors, rather than bony-muscular
ones.

(3) Nevertheless, differences in the syrinx do have statistically appreciable consequences for song.

(4) The most important, but not the only significantly variable, aspect of syringial structure is the number of pairs of internal muscles.

(In all perching birds there are also external syringial muscles, hence these may be abstracted from in comparisons.) This number varies in the Passeriformes from none in about 180 Suboscines to three in lyrebirds and four in Oscines.

Made with these considerations in mind, Table XV contains numerous facts from Ames's study, combined with some results of my reading and observation concerned with this order of birds. (Where a family is divided between groups, the number of its species in each group is given only very roughly, from such indications as I derive from Ames.)

Table XV classifies perching-bird families according to numbers of pairs of *intrinsic* syringial muscles (O, I, II), numbers of good singers, and numbers of species. The fractions under the family names are the number of good singers divided by the number of species in the family (or part of the family) in question.

It seems a reasonable hypothesis that the proportion of good singers in Suboscines is about the same as that of superior singers in Oscines, that is, about 5%, the anatomical difference producing the contrast between superior and merely good. In that case, if we were thoroughly familiar with these birds, our 30 good singers in the table would be raised to 50.

E. O. Willis (1966), with intensive experience of some of these birds, thinks that song develops better in species that live in unsettled shifting habitats, such as second growth or clearings, rather than in solid climax forest, of which there has been more in tropical America than elsewhere. The idea is that in settled habitats birds pair for life and have less trouble finding mates and so have less need for song. I have not been able to assimilate this idea. It may be worth investigation. If he is right, the 30 good singers given in Table XV may be more nearly the total than I incline to think.

We now turn to some particulars summed up in the table and to the ecological or ethological factors involved.

O(a). Why the New Zealand "wrens" do not need or produce noticeable song I do not know. But broadbills [Pt] are mostly gaudy and somewhat gregarious. Plantcutters are rather conspicuous, sitting often on bushtops in somewhat open country. They are not highly territorial; one species is brightly colored. Pittas [Pt] live in a manner usually favorable to song, hidden on the forest floor, and are not gregarious. However, they are brilliant in color. They have loud, but short and

TABLE XV

Syringial Equipment of Perching Birds

No. of muscle pairs	No. of good singers	No. of species					
0(a)	0	48	broadbills (Eurylaimidae) 0/14	NZ wrens (Acanthisittidae) 0/4	asities (Philepittidae) ?/4	plantcutters (Phytomidae) 0/3	pittas (Pittidae) 0/23
0(b)	4?	133	tyrants (Tyrannidae) 0/26?	manakins (Pipridae) 0/20?	cotingas (Cotingidae) 2/56?	antbirds (Formicariidae) 2/33	
I(a)	3+?	27	tapaculos (Rhinocryptidae) 2/26?	sharpbills (Oxyruncidae) 1/1			
I(b)	14+?	511	tyrants (Tyrannidae) 6/249	manakins 1/37	cotingas 3/34	antbirds 4/191	
II(a)	5++?	265	ovenbirds (Furnariidae) 3/215	woodcreepers (Dendrocolaptidae) 2/50			
II(b)	4+?	92	tyrants 4/90	manakins ?/2			
III	2	2	lyrebirds (Menuridae)	(possibly scrub-birds) (Atrichornithidae)			
IV	500?	4000	Oscines				

+ or ++ is insurance against our partial ignorance of these groups, taking ecological and anatomical factors into account.
Note: Nine families, designated as (a), are uniform in the number of muscle pairs, while four, designated as (b), are of mixed composition, two ranging all the way from no muscle pairs to two pairs.

scarcely musical, songs. Asities and false sunbirds (Madagascar) are said to have soft, seldom-heard "thrushlike" songs. (I interpret this to mean a sort of subsong.) They are arboreal forest birds.

O(b). Tyrant flycatchers sing about as well as might be expected from the OW flycatchers (their inferior equipment limiting the results), except that they have a fondness for restricting singing largely to dawn, or in a few cases to dawn and dusk. None of the family with no internal muscle pairs seems to sing well. The flycatcher habit is not favorable (Chapter 9), and the handicap of poor organs is, hence, not likely to be overcome. Such considerations apply also to manakins, gaudy, visually displaying, lek-type birds. They are hardly musical and their excuses for songs are not territorial in the distancing sense but are directed to the females. Cotingas are mostly treetop frugivorous birds, many of them gaudy. Most are rather quiet; some subsong and a few loud and striking utterances have been recorded. Some of these are unmusical, but a few are somewhat musical. This is very mildly the case with the plain-colored well-concealed Screaming Piha (*Lipaugus vociferans,* Beebe's "Goldbird"). Surprisingly, however, the Purple-throated Fruit Crow (*Querula purpurata*) has "one of the most beautiful songs in the Panama forests" (Skutch 1969: 93). It breeds territorially and is not so brightly colored as some other fruit crows and treetop cotingas.

O(b). Antbirds are mostly nongregarious, dull-colored (though dimorphous), and tend to live low in forests. Some "ground antbirds" or antthrushes (*Chamaeza* spp.), though with no internal muscle pairs, are, for Suboscines, outstanding singers. *Chamaeza ruficauda,* the Rufous-tailed Antthrush, has a splendid, long, and rather sweet-voiced song gradually rising in something like quarter tones, and taking from 15 to 30 or more seconds. If the bird reaches his highest pitch before he is ready to end the song, he continues it by repeating this highest pitch. Apparently, he cannot always make enough divisions of the pitch range he commands to make the song last as long as he wishes without repetition. The "Noonwhistle," as Fuertes called it, *C. ruficauda turdina,* had a "rising crescendo" of about 50 seconds. *Chamaeza campanisona,* the Short-tailed Antthrush, has a two-part song, each part monotonically reiterative.

I(a). Tapaculos are ground-dwelling, somber-colored, hard-to-see birds, highly vocal and in some species musical. Huet-huets (*Pteroptochos* spp.) (Chile) are said to be melodious (Sick, in Thomson

1964), and *Merulaxis ater,* the Slaty Bristlefront (southeastern Brazil, recording by Frisch), and other species to sing "strikingly pure scales," ascending or descending, while other tapaculos, namely, *Scytalopus* spp. (Panama to the Falklands), have rough voices. *M. ater* (recording by Frisch) is indeed a striking performer. I rate it 977.765:41. Thanks to Helmut Sick I have heard the Sharpbill (*Oxyruncus cristatus*) sing. It is a forest bird and has a sweet but simple song.

I(b). Hudson (1920) considered 28 and Skutch (1960, 1967) 37 species of the Tyrant family. Between them these authors single out five of the flycatchers with one muscle pair each for special praise: (1) the Vermilion Flycatcher (*Pyrocephalus rubinus*) [Hudson's Scarlet Tyrant]; (2) Hudson's Reed Tyrant, Warbling Doradito (*Pseudocolopteryx* [*Hapalocercus*] *flaviventris*), and three of Skutch's subjects— (3) Streaked Flycatcher (*Myiodynastes maculatus*), (4) Sulphur-bellied (*M. luteiventris*), (5) Golden-bellied (*M. hemichrysus*). (2) lives well hidden in bushes or weeds, where it forages much of the time "after the manner of wrens"; (5) lives in dense moist mountain forest. (3) and (4) are rather dull-colored. Thus only (1) seems puzzling. This species, found from Arizona to Argentina, seems rather conspicuous to be a "good" singer (which perhaps only Hudson has thought it to be) even by the standards of this family. Yet it is rather small and at least two others of Hudson's tyrants must be more readily identified by sight: the stout big-billed Bienteveo (*Pitangus* [*bolivianus*] *sulphuratus*) and the pure white and apparently rather silent Little Widow (*Xolmis* [*Taenioptera*] *irupero*). The Bienteveo has powerful calls with little musical quality. They *must* be powerful, since the pair members forage far apart but insist upon maintaining communication. Six of Hudson's 28 species sing duets, of which five are unmusical.

I(b). The Thrush-like Manakin (*Schiffornis turdinus*) is "always solitary," lives in forest undergrowth, is deep olive-brown, and has an "exquisitely musical tripartite song." It sings without monotony, since its pauses are from 3 to 14 times as long as the songs (Skutch 1969). Several cotingas in this part of their family (Ib) sing well. When I heard *Procnias nudicollis,* the Naked-throated Bellbird, in southeastern Brazil, it was low down in the forest. Its color did not seem concealing, but still it could be heard immensely farther than it could be seen. Presumably it needs to command a large territory. The outstanding features of the song include not only the great carrying power but also the nicety and complexity of the rhythmical variations. The bird gives both isolated and repetitive blows upon its "anvil." Also, as Greenewalt has shown, the bird utters two sounds simultaneously "exactly an octave apart." All this makes a rather better than merely mediocre song. The White-winged Becard (*Pachyramphus polychopterus*) is well up in trees, dimorphic, and scarcely protectively colored, but has a beautiful dawn song. It is, however, solitary and territorial. *Attila rufus,* the Gray-hooded Attila, foraging on the ground, sings 6–8 ascending notes in a minor key, the next to last note shorter and the last note several tones lower (Mitchell 1957). On the song of the Bright-rumped Attila (*Attila spadiceus*) see Skutch (1969). *Tijuca atra,* the Black-and-gold Cotinga, the Whistler ("Assobiador"), has a prolonged plaintive whistle, with first a crescendo, then a diminuendo. Its syrinx seems not to have been analyzed.

I(b). Ecologically the antbirds, especially the ground antbirds, should sing as well as anatomy permits. There is some evidence that they do so (for information additional to that given under O(b) see Fuertes 1914). The Dusky Antbird (*Cercomacra tyrannina*) has a "cosy little trill," according to Chapman; a "clear, mellow whistle which ascends in pitch" (Skutch 1969). The sexes duet, the female giving a higher-pitched version. They live low in dense growth and are dark in color. The Chestnut-backed Antbird (*Myrmeciza exsul*) has similar traits and habits. Willis, a specialist on the family, prefers the Bicolored (*Gymnopithys leucaspis*). His spectrograms (1966) show a rather simple song. The bird lives low in undergrowth; the sexes look alike. Antshrikes (arboreal) have loud songs, some harsh as in the Barred Antshrike (*Thamnophilus doliatus*), some more refined, as in *Taraba major,* the Great Antshrike, which has an almost musical descending song.

II(a). Ovenbirds (Furnariidae) are mostly dull-colored; some, however, are open-country birds, some treetop foragers, though many are terrestrial. Some of the latter sing rather well, e.g., the Rufous-fronted Thornbird (*Phacellodomus rufifrons*) and the Scaly-throated Leaf-scraper (*Sclerurus guatemalensis*). Both sexes of the latter species, which is very hard to see, sing "arrestingly beautifully" (Skutch 1969). The song lasts 5–6 seconds and sometimes there is only a slight pause between repetitions. Yet, says Skutch, the singing does not seem monotonous. This duplicates the case of the Winter Wren, considered in

Chapter 7. Some members of the family have lively duetting songs when mates come together after foraging apart. Hudson praises his Canastero (*Asthenes hudsoni*).

II(a). Woodcreepers (Dendrocolaptidae), behaving like Oscine creepers and somewhat like woodpeckers, have rather striking, sometimes mildly musical songs. In sharp contrast to woodpeckers they are very soberly colored and look much alike; also they mostly live in dense forest, and there are many species which must keep themselves distinct (compared to the few species of creepers in the entire Northern Hemisphere). Thus—considering their middling good organs—their middling musical output is about as one might expect. One species I heard in Ecuador had a male-female dual song, the male (?) taking the lead both in going up the tree and in singing his song. In this and some other species the notes descend the scale, and are rather sweet-sounding. Rhythmically fascinating is the Plain-brown Woodcreeper (*Dendrocincla fuliginosa*), with a monotonic song, something like an old-fashioned steam engine, now speeding up, now running steadily, now slowing down, and so on, nearly continuously for a minute or more (recording by Frisch). I have yet to hear a very poor song from this family. That of the Red-billed Scythebill (*Campylorhamphus trochilirostris*) may be the family's best (Skutch 1969).

II(b). Here are some of the best Suboscine singers: the Eastern Wood Pewee, a sober-colored woods bird; also Skutch's Vermilion-crowned Flycatcher (*Myiozetetes similis*) and his Scale-crested Pygmy-tyrant (*Lophotriccus pileatus*). The last lives low down in the forest, largely invisible, and the other, though rather brilliant, must, as Skutch remarks, be distinguished from a number of rather similar small species. The Olive-sided Flycatcher (*Nuttallornis borealis*) has a simple but mellow and powerful song. It likes open forest and is inconspicuously colored. The two manakin species in class II(b) seem not to be described as to song.

Note that the highest percentage of tyrants with good songs are in II(b) and the lowest in O(b), and that this *may* be true of the manakins; also that a higher percentage of good singers is found in I(b) than in O(b) cotingas. True, the O(b) antbirds show a higher percentage than the I(b) members, but this is perhaps sufficiently explained by the extreme ecological suitability of song in ground antbirds. Tapaculos in I(a) do even better, with similar ecology but better organs. The total for O(a,b) is 2.2%, for I(a,b) 3.3%. Also the probability of insufficient data is vastly greater for I than for O, in which half the species occur. There is a still greater probability of omissions in the list of 357 species in II. Here the percentage is 2.5. Probably it should be closer to 5% or more.

C. Discussion

Taking all birds with more primitive vocalizing equipment than lyrebirds, one finds many mediocre or poor songs, distributed roughly as ecological and anatomical factors imply they should be, and a smaller but substantial number of rather good songs, again in fair accordance with the intensity of the ecological need for song. But almost no song in the acoustically primitive families seems equal musically to the most highly developed 4 or 5% of the acoustically well-equipped birds.

It is perhaps arguable that a few of the former, say 10 or 15, belong with the 200 best singers, but even this would be but 0.003 of the primitive species, contrasted to 0.05 of the Oscines. (Those to be considered would be some tinamous, a few shorebirds, partridges, possibly a wood pigeon or two, the Potoo, and the Suboscines *Chamaeza ruficauda, Merulaxis ater, Procnias nudicollis,* and *Contopus virens*—all mentioned in this chapter.)

Thus human ratings of songs express objective physical facts of anatomical equipment. Yet this equipment was not taken into account in the ratings. Therefore, the correlation between the allegedly subjective or anthropomorphic aspect of "good" singing and the perfectly definite objective facts of anatomy, is, so far as it goes, a valid statistical refutation of the thesis of mere subjectivity.

If, instead of superior, one takes superb songs, say the 70–90 best, it does not seem reasonable to regard a single species with less than three syringial muscles as in this class. Yet more than half of all birds are primitives in this respect, 4600 or more, and one-third, perhaps one-half, of this half sing. There is no Hermit Thrush, Woodlark, Nightingale, Mockingbird, Blackbird, or Lyrebird with but one or two muscles for sound control.

It is quite possible to be very enthusiastic about some tinamous or the Potoo. But analyze the songs for variety and tonal purity, and they will probably not compare with the better oscinine productions. The

Potoo's song is very simple, and his voice slightly harsh though moving, while tinamous seem restricted essentially to one or two patterns without wide variations. But possibly a tinamou or two is superb. The statistical evidence still stands. Nothing like the Oscine proportion of superb singers can with any plausibility be claimed for the nonoscines. Add the fact that there are, in the latter, scores of cases of egregious violation of the aesthetic requirement of monotony avoidance, that is, reiteration ad nauseam, without appreciable pauses, of a single note or short phrase, though in the Oscines there is scarcely a single clear case of this. Thus, not only do the primitives sing less well, they exhibit behaviorally much less feeling for aesthetic requirements. They are even more remote from man than birds as a class are bound to be in degree of musical feeling. The evolution of song is to some extent toward a simple form or low degree of musical sense, with gulls and most birds of prey having virtually nothing of this sense and Hermit or Wood Thrushes, for example, having a good deal, tinamous and antbirds being perhaps nearest to them among the physiologically primitive families. Ecological theory gives an objective explanation of this. The thesis of subjectivity explains only some minor details of human judgments of song, not the broad outlines.

12

Some Conclusions and
Unsolved Problems

❧

A. Results of the Study

In this book I have attempted to relate biological to genuinely psychological aspects of the phenomenon of animal music, chiefly bird song,
following the analogy with human music. The analogy has at least
heuristic value, since it has led to the noticing of many otherwise
largely neglected facts, such as:

(1) The presence in animal music of all the simpler musical devices
(Chapters 2, 3, 5).

(2) The avoidance alike of mere regularity, unrelieved by deviations
or pauses, and mere randomness (Chapter 7).

(3) The relaxed leisurely sustained character of singing, also its mul-
tifunctional role, and its occurrence as youthful play, compared to the
emotional narrowness and strain associated with alarm notes and some
other innate cries (Chapter 3B).

(4) The shortness of the reiterated unit patterns (seconds rather
than minutes) compared to human hour-long patterns, showing that
the patterns correspond to the bird's limited attention span (Chapter
3A).

(5) The coincidence between the biological need for maximal distinctiveness of (territorial) song and the aesthetic value of definite,
complex patterns (Chapters 1, 2, 3).

(6) The fact that many a song usually described as a single pattern

is really a set of variations on a theme, or a repertoire of patterns
(Chapter 5C, D).

(7) The presence of imitativeness in singing as evidence of an interest in sounds as such, a somewhat different type of interest from that
at work in imitative "chatter," where the utterance is used as means of
quasi-conversational interchange with one or more companions, and is
less self-reinforcing or independent of immediate external stimuli
(Chapter 4).

(8) The statistical correlation of singing skill (as humanly judged)
with amount of singing per year, as well as with other objective features, physiological and ecological, showing that the human evaluations
have biological significance (Chapters 6, 8, 9, 11).

(9) The fact that the various indications of aesthetic sensitivity are
much more pronounced in Oscines than in birds physically less well
equipped for singing, showing that the evolution of organs for song has
been accompanied by a psychological evolution toward greater interest
in sounds and greater freedom, complexity, delicacy, flexibility, in the
feeling for them (Chapters 7, 10, 11).

(10) The fact that the principles used in interpreting bird songs
prove largely applicable to other classes of animals, including apes and
whales (Chapter 2G).

Concerning (7) I remark that chatterers are interested in sounds
much as human infants are. Children learn to talk, singing birds to
sing, and chattering birds to chatter partly by their inborn interest in
sounds. Not all interest in sounds is musical, but all musicians are interested in sounds.

Of course there are many unanswered or incompletely answered
questions. The singing habits of many, if not most, species are incompletely known. We have almost no evidence on the extent to which
birds without the Oscine syrinx, apart from parrots, learn their songs
or imitate. We do know that imitation is not prominent in such birds.
Naked-throated Bellbirds are caged in South America but have not
been reported to imitate. Hand-raising of singing nonoscines (other
than pigeons) seems not to have been extensively undertaken. If these
birds have no capacity at all to learn sound production by hearing
others sing, my principles would make me hesitate to call their utterances songs. Apparently deafening roosters or keeping them from hearing others crow does not affect the pattern of their own crowing. Craig's

pigeons could learn much from foster parents but not the latter's song. More recent work has not upset this result. We have no experiments designed to test the ability of frogs to learn by imitation, though we do have some for insects (with positive results).

I have tried to show that aesthetic ideas can be useful in ethology or comparative psychology. Harmonious, intense (sufficiently varied, not too regular) experience is what animals, including human beings, like when they have it and miss when they do not. Not to see this is to overlook much in one's view of life, including subhuman life of all kinds. Aesthetic blindness is more than a superficial defect. It makes all of our science less illuminating than it might be. The scorn of some of our youths for science is not unrelated to this deficiency. It also prevents us from understanding ethical problems properly. For the will to consider the good of others as equally important with our own good is empty if we do not know what either our or their good really is. Basically what are good are good experiences, harmonious and intense. Artists, more than others, directly aim to create such experiences, for themselves and others. It is a stupendous fact about nature that the territorial disputes of thousands of species are something like artistic contests—song duels. The struggle is mainly musical (countersinging), not pugilistic. If only human beings could do so well.

B. Some Philosophical Topics Not Discussed

My convictions about such ultimate questions of natural science as the evaluation of various forms of materialism, dualism, interactionism, determinism, positivism, and the like, I reserve for discussion elsewhere. Here I wish only to say that my views have much affinity with those of Whitehead—see the brief but sympathetic outline by Waddington (1969: 120f.), and see also E. H. Peters (1966, 1970). These views are scarcely majority opinions in any branch of inquiry. However, I am encouraged by partial agreements with Jordan (1951), Popper (1965), and Rescher (1970: 125ff.) among philosophers; Agar (1951), Wright (1953), Dobzhansky (1960: 425f.), Waddington (1961: 86f. and loc. cit.), and Rensch (1970) among biologists; Troland (1922), Allport (1955: 614–67), and Piaget (1970: 36–73) among psychologists; Whitehorn and Gendlin (oral communications) among psychiatrists; Margenau (1950: 443, 446), Pollard (1958: 47–61),

Munn (1960), Burgers (1965), Bohm (see Waddington 1969: 42f., 48), Lieber (ibid.: 315), and Wigner (oral communications) among physicists (see also Koerner, ed., 1957: 42, 47, 51, 60, 82, 218); and Gerard (1940, 1947) and Gomes (see Eccles 1966) among physiologists and biophysicists. I also take heart from some common ground with twenty-four centuries of Buddhist thought, the oldest and deepest continuous tradition of philosophical psychology, a "psychology without a soul," compatible with a reasonable behaviorism yet in principle nonmaterialistic, with a reasonable mechanism yet not mechanistic, with interaction yet not dualistic. I feel confident that religious truth is somewhere in the joint neighborhood of the Bodhisattva ideal of universal compassion and the more activistic Christian doctrine of love as both human and more than human. The elucidation of the foregoing cryptic remarks—and they can be elucidated—falls outside the plan of this book.

C. *Looking toward the Future*

I feel it a duty to record one somber reflection. In my judgment it is overwhelmingly probable that of the 5000 singing avian species (give or take a thousand, depending on the criteria of "sing"), at least many hundreds are doomed to extinction from man's destruction of them and their habitats—destruction arising from the human greed for luxuries, pleasure in destruction or in playing with technological toys (e.g., automobiles), and the refusal or failure to think responsibly and intelligently about the number of offspring. Everywhere, forests, swamps, and wild savannahs are shrinking; in some countries armed city people swarm into the country ready to shoot whatever flies. Industrial man has yet to exercise decent control over his ever-growing physical powers, puny in the astronomical universe, but overwhelming (in destructive, if not constructive, potential) on this planet.

When man emerged on the earth, he inherited a magnificent environment. At first, and locally, he somewhat appreciated this fact, although his admiration and reverence were heavily clouded by fears of other planetary powers, visible and invisible, real and imaginary. Now he has largely lost his fears, other than those relating to actions of his human fellows. But he has also tended to lose his sense of the inexhaustible beauty and glory of the web of life. Yet it is only now that this beauty and glory, in its planetary totality, is being made accessible by the very industrialism that tends to destroy it. Every naturalist hopes that some change of heart will emerge to counteract the gloomier aspect of this paradox.

Our machines have not, so far, enabled us to meet the basic challenge of rational animality, to find our place among the natural kinds —where possible, as an added level of value. Instead, we are more and more making human life an alternative to other forms of life, and in such a way as to threaten the endurance even of our own form. The privilege of enjoying wide glimpses of the inexhaustible beauty of the universe, never so apparent as now, carries with it the possibility— unless we revise our habits—of demolishing much of the portion of this beauty which is located on our planet. I salute the astronomers for giving us strong evidence that life on this planet is but a single pebble on the vast cosmic beach fostering animate existence. But even that pebble is not to be despised.

Nature apart from man is basically good. So is man, although he has unique capacities for evil as well as good. This is because every increase in freedom increases the dangers inherent in freedom. Man is the freest, hence most dangerous, of terrestrial animals. He needs to meditate upon this elementary but not trivial truth much more than he has. The Greek fear of human conceit, *hubris,* was entirely justified. We need to recover that fear. Technology makes man loom large in this solar system, but among the galaxies and island universes he is as small as ever. Science, given a balanced interpretation, fully justifies the old values of reverence and love toward what is other than, and in its encompassing aspect incomparably greater than, man and all his works, actual or potential.

APPENDIX A

Quality and Quantity
in 63 British Songbirds

(*See Chapter 8A*)

Q   Singing skill or quality   W   Song while wintering outside England
C   Continuity   V   Visitor
N   Nocturnal song

	Q	Months of song	Extras	Total extras
1. Robin *Erithacus rubecula*	6	11.0	CC	1
2. Hedge Sparrow *Prunella modularis*	3	9.9	C ½N?	½?
3. Starling *Sturnus vulgaris*	3	9.8	CCC (but mostly subsong)	?
4. Dipper *Cinclus cinclus*	4	9.8	CCC	2
5. Wren *Troglodytes troglodytes*	4	9.1	C-CC	½
6. Song Thrush *Turdus philomelos*	6	8.5	CCC 1/N	2½
7. Cirl Bunting *Emberiza cirlus*	4	7.9	½C	−½
8. Corn Bunting *Emberiza calandra*	3	7.7	C	0
9. House Sparrow *Passer domesticus*	1	7.7	CC (but performs little)	?
10. Skylark *Alauda arvensis*	6	7.4	CCC	2
11. Coal Tit *Parus ater*	2	7.3	CC	1
12. Blue Tit *Parus caeruleus*	2	7.2	?	?

	Q	Months of song	Extras	Total extras
13. Great Tit *Parus major*	2	7.1	CC	1
14. Linnet *Carduelis cannabina*	3	6.5	CCC (subsong)	2
15. Yellow Bunting *Emberiza citrinella*	4	6.4	C	0
16. Tree Creeper *Certhia familiaris*	4	6.2	¼C (1 sec. in 15)	−¾
17. Chaffinch *Fringilla coelebs*	4	6.0	C	0
18. Goldcrest *Regulus regulus*	3	6.0	C	0
19. Mistle Thrush *Turdus viscivorus*	4	5.9	CC	1
20. Lesser Redpoll *Carduelis flammea*	2	5.8	CC	1
21. Goldfinch *Carduelis carduelis*	3	5.6	CC (subsong)	1
22. Nuthatch *Sitta europaea*	4	5.5	CC	1
23. Blackbird *Turdus merula*	6	5.4	CC	1
24. Woodlark *Lullula arborea*	6	5.3	CC-CCC N	2½
25. Greenfinch *Chloris chloris*	2	5.2	C-CC	0–1
26. Dartford Warbler *Sylvia undata*	3	5.1	C	0
27. Reed Bunting *Emberiza schoeniclus*	3	4.8	C	0
28. Meadow Pipit *Anthus pratensis*	3	4.6	C-CC	½?
29. Chiffchaff *Phylloscopus collybita*	3 V	4.6	CC W	2
30. Marsh Tit *Parus palustris*	2	4.0	C	0
31. Rock Pipit *Anthus spinoletta*	3	4.0	?	?
32. Swallow *Hirundo rustica*	3 V	4.0	CC W	2?
33. Twite *Carduelis flavirostris*	2	4.0	?	?
34. Willow Warbler *Phylloscopus trochilus*	4 V	3.9	CC WW	3

QUALITY AND QUANTITY

	Q	Months of song	Extras	Total extras
35. Stonechat *Saxicola torquata*	2	3.6	?	?
36. Tree Pipit *Anthus trivialis*	4 V	3.4	CC	2
37. Sedge Warbler *Acrocephalus schoenobaenus*	5 V	3.2	CCC NN WW	7
38. Whitethroat *Sylvia communis*	4 V	3.2	C W	2
39. Hawfinch *Coccothraustes coccothraustes*	3	3.2	? ("Seldom heard")	?
40. Wheatear *Oenanthe oenanthe*	3 V	3.1	C-CC	2½
41. Sand Martin *Riparia riparia*	1 V	3.0	CC W	3
42. Blackcap *Sylvia atricapilla*	6 V	3.0	C-CC WW	3.5
43. Reed Warbler *Acrocephalus scirpaceus*	3 V	3.0	CCC N W	5
44. Crossbill *Loxia curvirostra*	2	2.9	CC	1
45. Ring Ouzel *Turdus torquatus*	4 V	2.8	C	1
46. Redstart *Phoenicurus phoenicurus*	4 V	2.7	C	1
47. Garden Warbler *Sylvia borin*	6 V	2.7	CC WW	4
48. Grasshopper Warbler *Locustella naevia*	3 V	2.6	? NN	3?
49. Wood Warbler *Phylloscopus sibilatrix*	4 V	2.6	C-CC W	1
50. Lesser Whitethroat *Sylvia curruca*	4 V	2.5	C	
51. Whinchat *Saxicola rubetra*	3 V	2.5	C	1
52. Willow Tit *Parus montanus*	3	2.4	C	0
53. Pied Wagtail *Motacilla alba*	2	2.3	CC	1
54. House Martin *Delichon urbica*	1 V	2.0	CC	2
55. Nightingale *Erithacus [Luscinia]* *megarhynchos*	6 V	2.0	CC NNN WW	7

	Q	Months of song	Extras	Total extras
56. Spotted Flycatcher *Muscicapa striata*	1 V	1.7	? ¼W "once"	1?
57. Pied Flycatcher *Muscicapa hypoleuca*	4 V	1.7	CC W	3
58. Marsh Warbler *Acrocephalus palustris*	6 V	1.5	CCC N ½W	4.5
59. Tree Sparrow *Passer montanus*	1	1.4	CC	1
60. Yellow Wagtail *Motacilla flava*	1 V	0.6	?	?
61. Grey Wagtail *Motacilla cinerea*	1	0.5	?	?
62. Bullfinch *Pyrrhula pyrrhula*	1	0.4	CC (subsong)	2
63. Red-backed Shrike *Lanius collurio*	1 V	0.2	CCC	3

Worldwide Statistical Sample of Quality and Quantity

(See Chapter 8C)

S   Number of days in the song season in the region in which the bird nests
F   Number of days of full or abundant song
L   Number of days with an excess or deficiency of daylight
N   Number of days of nocturnal song
W   Number of days of song while wintering
Cf Continuity fraction: Length of a song divided by the length of the song-pause cycle
ES Effective season

Country and Species	Rating	S	F	L	N	W	Cf	ES
	Very Good Singers (35 spp.)							
Australia								
Superb Lyrebird								
Menura superba	999.559:46	153	100	−30			1	108
Britain								
Skylark								
Alauda arvensis	989.576:44	295	197	60			1	250
Woodlark								
Lullula arborea	988.995:48	242	110	75	6		1	181
Marsh Warbler								
Acrocephalus palustris	899.657:44	53	38	38	9	8	1	60
Blackcap								
Sylvia atricapilla	976.995:45	93	85	85		45	1/3	44
Song Thrush								
Turdus philomelos	999.556:43	290	238				4/5	204
Blackbird								
Turdus merula	978.895:46	169	137	70			3/4	127
Nightingale								
Erithacus [Luscinia] megarhynchos	998.795:47	68	52	30	30	55	9/10	86

Country and Species	Rating	S	F	L	N	W	Cf	ES
Britain (continued)								
Robin								
Erithacus rubecula	888.785:44	344	306	−45			1/2	152
Europe								
Icterine Warbler								
Hippolais icterina	999.656:44	69	69	42	12	12	1	91
Thrush Nightingale								
Erithacus [Luscinia]								
luscinia	998.785:46	73	43	40	20	20	9/10	72
Bluethroat								
Erithacus svecicus	888.667:43	106	60	48	12	6	1	97
North America								
Bewick's Wren								
Thryomanes								
bewickii	877.894:43	280	90				3/5−	89
Carolina Wren								
Thryothorus								
ludovicianus	996.785:44	360	150				1/3+	75
Mockingbird								
Mimus polyglottos	999.668:47	270	110		35		9/10	157
Brown Thrasher								
Toxostoma rufum	989.775:45	75	40	40			1	65
Sage Thrasher								
Oreoscoptes								
montanus	879.775:43	100	70	25			4/5	70
Wood Thrush								
Hylocichla								
mustelina	967.995:45	105	80	50	6	6	1/2+	58
Hermit Thrush								
Catharus [Hylo-								
cichla] guttatus	978.995:47	101	85	70	6	6	3/5	71
Eastern Meadowlark								
Sturnella magna	986.885:44	240	112	60			1/3	58
Western Meadowlark								
Sturnella neglecta	985.995:45	300	140	50	12		1/5	43
Cardinal								
Pyrrhuloxia								
[Richmondena]								
cardinalis	977.884:43	220	100	20	6		1/2	74
Lark Sparrow								
Chondestes								
grammacus	788.785:43	170	60	15	3		9/10	92
Bachman's Sparrow								
Aimophila aestivalis	877.995:45	171	112	6			1/2	68
Song Sparrow								
Melospiza melodia	885.895:43	230	120	50	12		1/3−	54

Country and Species	Rating	S	F	L	N	W	Cf	ES
Mexico								
Slate-colored Solitaire								
Myadestes unicolor	987.995:47	280	150				3/5	112
Brown-backed								
Solitaire								
Myadestes obscurus	888.784:43	280	140				2/3	124
Costa Rica								
Blue-black Grosbeak								
Cyanocompsa								
cyanoides	867.994:43	212	140				2/5	66
Japan								
Bush Warbler								
Cettia diphone	977.885:44	135	100	60		15?	1/2	68
New Zealand								
Robin								
Petroica australis	978.884:44	275	105				3/5	93
Kenya								
Rüppell's Robin-chat								
Cossypha semirufa	999.678:48	330	90				1	170
Snowy-headed								
Robin-chat								
Cossypha								
niveicapilla	899.768:47	170	70				1	103
West Africa								
Blue-shouldered								
Robin-chat								
Cossypha								
cyanocampter	699.867:45	120					4/5	112
South Africa								
Chorister Robin-chat								
Cossypha dichroa	999.757:46	270	110				9/10	135
India								
Magpie Robin, Dyal								
Copsychus saularis	866.995:43	300	160				1/3+	74
Averages		200	110	20	3.3		0.69	103

Middling Singers (14 spp.)

Britain								
Starling								
Sturnus vulgaris	479.317:31	336	275	−60	3		1	297 (?)
Yellow Bunting								
Emberiza citrinella	854.562:30	198	175	90			1/4	53

Country and Species	Rating	S	F	L	N	W	Cf	ES
Britain (continued)								
Chaffinch								
Fringilla coelebs	856.453:31	222	144	40			1/3	61
Chiffchaff								
Phylloscopus collybita	847.442:29	178	117	85		9	3/5	101
Wood Warbler								
Phylloscopus sibilatrix	764.563:31	94	71	55		15	1/3	34
Ring Ouzel								
Turdus torquatus	654.664:31	88	82	40	3?		1/4	24
Redstart								
Phoenicurus phoenicurus	654.744:30	126	78	48	3?		1/4	28
United States								
House Wren								
Troglodytes aedon	756.553:31	104	72	60		12	1/3+	45
Short-billed Marsh Wren								
Cistothorus platensis	676.362:30	95	70	50	20		1/3+	48
Swainson's Warbler								
Limnothlypis swainsonii	943.672:31	154	74	20		6?	1/4−	24
Canada Warbler								
Wilsonia canadensis	855.542:29	70	55	55		6	1/4	21
Yellowthroat								
Geothlypis trichas	843.662:29	84	60	60	3?	6	1/5	18
Scarlet Tanager								
Piranga olivacea	955.452:30	76	50	50			1/4	19
Tufted Titmouse								
Parus bicolor	856.552:31	270	75	−25			1/3	45
Averages		150	101	41	2		0.43	58

Very Poor Singers (32 spp.)

Country and Species	Rating	S	F	L	N	W	Cf	ES
Britain								
Grasshopper Warbler								
Locustella naevia	624.221:17	125	0	1	24?		2/3?	33
Hawfinch								
Coccothraustes coccothraustes	623.321:17	93	76?				1/4?	22
Reed Bunting								
Emberiza schoeniclus	723.121:16	183	122				1/4	36

Country and Species	Rating	S	F	L	N	W	Cf	ES
Britain (continued)								
Grey Wagtail								
Motacilla cinerea	323.241:15	146	0				1/9	5
Tree Creeper								
Certhia familiaris	631.331:17	230	123	10			1/11	18
Marsh Tit								
Parus palustris	832.211:17	154	85				1/4	27
Goldcrest								
Regulus regulus	433.231:16	261	131				1/4+	48
North America								
Cactus Wren								
Campylorhynchus brunneicapillus	426.221:17	365	307				1/5+	30
Worm-eating Warbler								
Helmitheros vermivorus	233.121:12	67	50?	50		6	1/5−	13
Golden-winged Warbler								
Vermivora chrysoptera	332.221:13	67	50?	50		6	1/5	15
Blue-winged Warbler								
Vermivora pinus	342.132:15	80	60	60		6	1/7	13
Parula Warbler								
Parula americana	423.332:17	76	55	55		6	1/5−	14
Cape May Warbler								
Dendroica tigrina	243.123:15	70	50	50		6	1/4−	15
Blackburnian Warbler								
Dendroica fusca	522.221:14	62	45	45		6	1/5−	12
Bay-breasted Warbler								
Dendroica castanea	531.321:15	62	46	46		6	1/10	7
Blackpoll Warbler								
Dendroica striata	411.221:11	65	45	45		9?	1/6−	12
Palm Warbler								
Dendroica palmarum	332.221:13	67	50	50		6	1/7	12
Wilson's Warbler								
Wilsonia pusilla	622.321:16	67	50	50		6	1/5	17
Common Grackle								
Quiscalus quiscula	722.121:15	122	22	22		12	1/9	7
Bullock's Oriole								
Icterus bullockii	632.321:17	80	50	20			1/5?	16
Dickcissel								
Spiza americana	622.121:14	70	40	20		9	1/4	15
Abert's Towhee								
Pipilo aberti	433.321:16	70	40				1/5	10

Country and Species	Rating	S	F	L	N	W	Cf	ES
North America (continued)								
California Brown Towhee (subsp.) *Pipilo fuscus crissalis*	333.222:15	40	30				1/5	7
Spotted Towhee (subsp.) *Pipilo erythrophthalmus falcifer*	431.432:17	110	80	20			1/8	12
Grasshopper Sparrow *Ammodramus savannarum*	333.332:17	75	50	50	20?		1/5−	16
LeConte's Sparrow *Passerherbulus caudacutus*	412.221:12	75?	50	50			1/8	9
Henslow's Sparrow *Passerherbulus henslowii*	311.111:8	80	55	55	20?		1/15	6
Sharp-tailed Sparrow *Ammospiza caudacuta*	612.121:13	85	68	68			1/5	20
Clay-colored Sparrow *Spizella pallida*	534.131:17	90	70	70		18	1/5+	23
Rufous-crowned Sparrow *Aimophila ruficeps*	522.422:17	145	80	21			1/5	19
Costa Rica								
Hartlaub's Warbler *Vermivora superciliosa*	522.111:12	120	55				1/6?	13
Striped Brush Finch *Atlapetes torquatus*	446.111:17 +?	245	140?				1/4?	44
Averages		114	68	27	1.9		0.18	17

APPENDIX C

Some Staff Notations of Songs

(*transcribed by Frances Edwards*)

I. Slate-colored Solitaire. Each song is sung a few times in succession, with pauses of several seconds between reiterations. Some short songs are fragments of the longer songs—as in Cardinals and many other birds.

II. Heuglin's Robin-chat. Themes are not simply reiterated a number of times but are sung sharply crescendo, each reiteration usually louder than the previous one, so that the bird seems alternately far away and near. A repertoire has many themes, each sung crescendo. However, North and I found one bird that did not do this; probably the crescendo habit must be learned and some individuals fail to pick it up.

III. Rufous and White Wren. One of the most mellow-voiced, subtly musical of all small birds. To describe its voice as "owl-like" is odd, and has misled at least one knowledgeable ornithologist to fail to listen to the song as the superb animal music it is. Rather the voice is like a fairy bugle or clarinet. Note the theme and variations.

IV. Woodlark. This lark's oscillations are rather slower than normal trills. Its specialty is subtle modulations, as in the shift from the first to the second theme in the first song. The notations show but a fragment of the normal repertoire.

V. Banded Wren. Like IV and VI, this bird uses oscillatory trills more than mere reiterations (see notation for III). It strings the trills together with melodic transitions in a sweet voice. Anyone not charmed by this song must be unusual.

VI. Ryukyu Robin. This is one of the most musical complex songs. The bird is found only in a few subtropical isles, including Okinawa. Hence its future is problematic. Its song is less loud ("weaker") than the Japanese Robin to the north, but it has more scope. The recording is from a caged individual.

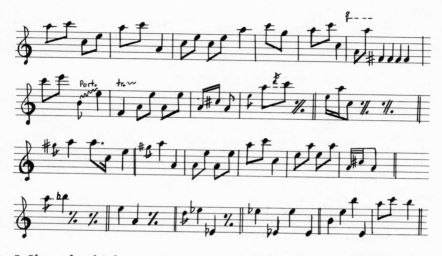

I. *Slate-colored Solitaire* (Mexico). *Recording by L. Irby Davis.* (See Chapters 3A; 10B, no. 95.)

II. *Heuglin's Robin-chat* (East Africa). *Recording by M. E. W. North.* (See Chapters 3A; 10B, no. 76.)

III. *Rufous and White Wren (Central America). Cornell Laboratory record-ing. (See Chapters 3A; 10B, no. 48.)*

IV. *Woodlark (Europe). Recorder not known. (See Chapters 5A; 10B, no. 10.)*

V. Banded Wren (Mexico). Recording by L. Irby Davis. (See Chapter 10B, no. 46.)

VI. *Ryukyu Robin (Islands south of Kyushu). Recording by K. Hoshino.*
(*See Chapter 10B, no. 75.*)

VIIA. *Western Meadowlark* (*Western North America*). *Recorder not known.* (*See Chapters 3C; 10B, no. 182.*)

VII. Western Meadowlark. These are gay, thrilling songs, with only a few hints of the plaintiveness of most songs of the Eastern Meadowlark. Some observers count a dozen or so songs in a repertoire, but Arlton found four times that number. Most people greatly prefer the Western to the Eastern species, yet both have songs that are highly musical and complex. The difference between the two ways of singing can be exaggerated. Both are of type 3 (Chapter 5C), i.e., "repertoire of repeated patterns," and therefore somewhat discontinuous, thanks to monotony avoidance (Chapter 7). The Western species puts more notes into each pattern but with its faster pace uses a similar amount of time. Both have good tones, the Western with a lower pitch limit.

All seven species have highly developed songs. Not one has become a literary or poetic celebrity. The Woodlark escaped this, I suppose, chiefly because it is much rarer than the Skylark. Its complexity is also subtler. It is not, like the more famous bird, a medleyist, and has a far higher standard of musical precision and excellence. Its more leisurely performance does not give a comparable impression of almost supernatural exuberance and tirelessness. But as musician the Woodlark, and not the Skylark, deserves the fame. The Skylark, as has been said, gives "more quantity than quality." Yet both species are among the wonders of nature, only some of which have much international and interlinguistic fame.

VIIB. *Western Meadowlark. Notations by Alexander Arlton. 49 Songs Sung by One Individual Bird in Mitchell, South Dakota.*

APPENDIX D

Some Spectrograms

I., II., and III., forms of the Nightingale Wren song (see Chapters 7C; 10B, no. 52), show that with a radical decrease in continuity (from essentially continuous to essentially discontinuous) comes a radical decrease in immediate variety (from an unusually large number of definite pitch changes to virtually none). In I. there are seven sounds (but only a small part of the song) lasting 2½ seconds, with a marked pitch change each time. The wide band version (a) is more accurate in the temporal dimension; the narrow band (b) is more accurate in pitch definition. In II. there are barely three sounds in 2½ seconds, and only slight pitch changes. In III. there is one sound and only part (less than half) of the preceding pause, and no appreciable change of pitch in the entire song. These three songs illustrate dramatically the correlation of versatility and continuity, or repetitiveness and discontinuity.

IV. represents one song of the repertoire of a Mountain Tailorbird (see Chapters 5D; 10B, no. 142). It shows the inaccuracy of the word "trill," which is sometimes used to describe this bird's song. There is neither a true trill, a rapid oscillation between two figures, nor (in this and in most of the songs) a rapid reiteration of one figure. Rather, the first brief sound (barely audible at normal speed) is reiterated in a somewhat prolonged version, then again in a much longer one with a slight break a third of the way through; then there is a higher and longer note, and finally a marked drop in pitch to a sound quickly reiterated in a shortened version. There are six or seven sounds in this song and no mere reiteration or oscillation, since pitch or timing, sometimes both, keep changing. The song (one of the shorter ones in the repertoire) takes about 1⅛ seconds, and the rate is 8–14 songs per minute. Just in itself a single song is not very much, but it is not to be taken simply in itself, for it is usually followed quickly by one of a number of contrasting songs. By some criteria this is immediately versatile, fairly continuous singing of a high order. The tones are flute-like, as one can demonstrate best by playing the recording at slow speed.

Spectrograms I–IV were made at the Balcones Research Center in Austin, Texas, by L. I. Davis and R. K. Selander.

V. Looked at casually, the Chipping Sparrow figures of spectrogram (a) seem vertical in the central portion, but actually they move a little to the right as they descend. Thus they record slurs, not noises. By contrast the "clicks" in spectrograms (e)–(g) are truly vertical and represent mere noises. In spectrograms (b)–(d) the pace is slowed and it becomes perfectly obvious that the figures consist of tones, not noises. Yet, we hear the sounds as noisy. And the bird? The argument is strong that the bird hears tones. To this extent our judgment of songs on the basis of the "harshness" or noisiness of the sounds may be subjective. So far as I can see, however, this has only a mild effect on our relative judgment of songs. Thus in Davis's account of the species of *Spizella*, the songs that have always seemed the poorest, those of the Chipping and Clay-colored Sparrows (*S. passerina* and *S. pallida*), still seem the poorest. The net result is to strengthen the argument for viewing bird song as pervasively musical, perhaps without effecting much change in our relative judgments between birds.

(a)

(b)

I. *Nightingale Wren. Recording by Ben B. Coffey, Jr., and E. P. Edwards in Mexico. Wide band above, narrow band below.*

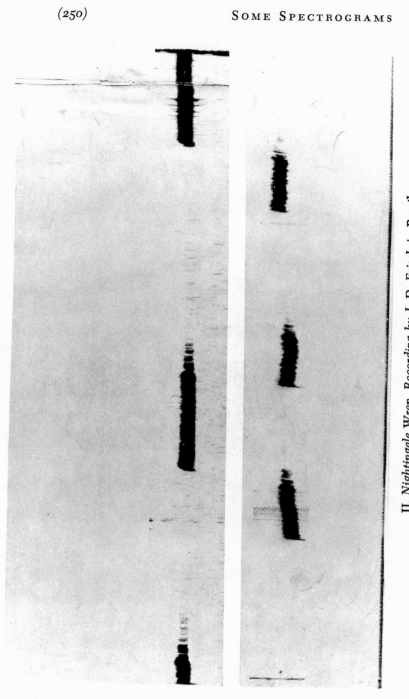

II. *Nightingale Wren. Recording by J. D. Frisch in Brazil.*

III. *Nightingale Wren. Recording by Hartshorne on Alexander F. Skutch's estate in Costa Rica.*

IV. *Mountain Tailorbird. Recording by Hartshorne in Malaya.*

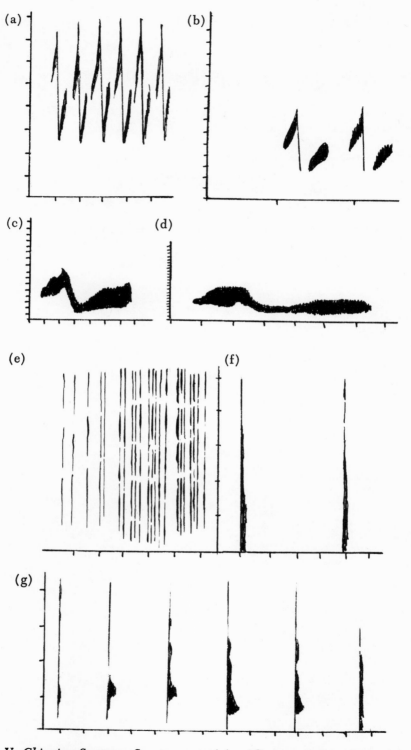

V. *Chipping Sparrow. Spectrograms* (a)—(d) *from Davis 1964b,* (e)—
(g) *from Davis 1964a.*

Glossary

aesthetic: Having to do with experienced or felt harmonies, discords, contrasts, cases of unity in variety (see *beauty*).

amount of singing: Number of hours of singing annually, not counting pauses between songs; or, the number of songs sung annually multiplied by the average length of the songs.

beauty: The enjoyed mean between monotony and chaos, mere order and mere disorder; also between trivial simplicity and baffling complexity —in both cases relative to the organism's capacity for assimilating order and complexity.

calls: Utterances other than *song*, but including *chatter*.

chatter: Partly imitative, usually unmusical, often not loud utterances identifying mates (or flock members) to each other, rather than advertising *territory* (where territory is involved, chatter tends to be louder and more musical and thus to lose its distinctiveness from *song*).

continuity: Relative shortness of pauses (intervals between songs) compared to the length of the songs (to be distinguished from *persistence*).

counter-singing: Said of rival males singing alternately from their respective territories.

cries: "Prewired" or unlearned utterances (e.g., alarm notes or scolds), in general simple and unmusical and not used to declare territory or sex (see *calls*). (Presumably, cries are the oldest forms of bird utterance, of which songs and chatter are evolutionary transformations.)

dimorphic: With conspicuous shape, size, or plumage differences between the sexes.

dual singing: Singing exhibited by two birds, usually mates, who cooperate in singing, whether singing simultaneously (duets) or antiphonally (one bird singing part of the song and the other the remainder).

ecological: Having to do with the interactions of diverse types of organisms occupying an area.

ethology: Study of behavior.

eventual variety: Said of a species with a repertoire of songs each in turn sung over and over, thus A,A,A, . . . , B,B,B, . . . , C,C,C (see *immediate variety*).

feeling: The generic term for sensation and emotion, including pleasure, pain, joy, distress, etc.

figure: A single continuous sound.

good singer: Bird with highly developed singing skill, as measured by degree of loudness, scope or complexity of patterns, continuity, tone, unity or *Gestalt* closure, and imitativeness.

gregarious: Opposite of *territorial*.

highly developed song: See *good singer*.

immediate variety: Avoidance of direct repetition of songs, e.g., singing A,B,C,A, . . . , not A,A,A, ...

monotony-threshold: Inhibition (most apparent in *Oscines*) upon direct repetition of a song until sufficient time (usually at least several seconds) has elapsed for intervening activities or experiences to give the next occurrence of the song the value of novelty. (There may be some analogy to, or even connection with, the refractory period in nerve action.)

musical: With certain acoustical characteristics including pitch definiteness or tonality, melody, rhythm, etc.; or, acting as if sensitive to such characteristics.

noise: Sound without definite organization of frequencies.

note: Sound on a single pitch (*figures* are either notes or slurs).

Oscines: See *Songbirds*.

pattern: A super*phrase*, one of the longer definite units of song which a bird repeats otherwise than by accident. (Patterns are either less than 20 seconds long or they are only approximately definite.)

pauses: Silent portions of a *performance*, measured in seconds, not minutes or fractions of a second (in the latter case silences are musical "rests").

perching birds: The order Passeriformes, containing more than half of all species and endowed with a special toe formation facilitating the grasping of small twigs and the like.

performance: A series of songs separated by *pauses* of less, usually much less, than a minute. Longer silences are periods of no singing, between, not within, performances.

persistence: Duration and frequency of *performances* through a day or season. (To be distinguished from continuity, which is proportion of a normal performance actually occupied by singing, including only silences less than a second or two in duration.)

phrase: A group of *figures* (sounds) with some degree of musical unity, and hence a natural subdivision of a song or pattern.

pitch: Nearly the same as frequency, different only because the impression of pitch depends somewhat upon intensity as well as upon frequency.

primitive birds: Those with simple *syrinxes* or none.

repertoire: Set of definite song *patterns,* each of which a bird sings many times during a performance, or at least during a day or two of *persistent* singing.

sequence: A more or less random succession of *phrases* or *patterns* (lasting, in some cases, many minutes).

singing birds: Species that actually do sing (see *Songbirds*).

song: Either a single *pattern* or a *repertoire*. All song, at least in the developed cases, is partly learned, if not by imitation, then by practice. It tends to be more musical than *cries* or *chatter,* and may be of various types, e.g., (a) primary or *territorial,* addressed to listeners at a distance; (b) courtship: may be soft (largely neglected in this book); (c) subsong: with less than normal volume, often fragmentary (largely neglected in this book); (d) whisper song: very faint (largely neglected in this book); (e) still other forms of more or less musical utterances not functioning territorially (largely neglected in this book).

Songbirds: In this book the suborder of perching birds (Passeriformes) called *Oscines,* set apart from other birds by much more elaborate muscular arrangements controlling voice production in the *syrinx.* (Some authors, including Austin, speak of perching birds in general as songbirds. The term is never restricted to species that actually sing.)

Suboscines: Those groups of *perching birds* that lack the highly developed syrinxes of *Songbirds* or *Oscines.*

syrinx: Vocalizing organ peculiar to birds (lacking in a few primitive species), forming the base of the windpipe, and most highly developed in the *Songbirds.*

territorial: Given to territorial defense and, in the most-developed cases, to habitual spatial separation, even of mates, still more of non-mates in the same or (sometimes) closely related species.

territory: "Any defended area," but in this book used only where the area is substantial; small nesting territories, as in many sea birds, are not considered.

tone: A sound sensation having a definite *pitch* (opposite of *noise*).

versatile: Said of a species of which each normal individual male has a variety of patterns or songs, a *repertoire.*

References

I. Books and Articles†

Agar, W. E. 1951. *A Contribution to the Theory of the Living Organism.* 2d ed. Carlton, Vic.: Melbourne University Press.

Alexander, R. D. 1957a. Sound production and associated behavior in insects. *Ohio J. Sci.* 57(2): 101–13.

————. 1957b. The song relationships of four species of ground crickets. Ibid. (3): 153–63.

————. 1960. Sound communication in Orthoptera and Cicadidae. In *Animal Sounds and Communication,* W. E. Lanyon and W. N. Tavolga, eds. Washington, D.C.: American Institute of Biological Sciences.

Ali, S. 1949. *Indian Hill Birds.* London: Oxford University Press.

————. 1962. *The Birds of Sikkim.* London: Oxford University Press.

————. 1964. *The Book of Indian Birds.* Bombay: Bombay Natural History Society.

Allport, F. H. 1955. *Theories of Perception and the Concept of Structure.* New York: Wiley.

Alpers, A. 1961. *Dolphins, the Myth and the Mammals.* Boston: Houghton Mifflin.

Altum, B. 1868. *Der Vogel und sein Leben.* Münster: Wilhelm Niemann.

Ames, P. L. 1971. The morphology of the syrinx in passerine birds. New Haven, Conn.: Peabody Museum of Natural History, Bull. 37.

Andrew, R. J. 1961. The displays given by passerines in courtship and reproductive fighting: a review. *Ibis* 103a: 315–48, 549–79.

Ansley, H. 1954. Do birds hear their songs as we do? *Proc. Linn. Soc. of New York* 63/65: 39–40.

Archer, G. F., and E. M. Godman. 1961. *Birds of British Somaliland and the Gulf of Aden.* Edinburgh: Oliver and Boyd.

Ardrey, R. 1966. *The Territorial Imperative.* New York: Atheneum.

Arlton, A. V. 1949. *Songs and Other Sounds of Birds.* Lithographed for Alexander V. Arlton of Parkland, Washington by Elkland Printing Co., Hoquiam, Wash.

† Including a few items which were consulted, but not referred to in the text.

Armstrong, E. A. 1955. *The Wren.* London: Collins.

———. 1963. *A Study of Bird Song.* London: Oxford University Press.

———. 1965. *Bird Display and Behavior.* New York: Dover.

Austin, O. L., Jr. 1961. *Birds of the World.* New York: Golden Press.

———. 1967. *Songbirds of the World.* New York: Golden Press. ("Song-birds" here includes the Suboscine perching birds.)

Austin, O. L., Jr., and N. Kuroda. 1953. The birds of Japan: their status and distribution. *Bull. Mus. Compar. Zool.* vol. 109, no. 4. Cambridge, Mass.

Baerg, W. J. 1930. Song period of birds of northwest Arkansas. *Auk* 47: 32–40.

Baker, E. C. S. 1942. *Cuckoo Problems.* London: Witherby.

Ball, S. C. 1945. Dawn calls and songs of birds at New Haven. *Trans. Conn. Acad. of Arts and Sciences* 36: 851–77.

Bannerman, D. A. 1953. *The Birds of West and Equatorial Africa.* 2 vols. Edinburgh: Oliver and Boyd.

———. 1953–54. *The Birds of the British Isles,* vols. I, II, III. London: Oliver and Boyd.

Barlow, G. W. 1968. Ethological units of behavior. In *The Central Nervous System and Fish Behavior,* D. Ingle, ed. Chicago: The University of Chicago Press.

Beebe, W. 1926. *Pheasants: Their Lives and Homes.* 2 vols. New York: Doubleday, Page and Co.

Benchley, B. 1942. *My Friends the Apes.* Boston: Little, Brown and Co.

Bent, A. C. 1946–68. *Life Histories of North American Birds.* Reprinted from Bulletins of the United States National Museum. New York: Dover.

1946. *Jays, Crows, and Titmice.* 2 vols. Bull. 191.

1948. *Nuthatches, Wrens, Thrashers, and Their Allies.* Bull. 195.

1949. *Thrushes, Kinglets, and Their Allies.* Bull. 196.

1950. *Wagtails, Shrikes, Vireos, and Their Allies.* Bull. 197.

1953. *Wood Warblers.* 2 vols. Bull. 197.

1958. *Blackbirds, Orioles, Tanagers, and Their Allies.* Bull. 211.

1968. *Cardinals, Grosbeaks, Buntings, Towhees, Finches, Sparrows, and Their Allies,* 3 vols. Bull. 237.

Bertram, B. 1970. *The Vocal Behavior of the Indian Hill Myna* Gracula religiosa. Animal Behavior Monographs 3, Pt. 2. Bridgwater, Somerset: Bigwood and Staple, Ltd.

Blake, E. 1953. *Birds of Mexico.* Chicago: The University of Chicago Press.

Blanchard, B. 1941. The White-crowned Sparrow (*Zonotrichia leucophrys*) of the Pacific seaboard: environment and renewal cycle. *University of California Publications in Zoology,* vol. 46, no. 1: 1–175.

Bond, J. 1936, 1947. *Field Guide to Birds of the West Indies.* New York: The Macmillan Company.

Bondesen, P., and L. I. Davis. 1966. Sound analysis within biological acoustics. *Natura Jutlandica* 12: 235–39. Aarhus, Naturhistorik Museum.

Borror, D. J., and K. C. Halafoff. 1969. Notes on song structure in Townsend's Solitaire. *Wils. Bull.* 81: 163–68.

Borror, D. J., and C. R. Reese. 1953. The analysis of bird song by means of a vibralyser. *Wils. Bull.* 65: 271–76.

———. 1956. Vocal gymnastics in Wood Thrush songs. *Ohio J. of Sci.* 56: 177–82.

Boswall, J. 1961. A world catalogue of gramophone records of bird voices. *Bioacoustics Bull.* 1(2): 1–12.

———. 1964. A discography of Palearctic bird sound recordings. *Brit. Birds* 57, Special Supplement: 1–63.

Boudreau, G. W. 1968. Alarm sounds and responses of birds and their application in controlling problem species. *The Living Bird,* Seventh Annual, 27–46.

Boulenger, F. G. 1936. *Apes and Monkeys.* London: George Harrop.

Broughton, W. B. 1965a. Song learning in grasshoppers? *New Scientist* 27: 338–41.

———. 1965b. Grasshoppers can learn to mimic others' songs. *Science News Letter* 88: 137 (August 28).

Burgers, J. M. 1965. *Experience and Conceptual Activity: A Philosophy Based on the Writings of A. N. Whitehead.* Cambridge, Mass.: M.I.T. Press.

Calder, N. 1970. *The Mind of Man.* New York: Viking.

Capranica, R. R. 1968. Vocal Repertoire of Bullfrog (*Rana catesbeiana*). *Behavior* 31: 302–25.

Carpenter, C. R. 1934. A Field study of the behavior and social relationships of Howling Monkeys. *Comp. Psych. Monogr.* 10 (ser. no. 48): 1–129.

———. 1940. Behavior and social relations of the gibbon. *Comp. Psych. Monogr.* 16: 1–200.

———. 1964. *Naturalistic Behavior of Nonhuman Primates.* (Includes the above monographs.) University Park: Pennsylvania State University Press.

Chapin, J. P. 1953. Birds of the Belgian Congo. *Bull. Am. Mus. Nat. Hist.* 75A. New York.

Chapman, F. M. 1936. *Autobiography of a Bird Lover.* New York: Appleton-Century.

Cheney, S. P. 1891. *Wood Notes Wild.* Boston: Lee and Shepard.

Cheng, T., ed. 1964. *Economic Birds of China.* Washington, D.C.: U.S. Dept. of Commerce, Office of Technical Services, Joint Publications Research Service. Bldg. T-30, Ohio Dr. and Independence Ave.

Chisholm, A. H. 1929. *Birds and Green Places.* London: Dent; New York: Dutton.

———. 1932. Vocal mimicry among Australian birds. *Ibis* 2(13): 605–24.

———. 1935. *Bird Wonders of Australia.* Sydney: Angus and Robertson.

Clark, A. 1938. Morning song commencement. *Brit. Birds* 31: 265–66.

Colquhoun, M. K. 1940. Visual and auditory conspicuousness in a woodland community. *Proc. Zool. Soc. of London* 110 (Ser. A): 129–48.

Craig, W. 1908. The voices of pigeons regarded as means of social control. *Amer. J. of Sociol.* 14: 86–100.

———. 1909. The expression of emotion in the pigeons. I. The Blond Ring-dove (*Turtur risorius*). *J. Comp. Neurol.* 19: 29–80.

———. 1911a. II. The Mourning Dove (*Zenaida macroura*). *Auk*, N.S. 28: 398–407.

———. 1911b. III. The Passenger Pigeon (*Ectopistes migratoria*). *Ibid.*, 408–27.

———. 1918. Appetites and aversions as constituents of instincts. *Biol. Bull.* 34: 91–107.

———. 1943. The song of the Wood Pewee (*Myiochanes virens* Linnaeus): a study of bird music. *New York State Mus. Bull.* 334: 1–186.

Darling, F. 1952. Social behavior and survival. *Auk* 69: 183–91.

Davis, L. I. 1964a. Biological acoustics and the use of the sound spectrograph. *S. W. Naturalist*, 9(3): 118–45.

———. 1964b. Voice structure in *Spizella*. *S. W. Nat.* 9(4): 255–69.

———. 1972. *A Field Guide to the Birds of Mexico and Central America*. Austin and London: University of Texas Press.

Deignan, H. G. 1945. *The Birds of Northern Thailand*. Washington, D.C.: Smithsonian Institution.

Delacour, J. 1947. *The Birds of Malaysia*. New York: Macmillan.

Dementiev, G. P., and N. A. Gladkov. 1966. *Birds of the Soviet Union*. Published for the Smithsonian Institution by the Israeli Program for Scientific Translations.

Dickey, D. R., and A. J. van Rossem. 1938. *The Birds of El Salvador*. Chicago: Field Museum of Natural History.

Dixon, K. L. 1969. Patterns of singing in a population of the Plain Titmouse. *Condor* 71: 94–101.

Dobzhansky, Th. 1960. Evolution and environment. In *The Evolution of Life*, Sol Tax, ed. Chicago: The University of Chicago Press.

———. 1967. *The Biology of Ultimate Concern*. New York: New American Library.

Eccles, J. C., ed. 1966. *Brain and Conscious Experience*. New York: Springer-Verlag.

Eccles, J. C. 1970. *Facing Reality: Philosophical Adventures by a Brain Scientist*. New York: Springer-Verlag.

Eisenmann, E. 1955. The species of Middle American birds. *Trans. Linn. Soc. of New York*, vol. 7.

Evans, W. E. 1968. *Communication in the Animal World*. New York: Thomas Crowell and Company.

Fenis, F. de. 1921. *Les Langages des animaux et de l'homme considérés comme un fait biologique*. Hanoi: Imprimerie d'Extrême Orient.

Ficken, M. S. and R. W. 1962. Comparative ethology of the wood warblers. *The Living Bird* I: 102–21.

Finn, F. 1919. *Bird Behaviour.* London: Hutchinson.

Fisher, J., and R. T. Peterson. 1966. *The World of Birds.* New York: Doubleday and Co.

Fokker, A. D. 1955. Equal temperament and the thirty-one-keyed organ. *Sci. Monthly* 81: 161–66.

Forsythe, D. M. 1970. Vocalizations of the Long-billed Curlew. *Condor* 72: 213–24.

Friedman, H., and F. D. Smith. 1955. A contribution to the ornithology of Venezuela. *Proc. of the U.S. Nat. Mus.,* vol. 104, no. 3345.

Fuertes, L. A. 1913–14. Impressions of the voices of tropical birds. *Bird-Lore* 15: 341–44; 16: 1–6; (3) 1–9; (5) 1–8; (6) 1–6.

Gannon, G. R. 1953. Group nesting of the same species of passerine birds. *Emu* 53: 295–302.

Gardner, R. A. and B. T. 1969. Teaching sign language to a Chimpanzee. *Science* 165^1: 664–72 (August 15).

Garstang, W. 1923. *Songs of the Birds.* London: John Lane.

Gerard, R. W. 1940. Organism, science and society. *Sci. Monthly* 50: 340–50.

————. 1947. The scope of science. Ibid., 64: 500ff.

Géroudet, D. 1961. *Les Passereaux.* Neuchâtel and Paris: Delachau et Niesle.

Gomperz, T. 1961. The vocabulary of the Great Tit. *Brit. Birds* 54: 369–94, 409–18.

Greenewalt, C. H. 1960. *Hummingbirds.* New York: Doubleday and Co.

————. 1968. *Bird Song: Acoustics and Physiology.* Washington, D.C.: Smithsonian Institution.

Griscom, L., and A. Sprunt, Jr. 1957. *The Warblers of America.* New York: Devin-Adair.

Groos, K. 1901. *The Play of Animals.* New York: D. Appleton and Co.

Gwinner, E., and J. Kneutgen. 1962. Über die biologische Bedeutung der zweckdienlichen Anwendung erlernter Laute bei Vögeln. *Z. Tierpsychol.* 19: 692–96.

Haecker, V. 1900. *Der Gesang der Vögel.* Jena: G. Fischer.

Haldane, J. B. S. 1959. Natural selection. In *Darwin's Biological Work,* P. R. Bell, ed. Cambridge: Cambridge University Press.

Hall, H. M., and R. C. Clement. 1960. *A Gathering of Shore Birds.* New York: Devin-Adair.

Hall-Craggs, J. 1962. The development of song in the blackbird *Turdus merula. Ibis* 104: 277–99.

Hann, H. W. 1937. Life history of the Ovenbird in Southern Michigan. *Wils. Bull.* 49: 145–237.

Hardy, J. W. 1966. Physical and behavioral factors in sociality and evolution of certain parrots. *Auk* 83: 66–83.

Hartert, E. 1910–1923. *Die Paläarktische Fauna*. Berlin: R. Friedländer und Sohn.

Hartshorne, C. 1934. *The Philosophy and Psychology of Sensation*. Chicago: The University of Chicago Press.

————. 1968. Reissued. Port Washington, N.Y.: Kennikat Press, Inc.

————. 1942. Mind, matter, and freedom. *Scientific Monthly* 78: 314–20.

————. 1953. Musical values in Australian bird songs. *Emu* 43:109–28.

————. 1956a. The monotony-threshold in singing birds. *Auk* 83: 176–192.

————. 1956b. The phenomenon of bird song. *Emory University Quarterly* 12: 139–47.

————. 1958a. Some biological principles applicable to song-behavior. *Wils. Bull.* 70: 45–56.

————. 1958b. The relation of bird song to music. *Ibis* 100: 421–45.

————. 1961. Sketch of a theory of imitative singing. *The Oriole* 26: 23–27.

————. 1967. Psychology and the unity of knowledge. *Southern Journal of Philosophy* 5: 81–90.

————. 1970. *Creative Synthesis*. London: SCM Press; LaSalle, Ill.: Open Court.

Hassman, M. 1952. Vom Erlernen unbenannten Anzahlen bei Eichörnchen. *Z. Tierpsychol.* 9: 294–321.

Hazen, H. 1928. Nocturnal song of migrants. *Auk,* 45: 230.

Heckenlively, D. B. 1970. Song in a population of Black-throated Sparrows. *Condor* 72: 24–36.

Herzog, G. 1941. Do animals have music? *Bull. Amer. Musicological Soc.* 5: 3–4.

Hinde, R. A. 1958. Alternative motor patterns in Chaffinch song. *An. Beh.* 6: 211–18.

————. 1966. *Animal Behavior: A Synthesis of Ethology and Comparative Psychology*. New York: McGraw-Hill.

Hinde, R. A., ed. 1969. *Bird Vocalizations: Their Relation to Current Problems in Biology and Psychology*. Cambridge: Cambridge University Press.

Hjorth, I. 1970. A comment on graphic displays of bird sounds and analyses with a new device, the Melograph Mona. *J. Theoret. Biol.* 26: 1–10.

Hoffman, B. 1908. *Kunst und Vogelgesang*. Leipzig: Quelle und Meyer.

Hoffman, R. 1927. *Birds of the Pacific States*. Boston and New York: Houghton Mifflin.

Hold, T. 1970. The notation of bird-song: a review and recommendation. *Ibis* 112: 151–72.

Howard, E. 1920. *Territory in Bird Life*. London: John Murray.

————. 1935. *The Nature of a Bird's World*. Cambridge: Cambridge University Press.

————. 1968. *Territory in Bird Life*, with Foreword by James Fisher and Julian Huxley. New York: Atheneum.

Howard, L. 1953. *Birds as Individuals*. New York: Doubleday.

Hudson, W. H. 1920. *Birds of La Plata.* 2 vols. London: Dent and Sons.

Huxley, J. 1964. *Animal Language.* New York: Grosset and Dunlap.

Immelmann, K. 1969. Song development in the Zebra Finch and other estrilid finches. In *Bird Vocalizations: Their Relation to Current Problems in Biology and Psychology,* R. A. Hinde, ed. Cambridge: Cambridge University Press.

Ingraham, S. E. 1938. Instinctive music. *Auk* 55: 614–28.

Jackson, F. J., and W. L. Sclater. 1938. *The Birds of Kenya and Uganda.* 3 vols. London: Gurney and Jacks.

Jacobsen, C. F., M. M. Jacobsen, and J. G. Yoshioka. 1932. Development of an infant Chimpanzee during her first year. *Comp. Psychol. Monogr.* 9(1): 1–92.

Jaeger, E. C. 1951. Pebble-dropping by House Sparrows. *Condor* 53:207.

Jordan, R. 1951. *The New Perspective.* Chicago: The University of Chicago Press.

Kawamura, T. 1948. *Tori no Uta no Kagaku.* Kyoto: Usui Shobo.

Kellogg, W. N. 1961. *Porpoises and Sonar.* Chicago: The University of Chicago Press.

Kendeigh, S. C. 1945. Nesting of wood warblers. *Wils. Bull.* 57: 145–64.

Kilham, L. 1959. Mutual tapping of the Red-headed Woodpecker. *Auk* 76: 235–36.

Kleinenberg, S. E., et al. 1969. *Beluga (Delphinapterus leucas).* Translated for the Smithsonian Institution and the National Science Foundation by the Israeli Research Translation Service.

Knecht, S. 1940. Über den Gehörsinn u. die Musikalität der Vögel. *Z. vergl. Physiol.* 27: 171–232.

Koehler, O. 1951. Der Vogelgesang als Vorstufe der Musik. *J. Ornithol.* 93: 3–20.

―――. 1953. Tierpsychologische Versuche zur Frage des "unbenannten Denkens." *Vjschr. Naturf. Ges. Zürich.* 98: 242–51.

―――. 1954. Vorbedingungen u. Vorstufen unserer Sprache bei Tieren. *Verh. Deut. Zool. Ges.* 48: 327–41.

Koerner, S., ed. 1957. *Observations and Interpretations.* London: Butterworth's Scientific Publications.

Konishi, M. 1963. The role of auditory feedback in the vocal behavior of the domestic fowl. *Z. Tierpsychol.* 20: 349–67.

Lack, D. 1968. *Ecological Adaptation for Breeding in Birds.* London: Methuen.

Langer, S. 1957. *Philosophy in a New Key: A Study in the Symbolism of Reason, Rite, and Art.* 3d ed. Cambridge: Harvard University Press.

Lanyon, W. E. 1957. *The Comparative Biology of the Meadowlarks (Sturnella) in Wisconsin.* Cambridge, Mass.: Nuttall Ornithological Club.

―――. 1960. The ontogeny of vocalizations in birds. In *Animal Sounds and Communication*. W. E. Lanyon and W. N. Tavolga, eds. Washington, D.C.: American Institute of Biological Sciences.

Laskey, A. R. 1936. Fall and winter behavior of Mockingbirds. *Wils. Bull.* 48: 241–45.

Lemon, R. E. 1965. Song repertoires of Cardinals. *Canadian J. of Zool.* 43: 559–69.

———. 1968. Coordinated singing by Black-crested Titmice. Ibid. 46: 1163–67.

———. 1969. The Relation between organization and function of song. *Behaviour* 32: 158–78.

Lemon, R. E., and A. Herzog. 1969. The vocal behavior of Cardinals and Pyrrhuloxias in Texas. *Condor* 71: 1–15.

Leopold, A. S. 1959. *Wildlife of Mexico: the Game Birds and Mammals*. Berkeley: University of California.

Lewis, E. S. 1940. The 'Sambar' call of the tiger and its explanation. *J. Bombay Nat. Hist. Soc.* 41: 889–90.

Lilly, J. C. 1962. *Man and Dolphin*. London: Gollancz.

Linsdale, J. M. 1938a. Bird life in Nevada with reference to modifications in structure and behavior. *Condor* 40: 173–80.

———. 1938b. Environmental responses of vertebrates in the Great Basin. *Amer. Midl. Nat.* 19: 1–206.

Lögler, P. 1959. Versuche zur Frage der "Zahl"-vermögens an einem Grau Papagei. *Z. Tierpsychol.* 16: 179–217.

Lorenz, K. 1943. Die angeborenen Formen möglicher Erfahrung. *Z. Tierpsychol.* 5: 235–409.

———. 1966. *On Aggression*. M. Latzke, tr. London: Methuen.

McCann, C. 1931. Notes on the Whistling Schoolboy or Malabar Whistling Thrush. *Bombay Nat. Hist. Soc.* 35: 202–204.

Manniche, A. L. V. 1912. Terrestrial mammals and birds of north-east Greenland. In *Meddelelser om Grønland*. Copenhagen.

Margenau, H. 1950. *The Nature of Physical Reality*. New York: McGraw-Hill.

Marler, P. 1955. Characteristics of some animal calls. *Nature* 176: 6–7.

———. 1959. Developments in the study of animal communication. In *Darwin's Biological Work: Some Aspects Reconsidered*, P. R. Bell, ed. Cambridge: Cambridge University Press.

———. 1960. Bird songs and mate selection. In *Animal Sounds and Communication*, W. E. Lanyon and W. N. Tavolga, eds. Washington, D.C.: American Institute of Biological Sciences.

———. 1961. The logical analysis of animal communication. *J. Theoret. Biol.* 1: 295–317.

Marler, P., and D. Isaac. 1960. Song variation in a population of Brown Towhees. *Condor* 62: 272–83.

———. 1961. Song variation in a population of Mexican Juncos. *Wils. Bull.* 73, no. 2: 193–206.

————. 1963. Ordering of sequences of singing behavior of Mistle Thrushes in relation to timing. *Anim. Beh.* 11: 179–88.

Marler, P., and M. Tamura. 1962. Song "dialects" in three populations of White-crowned Sparrows. *Condor* 64: 368–77.

Marler, P., M. Kreith, and M. Tamura. 1962. Song development in hand-raised juncos. *Auk* 79: 12–30.

Marshall, A. J. 1954. *Bower Birds.* London: Oxford University Press.

Mathews, F. S. 1921. *Field Book of Wild Birds and Their Music.* New York: G. P. Putnam's Sons.

Matthiessen, P., and R. S. Palmer. 1967. *The Shorebirds of North America.* New York: Viking.

Mayfield, G. R. 1940–41. August the silent month for bird songs. *The Migrant* 11: 62–65.

Mayfield, H. 1966. Hearing loss and bird song. *The Living Bird* 5: 174.

Mayr, E. 1945. *Birds of the Southwest Pacific.* New York: The Macmillan Co.

Mead, G. H. 1909. Social psychology as counterpart to physiological psychology. *Psychol. Bull.* VI: 401–408.

————. 1964. *Selected Writings.* A. Reck, ed. Indianapolis and New York: Bobbs-Merrill Co.

Messmer, E. and I. 1956. Die Entwicklung der Lautäusserungen u. einiger Verhaltensweisen der Amsel. *Z. Tierpsychol.* 13: 341–441.

Meyer, L. B. 1956. *Emotion and Meaning in Music.* Chicago: The University of Chicago Press.

Meyer de Schauensee, R. 1966. *The Species of Birds of South America with Their Distribution.* Narberth, Pa.: Livingston Publishing Co.

Meyer-Holzapfel, M. 1950. Verhalten einer Gibbonfamilie. *Zoolog. Garten* (NF) 17: 10–27.

————. 1956. Über die Bereitschaft zu Spiel-u. Instincthandlung. *Z. Tierpsychol.,* 13: 442–62.

Mills, E. A. 1931. *Bird Memories of the Rockies.* Boston: Houghton Mifflin.

Mitchell, M. H. 1957. *Observations on the Birds of Southeastern Brazil.* Toronto: University of Toronto Press; London: Oxford University Press.

Morris, S. 1925. *Bird-Song: A Manual for Field Naturalists on the Notes and Songs of some British Birds.* London: Witherby.

Mott, F. 1924. A study by serial sections of the larynx of *Hylobates syndactylus* (siamang gibbon). *Proc. Zool. Soc. of London* 1161–70.

Mowrer, O. H. 1952. Speech development in the young child. *J. Speech and Hearing Disorders* 17: 263–68.

Mulligan, J. A. 1963. A description of Song Sparrow song based on instrumental analysis. *Proc. XIII Intern. Ornith. Congress:* 272–84.

————. 1966. Singing behavior and its development in the Song Sparrow, *Melospiza melodia. Univ. of Calif. Publ. in Zool.* 81: 1–75.

Mundinger, P. C. 1970. Vocal imitation and individual recognition in finch calls. *Science* 168: 480–82.

Munn, A. M. 1960. *Free Will and Determinism*. Toronto: University of Toronto Press.

Nice, M. M. 1931. Two nests of the Ovenbird. *Auk* 48: 215–28.

———. 1943, 1964. Studies in the life history of the Song Sparrow II. *Trans. Linn. Soc. of New York* 6: vii–328.

———. 1945. How many times does a Song Sparrow sing one song? *Auk* 62: 302.

Nice, M. M. and L. B. 1931. *The Birds of Oklahoma*. Norman: University of Oklahoma Press.

———. 1932. Two nests of the Black-throated Green Warbler. *Bird Banding* 3: 157–71.

Nichols, E. G. 1937. Birds of the Kodaikanal and how to name them. *J. Bombay Nat. Hist. Soc.* 39: 817.

Nicholson, E. M. 1929. *How Birds Live*. London: Williams and Norgate.

Nicholson, E. M., and L. Koch. 1936. *Songs of Wild Birds*. London: Witherby.

———. 1937. *More Songs of Wild Birds*. London: Witherby.

North, M. E. W. 1950. Transcribing Bird-song. *Ibis* 92: 99–114.

North, M. E. W., and E. Sims. 1958. *Witherby's Sound Guide to British Birds*. London: Witherby.

Nottebohm, F. 1970. Ontogeny of bird song. *Science* 167: 950–56 (February).

Nottebohm, F. and M. 1969. The Parrots of Bush Bush. *Animal Kingdom* 11: 19–23 (February).

Ogburn, C. 1953. The meaning of birds. *Atlantic Naturalist*. Reprinted in *The Bird Watcher's Anthology*, R. T. Peterson, ed. New York: Harcourt Brace and Co., 1957.

Ogden, C. K., I. A. Richards, and J. Wood. 1925. *Foundations of Aesthetics*. New York: International Publishers.

Oring, L. W. 1968. Vocalizations of the Green and Solitary Sandpipers. *Wils. Bull.* 80(4): 395–420.

Payne, R. B., and N. J. Skinner, 1969. Temporal patterns of duetting in African barbets. *Ibis* 112: 173–83.

Payne, R. S., and F. Watlington. 1970. *Songs of the Humpback Whale*. (With record.) Del Mar, Cal.: CRM Records.

Payne, R. S., and S. McVay. 1971. Songs of the Humpback Whale. *Science* 173 (3997): 585–97.

Peirce, G. W. 1949. *The Songs of Insects*, pp. 128f. Cambridge: Harvard University Press.

Pepper, S. C. 1937. *Aesthetic Quality*. New York: Scribner's.

———. 1970. Autobiography of an aesthetics. *J. of Aesthetics and Art Criticism*, 28: 275–86, esp. 277–78.

Perry, R. 1964. *The World of the Tiger*, London: Cassell.

Peters, E. H. 1966. *The Creative Advance*. St. Louis: Bethany Press.

————. 1970. *Hartshorne and Neoclassical Metaphysics: An Interpretation.* Lincoln: University of Nebraska Press.

Peters, J. L. 1931–70. *Check-list of Birds of the World.* Cambridge: Harvard University Press.

Piaget, J. 1970. *Structuralism.* Trans. by C. Maschler. New York: Basic Books.

Pollard, W. G. 1958. *Chance and Providence.* New York: Scribner's.

Popper, K. 1965. *Of Clouds and Clocks: An Approach to the Problem of Rationality and the Freedom of Man.* St. Louis: Washington University Press.

Potter, P. E. 1972. Territorial behavior in Savannah Sparrows in southeastern Michigan. *The Wilson Bulletin* 84: 48–59.

Power, D. 1966. Antiphonal duetting and evidence for auditory reaction time in the Orange-Chinned Parakeet (*Brotogeris jugularis*). *Auk* 83: 314–19.

Premack, D. 1970a. A functional analysis of language. *J. of the Experimental Analysis of Behavior.* 14: 107–27.

————. 1970b. The education of S°A°R°A°H. *Psychology Today* 4(4): 54ff.

Quaintance, C. W. 1938. Content, meaning and possible origin of male song in the Brown Towhee. *Condor* 40: 97–101.

Rand, A. L. 1967. *Ornithology, an Introduction.* New York: Norton.

Rand, A. L. and R. M. 1943. Breeding notes on the Phainopepla. *Auk* 60: 333–41.

Redfield, J. 1935. *Music: A Science and an Art.* New York: Tudor.

Reinert, J., and W. Reinert-Reetz. 1962. Das Erkennen erlernter Tonfolgen in abgewandelter Form durch einen Wellensittich. *Z. vergl. Physiol.* 19: 728–40.

Rensch, B. 1954. Increase of learning capacity with increase of brain-size. *Amer. Naturalist* 90: 81–95.

————. 1970. *Biophilosophie auf erkenntnisstheoretischer Grundlage (Panpsychistischer Identismus).* Stuttgart: Gustav Fischer.

Rescher, N. 1970. *Scientific Explanation.* New York: Free Press.

Reynard, G. B. 1963. The cadence of bird song. *The Living Bird* 2: 139–48.

Reynolds, V. 1967. *Apes: Gorilla, Chimpanzee, Orangutan and Gibbon. Their History and Their Ways.* New York: E. P. Dutton.

Ripley, S. D. 1952. The Thrushes. *Postilla Yale Peabody Museum*, no. 12.

Robbins, C. S., B. Bruun, and H. S. Zim. 1966. *Birds of North America.* New York: Golden Press.

Roberts, A. 1957. *Birds of South Africa.* Rev. by McLachlan and Liversidge. Capetown: Cape Times, Ltd.

Robinson, A. 1949. The biological significance of bird song in Australia. *Emu* 48: 291–315.

————. 1956. The annual reproductive cycle of the Magpie, *Gymnorhina dorsalis* Campbell, in southwestern Australia. *Emu* 56: 233–336.

Rollin, N. 1943a. Skylark song. *Brit. Birds* 36: 146–50.

———. 1943b. Output of Skylark and Willow Warbler. *Brit. Birds* 37: 85–87.

———. 1945. Song Thrush song. *Brit. Birds,* 38: 262–70; 51: 290–303.

Sachs, C. 1953. *Rhythm and Tempo.* New York: Dent.

Sanderson, I. 1957. *The Monkey Kingdom.* New York: Doubleday and Co.

Sauer, F. 1954. Die Entwicklung d. Lautausserungen v. Ei ab Schalldicht gehalten Dorngrasmücken (*Sylvia communis* Latham). *Z. Tierpsychol.* 11: 10–93.

———. 1955. Über Variationen der Artgesänge bei Grasmücken. *J. Ornithol.* 96: 129–46.

———. 1956. Über das Verhalten junger Grasmücken (*Sylvia borin*). *J. Ornithol.* 97: 156–89.

Saunders, A. A. 1929. *Bird Song.* Albany: New York State Museum Handbook 7.

———. 1947. The seasons of bird song: the beginning of song in spring. *Auk* 64: 97–114.

———. 1948. The seasons of bird song: the cessation of song after the nesting season. *Auk* 65: 19–30.

———. 1951. *A Guide to Bird Songs.* Revised ed. New York: Appleton-Century.

Schaller, G. B. 1967. *The Deer and the Tiger.* Chicago: The University of Chicago Press.

Schmid, B. 1937. *Interviewing Animals,* trans. M. Miall. Boston: Houghton Mifflin.

Schmitt, C., and H. Stadler, 1919. *Die Vogelsprache.* Stuttgart: Franckh.

Schubert, M. 1967. Probleme der Motivwahl u. der Gesangsaktivität bei *Phylloscopus trochilus. J. Ornithol.* 108:265–334.

Schwarzkopf, J. 1955. On the hearing of birds. *Auk* 72: 341–47.

Sebeok, T. A., ed. 1968. *Animal Communication: Techniques of study and results of research.* Bloomington: Indiana University Press.

Selander, R. K. 1964. Speciation in Wrens of the genus *Campylorhynchus. University of California Public. in Zool.* 74.

———. 1971. Sexual selection and dimorphism in birds. In *Sexual Selection and the Descent of Man,* B. G. Campbell, ed. Chicago: Aldine Press.

Shaw, K. C. 1968. An analysis of the phonoresponse of males of the true Katydid *Pterophila camellifolia* (Orthoptera). *Behavior* 31:203–60.

Sibley, C. G. 1952. The birds of the South San Francisco Bay region. Mimeographed.

Skutch, A. F. 1954. *Life Histories of Central American Birds.* Part I. Berkeley, Cal.: Cooper Ornithological Society.

———. 1960. *Life Histories of Central American Birds.* Part II. Berkeley, Cal.: Cooper Ornithological Society.

———. 1967. *Life Histories of Central American Highland Birds.* Cambridge, Mass.: Nuttall Ornithological Club.

————. 1969. *Life Histories of Central American Birds.* Part III. Berkeley, Cal.: Cooper Ornithological Society.

Slijper, E. J. 1962. *Whales.* Trans. from the Dutch. London: Hutchinson.

Slud, P. 1958. Observations on the Nightingale Wren in Costa Rica. *Condor* 60: 243–51.

————. 1960. The birds of Costa Rica. *Bull. Amer. Mus. Nat. Hist.* New York.

Smythies, B. E. 1953. *The Birds of Burma.* Edinburgh: Oliver and Boyd.

————. 1960. *The Birds of Borneo.* Edinburgh: Oliver and Boyd.

Snow, D. W. 1968. The singing assemblies of Little Hermits. *The Living Bird* 7:47–55.

Stadler, H. 1929. Die Vogelstimmenforschung als Wissenschaft. *Verh. 6te Int. Orn. Congr. Copenhagen,* 1926: 338–57.

————. 1934. Der Vogel kann transponieren. *Orn. Monatschr.* 59: 1–9.

Stevenson, J. 1969. Song as a reinforcer. In *Bird Vocalizations: Their Relation to Current Problems in Biology and Psychology,* R. A. Hinde, ed. Cambridge: Cambridge University Press.

Summers-Smith, J. D. 1963. *The House Sparrow.* London: Collins.

Swarth, H. S. 1930. Nesting of the Timberline Sparrow. Condor 32: 255 ff.

Szöke, P. 1962. Zur Entstehung u. Entwicklungsgeschichte der Musik. *Studia Musicologia,* Tom. 2, fasc. 1–4: 33–85.

Szöke, P., W. W. H. Gunn, and M. Filip. 1969. The musical microcosm of the Hermit Thrush. *Studia Musicologia Academiae Scientarum Hungaricae* 11.

Taczanowski, L. 1884. *Ornithologie de Pérou.* Paris: Typographie Oberthur.

Tavolga, W. N., ed. 1966. *Second Symposium on Marine Bio-Acoustics.* London and New York: Pergamon Press.

Thielcke, G., and K. E. Linsenmair. 1963. Zur geographischen Variation des Gesanges des Zilpzalps *Phylloscopus collybita* in Mittel-und-Sudwesteuropa. *J. Ornithol.* 104: 372–402.

Thomson, A. L., ed. 1964. *A New Dictionary of Birds.* London: Nelson.

Thorpe, W. H. 1954. The process of song-learning in the Chaffinch as studied by means of the sound spectrograph. *Nature* 173: 465–69.

————. 1955. Comments on 'The Bird Fancier's Delight' together with notes on imitation in the sub-song of the Chaffinch. *Ibis* 97 (2): 247–51.

————. 1959. Talking birds and the mode of action of the vocal apparatus of birds. *Proc. Zool. Soc. Lond.* 132: 441–55.

————. 1961. *Bird-song: The Biology of Vocal Communication and Expression in Birds.* Cambridge: Cambridge University Press.

————. 1963. *Learning and Instinct in Animals.* 2d ed. London: Methuen.

————. 1965a. *Science, Man and Morals.* London: Methuen.

————. 1965b. The ontogeny of behavior. In *Ideas in Modern Biology,* J. A. Moore, ed. 16th International Congress of Zoology. Garden City, N.Y.: Natural History Press.

————. 1966a. Ethology and consciousness. In *Brain and Conscious Experience,* J. C. Eccles, ed. New York: Springer-Verlag.

————. 1966b. Ritualization in ontogeny. *Philos. Trans. of the Royal Soc. of London,* B. 251: 311–19, 351–58.

————. 1967. Vocal imitation and antiphonal song. *Proc. XIVth Intern. Ornith. Congress:* 245–63.

————. 1969. The significance of vocal imitation in animals with special reference to birds. *Acta Biol. Exp.* 29: 251–69.

Thorpe, W. H., and B. I. Lade. 1961. Songs of some families of Passeriformes. *Ibis* 103a: 231–59.

Thorpe, W. H., and M. E. W. North. 1966. Origin and significance of the power of vocal imitation. *Nature* 208, no. 5007: 219–22.

Thorpe, W. H., and P. M. Pilcher. 1958. The nature and characteristics of sub-song. *Brit. Birds* 51: 509–14.

Tiessen, H. 1953. *Musik der Natur:* über den Gesang der Vögel, insbesonders über Tonsprache und Form des Amselgesanges. Freiburg (Br.): Atlantis Verlag.

Tretzel, E. 1967. Imitation und Transposition menschlicher Pfiffe durch Amsel (*Turdus merula merula*). Nachweis relativen Lernens und akustischer Abstraction bei Vögel. *J. Tierpsych.* 24: 137–61.

Troland, L. T. 1922. Psychophysics as related to the mysteries of physics and metaphysics. *J. Washington Acad. Sci.* 12: 141–62.

Turnbull, A. L. 1943. *Bird Music.* London: Faber and Faber.

Vaurie, C. 1959. *The Birds of the Palearctic Fauna: Passeriformes.* London: Witherby.

Verner, J. 1965. Time budget of the male Long-Billed Marsh Wren during the breeding season. *Condor* 67: 125–39.

Waddington, C. H. 1961. *The Nature of Life.* London: Allen and Unwin.

————, ed. 1969. *Toward a Theoretical Biology,* Vol. 2. Edinburgh: Edinburgh University Press.

Warner, D. W., and B. E. Harrell. 1957. The systematics and biology of the Singing Quail, *Dactylortyx thoracicus. Wilson Bull.* 69: 123–48.

Wayne, A. T. 1910. *Birds of South Carolina.* Charleston, S.C.: Contribution of the Charleston Museum.

Welty, J. C. 1962. *The Life of Birds.* Philadelphia and London: W. B. Saunders.

White, L. A. 1949. *The Science of Culture.* New York: Grove Press.

Wildash, P. 1968. *Birds of South Vietnam.* Rutland, Vt. and Tokyo: Charles E. Tuttle Co.

Willard, F. C. 1908. Three Vireos: nesting notes from the Huachuca Mts. *Condor* 10: 230–34.

Willis, E. O. 1966. The role of migrant birds at swarms of army ants. *The Living Bird* 5: 187–232.

Wing, A. H. 1951. Notes on song series of a Hermit Thrush. *Auk* 68: 189–93.

Witherby, H. F., F. C. R. Jourdain, N. F. Ticehurst, and B. W. Tucker. 1938, 1943. *Handbook of British Birds,* vols. I, II. London: Witherby.

Wright, S. 1953. Gene and organism. *The Amer. Naturalist* 57(5).

Yerkes, R. M., and A. Petrunkevitch. 1925. Studies of Chimpanzee vision by Nadie Kohts. *J. Comp. Psych.* 5: 99–108.

Yerkes, R. M. and A. W. 1929. *The Great Apes: A Study of Anthropoid Life.* New Haven: Yale University Press; London: Oxford.

Zahl, P. A. 1971. Nature's night lights. *National Geographic* 140: 46, 50.

II. Sound Recordings
(see also Boswall, References I)

A. Tapes

Research Libraries: The largest collection of animal sounds is at the Laboratory of Ornithology, Cornell University, Ithaca, N.Y. There are smaller collections at the Department of Zoology, The Ohio State University, Columbus, Ohio; at the BBC, England; and at the Japanese NHK. L. Irby Davis has an important collection at Balcones Research Center, The University of Texas at Austin.

Commercial Sources: Dan Gibson Productions Ltd., 196 Bloor St., West Toronto 5, Canada. The following tapes can be ordered from A-V Explorations, Inc., 505 Delaware Ave., Buffalo, New York:

T1. Song Sparrow, Bobolink, Wood Thrush, Brown Thrasher, etc.
T2. Mockingbird, Carolina Wren, Cardinal, Eastern Meadowlark, etc.
T3. Bewick's Wren, Western Meadowlark, etc.
T4. Some non-Oscine species.
(Also available as cassettes C1, C2, C3, C4.)

B. Phonograph Records

Borror, D. J., and W. W. H. Gunn. Sounds of Nature Series. Federation of Ontario Natu ralists, Edwards Gardens, Don Mills, Ontario; also available from Curtiss and Wei, 54 Priscilla Place, Trumbull, Conn.

Vol. 4. Warblers (of the U.S. and Canada).
Vol. 6. Finches (birds of the finch type of the U.S. and Canada).
Vol. 8. Thrushes, Wrens, Mockingbirds of Eastern North America (most of the nontropical North American species in these families).

Davis, L. I. "Mexican Bird Songs." Representative selection of species in the North American tropics, including the Slate-colored and Brown-backed Solitaires and the Banded Wren. Laboratory of Ornithology, Cornell University, Ithaca, N.Y.

Frisch, J. D. "Bird Songs of Brazil." Som, S/A, Av. Casper Libero, 58, São Paulo, Brazil.

"Cantos do Aves do Brasil." (Portuguese commentary, scientific names given.) SCLP 10502
"Ecos do Inferno Verde." SCLP 10513
"Vozes de Amazonia." SCLP 10525
"Vozes de Selva Brasileira." SCLP 10527

Kellogg, P. P., and A. A. Allen. "A Field Guide to Western Bird Song," to accompany R. T. Peterson, *A Field Guide to Western Birds*. Laboratory of Ornithology, Cornell University, Ithaca, N.Y.

North, M. E. W., and D. S. McChesney. "More Voices of African Birds." (White-browed, Rüppell's, and Snowy-headed Robin-chats.) Booklet, with notes on the 80-odd species. Laboratory of Ornithology, Cornell University, Ithaca, N.Y.

Roché, J.C. "L'Oiseau Musicien" [The Bird as Musician]. L'Oiseau Musicien, 04 Aubenas-les-Alpes (Haute-Provence), France. A series of small 45 rpm records with two species on each.

1. Blackbird and Skylark.
3. Woodlark and Nightingale.
5. Bluethroat and Thrush Nightingale.
7. Rufous-throated (Jamaican and Haitian) Solitaire and Bare-eyed Thrush.
9. Bifasciated Lark and Desert Warbler.

(Roché also directs the nonprofit organization Institut Echo, whose members have received many recordings of European and African birds. Same address as above.)

Schwarz, P. "Bird Songs from the Tropics." (Venezuela) Instituto Neotropical, Apartado 4640 Chacao, Caracas, Venezuela.

Vol. I. 40 Neotropical species.
Vol. II. 70 birds and animals. (With English narration.)
Vol. III. Additional species. (Without narration, but with accompanying text.)

Stannard, J., and P. Niven. Bird Song Series. Sound Recording Division, Percy Fitzpatrick Institute of African Ornithology, 3 Prospect Road, Port Elizabeth, Cape Province, South Africa.

No. 1. "Bird Songs of Amanzi."
No. 2. "Bird Songs of the Forest."

Verlag Paul Parey, Hamburg-Berlin. "Singvögel unserer Heimat." E 40 990.

Walker, A. "Birdsong of Southern Africa." Wildlife Series, no. 6. The African Music Society, MSAHO, Box 138, Roodepoort, Transvaal, South Africa.

Index of Birds

Acanthis [Carduelis] cannabina, Linnet, 187, 231
Acanthisittidae, New Zealand wrens, 217, 218
Acanthiza pusilla, Brown Thornbill, 196
A. uropygialis, Chestnut-tailed Thornbill, 196
accentors, 159, 163, 167f., 177
Accipitridae, hawks, 162
Acridotheres tristis, Common Myna, 18
Acrocephalus spp., reed warblers, 75, 126
A. aedon, Thick-billed Reed Warbler, 195
A. agricola, Paddy-field Warbler, 195
A. dumetorum, Blythe's Reed Warbler, 75, 195
A. palustris, Marsh Warbler, 53, 74, 75, 143, 146, 195, 233, 234
A. schoenobaenus, Sedge Warbler, 53, 138, 187, 232
A. scirpaceus, Reed Warbler, 232
A. stentoreus, Southern Great Reed Warbler, 195
Aechmophorus occidentalis, Western Grebe, 95
Aegolius acadicus, Saw-whet Owl, 210
A. funereus, Boreal Owl, 210
Aimophila aestivalis, Bachman's, Pine-woods, Sparrow, 42, 90, 94, 129, 146, 169, 181, 198, 235
A. cassinii, Cassin's Sparrow, 94
A. ruficeps, Rufous-crowned Sparrow, 239
Alaemon spp., larks, 75
A. alaudipes, Bifasciated Lark, 23, 36, 37, 166, 190
Alauda spp., larks, 75

Alauda arvensis, Skylark, 74, 104f., 115, 135, 140, 143, 151, 190, 230, 234, 245
A. gulgula, Indian Skylark, 190
Alaudidae, larks, 76, 126, 159f., 162, 164, 167ff., 180, 188
albatrosses, 203
Alcedo atthis, Eurasian Kingfisher, 212
Alcippe abyssinica, Abyssinian Hill-babbler, 191
A. nipalensis, Nun Babbler, 191
Amaurornis phoenicurus, White-breasted Waterhen, 204
Amazilia tzacatl, Rufous-tailed Hummingbird, 211
Amazon, Orange-winged, 67
Amazona amazonica, Orange-winged Parrot, Orange-winged Amazon, 67
Ammodramus bairdii, Baird's Sparrow, 182
A. savannarum, Grasshopper Sparrow, 23, 120f., 182, 239
Ammospiza caudacuta, Sharp-tailed Sparrow, 181f., 239
Amphispiza bilineata, Black-throated Sparrow, 129, 166
Anatidae, ducks, 205
Anhimidae, screamers, 205f.
anis, 213
Anseriformes, waterfowl, 205f.
Anserinae, geese and swans, 206
Antbird: Bicolored, 221; Chestnut-backed, 221; Dusky, 221
antbirds, 218, 219, 221, 222, 224; ground, 219, 221f.
Ant-chat, Sooty, 194
Anthornis melanura, New Zealand Bellbird, 170, 197
Anthus spp., pipits, 167f., 180

121; Fox, 23, 89, 147, 181, 187;
Grasshopper, 23, 120f., 182, 239;
Hedge, 141, 143, 230; Henslow's,
23, 88, 94, 108f., 113, 146, 181f.,
239; House, 143, 148, 230; Lark,
92ff., 128f., 181f., 198, 235; Le-
Conte's, 23, 109, 146, 181f., 239;
Pine-woods (see Bachman's); Ru-
fous-crowned, 239; Savannah, 182;
Sharp-tailed, 181f., 239; Song, 69,
90, 108, 129, 152f., 181f., 198, 235;
Tree, 233; Vesper, 121; White-
crowned, 20, 183; White-throated,
127, 181, 187
sparrows, New World, 128, 146f.,
148, 164, 167ff., 181
sparrows, true, 167ff.
Speirops, Black-capped, 197
Speirops lugubris, Black-capped Spei-
rops, 197
Spheniscidae, penguins, 203
Sphenostoma cristatum, Wedgebill,
Chimes-bird, 188
Spiza americana, Dickcissel, 238
Spizella breweri, Brewer's Sparrow,
129
S. *pallida,* Clay-colored Sparrow, 239,
248
S. *passerina,* Chipping Sparrow, 108,
133, 247f., 252
S. *pusilla,* Field Sparrow, 42, 121
Spot-throat, 193
Starling, 46, 74, 76, 230, 236
starlings, 111, 158, 159, 165, 167ff.,
179, 181
Stercorariidae, skuas, 203
Stilt, Black-necked, 206
Stonechat, 232
storks, 202
Strigiformes, owls, 210
Struthio camelus, ostrich, 202
Sturnella spp., meadowlarks, 49, 108,
146, 179
S. *magna,* Eastern Meadowlark, 45,
72, 120, 166, 197, 235, 245
S. *neglecta,* Western Meadowlark, 49,
116, 145, 147, 166, 197, 235, 245,
246
Sturnidae, starlings, 111, 158, 159,
165, 167ff., 179, 181
Sturnus vulgaris, Starling, 46, 74, 76,
230, 236
Sunbird, Olive, 197
sunbirds, 111, 126, 160, 165, 167,
170, 197
sunbirds, false, 218, 219

Swallow, Barn Swallow, 231
swallows, 107, 110, 111, 138, 159,
164, 167ff.
swans and geese, 206
Swift, Chimney, 107
swift-like birds, 211
swifts, 107, 138, 154, 203, 211, 216
Sycalis luteola, W. H. Hudson's Misto
Seed-finch, 42
Sylvia atricapilla, Blackcap, 88, 101,
141, 143, 195, 232, 234
S. *borin,* Garden Warbler, 143, 195,
232
S. *communis,* Whitethroat, 70, 232
S. *curruca,* Lesser Whitethroat, 144,
232
S. *hortensis,* Orphean Warbler, 195
S. *nisoria,* Barred Warbler, 75, 195
S. *undata,* Dartford Warbler, 231
Sylviidae, Old World warblers, 111,
126, 157, 159f., 163, 167ff., 171,
179, 180, 181, 188, 195

Tailorbird: Common, 100; Mountain,
46, 100f., 196, 247, 251
Tanager, Gray-headed, 169; Scarlet,
169, 237; Scarlet-rumped, 169;
Swallow, 165, 167ff.; Thrush, 169
tanagers, 152, 160, 167, 169, 181
Tanagridae, tanagers, 106
tapaculos, 218, 219f., 222
Taraba major, Great Antshrike, 221
Teretistris fernandinae, Yellow-
headed Warbler, 174
T. *fornsi,* Oriente Warbler, 174
Tersina viridis, Swallow Tanager,
165, 167ff.
Thamnolaea cinnamomeiventris, Cliff-
chat, 194
Thamnophilus doliatus, Barred Antshrike, 221
Thornbill: Brown, 196; Chestnut-
tailed, 196
Thornbird, Rufous-fronted, 221
Thrasher: Bendire's 187; Brown, 105,
121, 123, 145, 146, 150, 167, 192,
235; California, 74, 187; Crissal,
192; Curve-billed, 187; Long-
billed, 187; Sage, 145, 146, 192,
235
thrashers, 74, 126, 128, 159, 163, 166,
192
Thraupidae, tanagers, 152, 160, 167ff.,
181
Threnetes ruckeri, Band-tailed Barbthroat, 211

Index of Persons

Index of Topics

116, 118, 121, 151; degenerates under stress, 53; functions of, 15, 20, 57, 161, 202; identifies individuals, 62; indicates sex, 5, 15, 20; indicates species, 5, 20; individual variations in, 81; a bird's most informative utterance, 20; partly learned, 23, 33; reproductively isolates, 60; relation to stimuli, 226; sexual stimulus to males, 55; and territory, 2, 15ff. (*see also* Separation of individuals; Territory); as warning, 47, 202. *See also* Calls; Chatter; Communication; Complexity in songs; Dialects; Music; Organization in song; Outcries; Scope; Territory; Tone; Utility of song
Songbirds, 16, 134, 201. *See also* Oscines
Song-development, 112; degrees of, 112, 183; dimensions of, 112ff., 157, 176, 185; ecological (ethological) factors affecting, 15ff., 111; and habits, 163–67, 200; and habitats, 94, 163–67, 200; judgments of, 117f., 202–24 passim; selective pressure for, 111; and size, 184; and territory (*see* Territory). *See also* Skill, in singing
Song duels, 227
Song lengths, 140
Songless: birds, 200; Oscines, 201f.
Song-pause cycles, 152
Songs: some easily describable, 83f.; courtship, 68 (*see also* Courtship; Mating); good, 107, 109; highly developed, 108, 158; human estimates of, 148; kinds of, 91; long, 32, 40, 219 (*see also* Patterns in song); parts of, 88; poor, 107, 108, 109; of "power and variety," 117, 138; primitive, 13, 94, 131, 182, 214; short, 88, 172; territorial, 52; unmusical, 5, 116; war, 46
Songsters, world's outstanding, 186.
Sound, controllability of, 14, 33
Soundproof chambers, 64
Sounds: birds' brief, 36; birds' interest in, 60f., 68, 226; emotional meanings of, 54; sustained, 37, 44, 131
South America, 186, 201. *See also* Regions
Specialization, law of. *See* Exclusive specialization

Species limitation. *See* Exclusive specialization
Spectrograms, 24, 43, 78f., 94, 140, 152, 172
⁕ Species, 158ff., 190–99 passim
Speech: parts of, 4, 40; learning of (*see* Learning)
Stability of songs through generations, 49
Staff, musical. *See* Notation
Statistical: analysis, 103; evidence, 11, 104f., 105, 109, 115, 118, 125f., 143, 153, 216, 226; sample, 234ff.
Stimulus: for chatter, 66, 68; for singing, 51; song as, 60; unvarying, birds adapt to, 121, 151
Stridulate, 28
Subfamilies, 157
Subjectivity: in aesthetic matters, 6, 107, 109, 185; of biological concepts, 183; "thesis of," 110
Sublime, the, 7, 8
Suboscines, 186, 201
Subsong, 43, 143, 148
Subspecific differences in song, 36, 44, 82
Superior singers, 94, 160; list of, 190–98. *See also* Outstanding songsters; Singers
Superlative singers, 198
Survival value, 6
Suspense, musical, 100
Swamp birds, 181, 203
Symbolic power, man's, 8, 40, 54, 59
Symbols, visual, 25
Synchronization: of song, 24, 47; of visual display, 23. *See also* Duetting
Syringial muscles, 66, 111, 157, 201, 202, 209, 216–23
Syrinx, 28, 145, 155

Tape recordings. *See* Recordings
Tapping, by woodpeckers, 28
Taste, musical, in birds, 49, 56, 60f.
Taxonomic groups, 161
Technology, 228f.
Template, 69
Tempo, birds' fast, 36, 40
Territorial birds, 17, 65, 162–71 passim, 178, 180, 184, 202–25 passim
Territoriality, 111, 202; ambiguity of, 162, 183; in amphibians, 17; degrees of, 17, 183, 184; in insects, 17; miscellaneous, 61; in whales, 30; year-round, 137